Modernity, Domesticity and Temporality in Russia

Modernity, Domesticity and Temporality in Russia

Time at Home

Rebecca Friedman

BLOOMSBURY ACADEMIC
LONDON • NEW YORK • OXFORD • NEW DELHI • SYDNEY

BLOOMSBURY ACADEMIC
Bloomsbury Publishing Plc
50 Bedford Square, London, WC1B 3DP, UK
1385 Broadway, New York, NY 10018, USA

BLOOMSBURY, BLOOMSBURY ACADEMIC and the Diana logo are trademarks
of Bloomsbury Publishing Plc

First published in Great Britain 2020

Cover design by: Tjaša Krivec
Cover image: Photo shows Russian women on the assembly line for the
manufacture of alarm clocks. (© George Rinhart/Getty Images)

A catalogue record for this book is available from the British Library.

Library of Congress Cataloging-in-Publication Data
Names: Friedman, Rebecca, 1968- author.
Title: Modernity, domesticity and temporality in Russia : time at home / Rebecca Friedman.
Description: London, UK ; New York, NY : Bloomsbury Academic, 2020. | Includes
bibliographical references and index.
Identifiers: LCCN 2020015217 (print) | LCCN 2020015218 (ebook) | ISBN 9781350112438
(hardback) | ISBN 9781350112445 (ebook) | ISBN 9781350112452 (epub)
Subjects: LCSH: Home–Russia–History–19th century. | Home–Russia–History–20th
century. | Russia–Social conditions–1801-1917.
Classification: LCC HN523 .F75 2020 (print) | LCC HN523 (ebook) | DDC 306.0947–dc23
LC record available at https://lccn.loc.gov/2020015217
LC ebook record available at https://lccn.loc.gov/2020015218

ISBN: HB: 978-1-3501-1243-8
          ePDF: 978-1-3501-1244-5
          eBook: 978-1-3501-1245-2

Typeset by Integra Software Services Pvt. Ltd.

To find out more about our authors and books visit www.bloomsbury.com
and sign up for our newsletters.

I dedicate this book to my parents, Ellen and Max Friedman. They have always provided me with a home and given me whatever time I have needed.

Contents

List of Illustrations   viii

Acknowledgments   ix

Introduction: Why Time and Home?   1

1   Russian Modernity through Time and Space   9

2   Present Time, Hygiene and the Urban Apartment   35

3   The Past in the Present: Nostalgic Portraits of the Russian Home   81

4   Revolutionary Time   127

Coda: Timelessness Today: A Few Observations   169

Notes   184

Bibliography   210

Index   219

Illustrations

1 "Humorous Album," *Zhenshchina*, 1907. 39

2 "Child's Sleeping Quarters," *Zhenshchina*, 1908. 75

3 "Kitchen in the Room," *Dom i khoziastvo*, 1928. 144

4 "Sweeping," *Bezgodnik i stanka*, 1926. 148

5 Candy box. Rebecca Friedman, May 2019. 173

6 Mechanical time. Rebecca Friedman, May 2019. 174

7 Alexander Herzen's literature. Rebecca Friedman, May 2019. 175

8 Pages of *Pravda*. Rebecca Friedman, May 2019. 175

9 A family watching TV in their living room. Rebecca Friedman
   in GUM, May 2019. 178

10 Book by Vladimir Mayakovsky. Rebecca Friedman in GUM, May 2019. 179

11 Mechanical clock. Rebecca Friedman in GUM, May 2019. 180

12 Mother, father and child. Rebecca Friedman in GUM, May 2019. 181

13 A Soviet-era Melodiya record. Rebecca Friedman in GUM, May 2019. 182

14 Store front. Rebecca Friedman, May 2019. 183

Acknowledgments

This book has been a struggle. A real daily struggle over a very long period of time, so much so that my own sense of home has changed since I began this project. But I do not wish this to be a confessional but rather a heartfelt thanks. It is nothing short of a miracle that after all this time, I still have family and friends and colleagues who have stuck around in my life long enough that I have the pleasure of saying "thank you." But I do. In spades ....

I have said many times to anyone who would listen that I have the most amazing collection of friends, each of whom has listened and distracted and cared for me during these many years. I will simply list them all here with a huge thank you: Kristin McGuire, Amy Randall, Tracy McDonald, Ali Hernandez, Stephanie Doscher, Ana Lucsczynzka, Heather Russell, Jessica Adler, Deirdre Harshman, Meredith Newman, Michelle Walsh, Ana Menendez, Maite Morales, Lorie de la Fe, Martha Sesin, Renata Benedini and Jill Kaplan. And a few good men. Jon Mogul, who always made the space for my work and was there from the start. Bill Anderson, David Rifkind, Mark Edele, Markus Thiel, Eddy Gallo and Julio Capo and to all of those of you who have added sugar and spice, including nutmeg. And to one Miami friend, I owe a particular debt of gratitude. You have all made me laugh, without which there would be no book.

A special thank you to the inspiring and always generous Mark Steinberg. You encouraged me early on, introduced me to the wonderful Deirdre Harshman and read and offered comment along the way. A particularly sincere "I never would have crossed the finish line without you" goes to Amy Randall. Let's just say once we discovered that we could go to Moscow together to do our research, all bets were off. Tracy McDonald, you have kept me (albeit virtually) company every day these past couple of years. Thank you. Each of these two stellar scholars, Amy and Tracy, have read and provided comment on parts of this book. I also thank Mark Edele, although our paths did not cross until late in the day, I am grateful for your willingness to read much of this manuscript, for your friendship, your encouragement and your smile.

Thanks go to family of various kinds, from my sister and brother-in-law, Sonia Friedman and Jerry Weinhouse, and their kids Sam and Angela, who let me live with them for many weeks at a time so I could use the library at Harvard; to Kathy and Louis Mogul who allowed me the same; and the Kroguls and Poguls, who provided me company and never stopped showing interest in this book, Christmas after Christmas, Fourth of July after Fourth of July, and around again. A rather ethereal thank you to Jack and Lola Glazer and David and Ida Friedman, because that matters.

Friends. Colleagues. More friends. Twelve years is a lifetime and so I give a huge thank you to anyone who has sat on a panel with me, enduring my half thoughts. And to my friends and colleagues in Miami and at Florida International University (FIU). To Ken Furton, our Provost, and his team. To everyone who worked together in the very special Office for Faculty and Global Affairs (OFGA) at FIU, who made coming in to the office a place of friendship and joy each day (or whenever I managed to come in). To Meredith Newman, for her mentorship and friendship. To colleagues and friends in the Department of History at FIU, and finally to Bloomsbury Press, most especially Rhodri Mogford and Laura Reeves for all of your support and help, and believing this manuscript worth a wider audience. And thank you too to the anonymous reviewers and the National Endowment for the Humanities (NEH) for a faculty research grant so long ago.

And finally, to my three wonderful children, Simon, Joseph and Iris. You, of course, will always be my greatest accomplishments. You have lived with this project for way too long. Iris has never known life without this book. Iris: this book, about time and home, is as old as you. I was awarded a NEH grant the very moment you were born. To Joseph, such an inspiring young man, launched and in college: thank you for always making me laugh. To Simon, our family's musician: thank you for guaranteeing there is music in my days and for always making me smile. And to Iris, my one and only daughter: thank you for keeping me on my toes and making me be the best mother and person I am capable of being. All three of you bring laughter, happiness and accountability into my life each and every day.

And finally, to my parents, Ellen and Max Friedman, I dedicate this book to you.

Of course, all of the mistakes, errors, poor writing and incomplete observations, are all my own.

Introduction: Why Time and Home?

Home can be a site for time travel. Home can be a space where layered temporal narratives reside, where memories of the past, struggles in the present and dreams for the future are each projected onto the contours of the corridors and the texture of the cushions. Sometimes, though, you simply cannot go back, try as you might. Ana Menendez reminds us of this in her beautiful story "Her Mother's House," where the narrator travels to Havana from Miami in search of a childhood imagined frozen in time. The protagonist mourns that "the past wasn't something you could play again, like an old song."[1] Time has moved forward even as dreams of her mother's house remain in her present consciousness. Even when unattainable, though, the past continues to haunt the present, to walk its gardens and to wear its clothes.

In this sense, past and present reside, completely interwoven, in the hallways and parlors and kitchens of home, of memory and of representation. The past is, in modern narratives, necessarily constitutive of the present, even as it eludes one's grasp. Temporal and domestic narratives, such as the one Menendez provides, too are always interwoven, whether in Havana, Miami, Moscow or St. Petersburg. Home—the material place (an estate, an apartment or the corner of a room) and the imagined space of childhood dreams and adult nightmares— serves as a site for the projection of a past, a reordering of the present and a hope for the future.

In the early part of the twentieth century, as populations shifted, professions emerged and mass politics took to the streets, new narratives of time and home spread throughout Europe. Architects, tastemakers, writers and state agencies contemplated and defined idealized normative narratives of everyday life and domestic spaces became reimagined in paintings, literary portraits, magazines, state propaganda and prescriptive booklets, to name a few. Narratives of progress and technological innovation undergirded discussions of domestic space in the modern present. The home, thus, contained not only the past, as Menendez shows us, but also the present with its dreams and future desires.

The book is about the intersection of time and space. Each of the substantive chapters takes the reader through the ways in which notions of temporality—all from the vantage point of 1900 to 1930 in Russia—were refracted through the home, whether the urban apartment, the gentry estate or the communal ideal. This was a time, of course, of tremendous transformation and movement, from countryside to city, from political underground to mass politics (if still tempered by the autocracy), from monarchy to socialism, from estate to apartment. Although neither overnight nor uniform, the twentieth century brought with it substantive change. The dawn of the twentieth century saw new professions, artistic experiments, and new social and economic stratifications. Included in these transitions emerged new temporal narratives, from nostalgia to utopia to speed.

Modernity, Domesticity and Temporality in Russia: Time at Home begins at this moment, the turn of the twentieth century. This study begins where others have left off, bringing the reader not only across the revolutionary divide but also into the homes and apartments of newly urban Russians, whether impoverished and aspirational or comfortable and middling class. The substantive sections of this book begin with a chapter that outlines historical and philosophical ideas about modern domesticity and temporality in the pan-European context, locating Russia's place within these narratives. Chapter 1 traces the writings of scholars and philosophers of modern temporality, from Henri Bergson to Svetlana Boym, from the nineteenth century until today to piece together narratives of temporality and domesticity—both separately and together—in the Russian context in the early decades of the twentieth century. During the 1890s and beyond, across much of Europe and in the United States, new and modern notions of time were emerging. Railroad companies and governments created standard time zones and coordinated ideas about time. Clocks themselves, detaching time from nature, helped to externally impose a sense of mechanized and standardized time. By the late nineteenth century, thus, the now, the present, was being understood in increasingly standardized and unified ways. Against this backdrop and given their own fast-paced modernizing attempts, Russians too experienced a new sense of historical time at the fin de siècle. Modernist thinkers, both Russian and more generally European, who traded in disparate fields of knowledge, challenged ideas about the teleological and unidirectional movement of time, based on the ticking of a clock and instead highlighted time that relied on reversals, movements that were in irregular rhythms, where the past flowed into the present with an eye toward the future. The two concepts of duration and simultaneity held currency in Russia as they did throughout

Europe. Readers and writers, on the one hand, imagined time frames as malleable and fluid, and feared that the past might bleed into the present and the present into the future. The threat of intrusion loomed large. The stretch of a moment or duration of a period of seconds, minutes or hours might include the residue of the moments that came before, always potentially flowing into the now. Authors of domestic discourses, in their writings and production of images, expressed anxieties about the present and its relationship to the past, whether in the form of imaginary peasants, dirt and grime, or general disorder. The past was always felt to be proximate: lurking in the shadows; around the corner; and within sight. At the same moment, the urge toward uniformity—the syncretizing of time—presented a solution to combat the past and its seeping into the present. A uniform, well-ordered, clean and efficient daily life could ward off the backwardness of what came before.

And yet, many Russians glanced nostalgically backwards, if only as a means to grapple with the present. This is the context in which nostalgia found its way into the pages of magazines and memoirs written in the last years of the Russian tsarist regime, a time of rapid industrial growth, urban migration and tentative political transformation. Expressions of nostalgia for an imagined past mixed with a rapidly changing environment, where peasants became landlords and intelligentsia families fled. As a phenomenon of the late nineteenth and early twentieth centuries, nostalgia exposed not the past but rather a fractured and modern present. In other words, despite the glancing backwards, the portraits of gentry estates created in the self-writings and journals of this era are both reflective and constitutive of Russians' modern notions of time and space, and part of modernity itself. Nostalgia, as a sentiment, requires a sense of historicity, an investment in the movement of time and the flow of human activity and its environment. In the case of late tsarist Russia, nostalgia inspired writers to show their readers how time embodies space, and especially domestic space. And, too, given the emergent Soviet context, with its commitment to communal domestic arrangements and always with an eye toward tomorrow, utopian visions injected anxieties about the future into the now, as all three frames coexisted and overlapped as Russia stumbled toward the modern age. This theme weaves its way throughout this study.

The urban apartment, a quintessentially modern space, embodied the anxieties and dreams of this present moment with its emergent temporal narratives. Spatially, apartment living inevitably demanded living in close quarters with one's neighbors and often not those of the same life circumstances. It created a proximity in daily life, although separate and compartmentalized. Moreover, the dangers of the past—the dirt, the old habits of food and living, the inefficiencies—were just next door in the apartment buildings. Anyone could be living next door; the potential for overcrowding, dirt and general "backwardness" were omnipresent. The phenomenon of the migration of the peasants from the countryside into the cities and into apartments was, in effect, bringing the past into the present. Whether or not most peasants actually stayed in the cities or lived in apartments is another matter; peasants' presence in the urban imaginary impacted the narratives of modernity. They had to be transformed to conform to modern expectations. The past, in other words, was partly embodied by the countryside, its peasantry and the Russian particularism of those arrangements. By contrast, the present was the city, which necessitated routine and synchronicity, and finally efficiency.

New modern scientific approaches to domestic dilemmas could be found in the prescriptive literature of the day, from Maria Redelin's aspirational guide to household management to editorial columns in women's magazines. Readers were inundated with advice about how to combat the past and build environments that conformed to present ideas of efficiency and uniformity. Readers were advised that as peasants left the countryside and members of fading gentry families migrated to Moscow and St. Petersburg to find work and new residences, they should adopt daily domestic practices that reflected modern definitions of time, of the present and of proper, modern home life. The domestic became one central repository for ideas about the now, both its large-scale seismic shifts and its everyday mundane manifestations. In Russia, perhaps even more so than in other parts of Europe, the past did not recede so delicately, as the countryside continued to dominate the landscape and recent migrants from peasant villages populated the city. The urban infrastructure could not keep up and modern standards were hard to implement in any widespread way. Yet, that did not stop those who worked for the aspirational press from publishing issue after issue and writing column after column instructing Russians how to live in the modern, present day.

This book attempts to make an intervention into the scholarship on Russian private life and domesticity. By using temporality as the main conceptual lens, *Modernity, Domesticity and Temporality in Russia: Time at Home*, finds that even as readers and writers focused longingly backwards to the eighteenth and nineteenth centuries, they also embraced present-day and future-oriented desires steeped in bourgeois norms attached to modern, hygienic practices in urban apartments. The proliferation of actual apartments, combined with the whirlwind effect of the publication of prescriptive tracts and autobiographical reflections instructing newly urban Russians how to decorate and set up their homes, relied on a temporality that focused not on the past but on the present and its aspirations for scientific, efficient and hygienic homes. The great emphasis placed on efficiency at home, including getting the kitchen clean and the sheets dried, became especially crucial at the very moment when there appeared a growing urban culture and broader public discourses about leisurely pursuits and consumption practices.

This study's insistence on time grew organically from the sources, whether autobiographical or prescriptive, fiction or nonfiction, textual or visual. Time, of course, is at the heart of any historical study. Yet, it is rarely the focus. Time "defines history as a discipline." And, in the words of Reinhart Koselleck, the past itself is understood as the "sediments or layers of time," which reflect the multiplicity of not only historical narratives but also temporal ones.[2] In this instance, the magazines, the prescriptive texts and autobiographies reflected temporal themes of efficiency and speed, nostalgia and longing, and utopian dreaming. This study relies on a multitude of printed and visual sources. The first substantive chapter, Chapter 2, centers on the multifaceted representations of the emerging urban apartment. This imagery was found in the pages of women's magazines and journals—including *Zhenshchina, Zhurnal dlia zhenshchin, Damskii mir, Zhurnal dlia khoziaek* and *Zhenskii vestnik*—as well as the volumes of prescriptive texts and advertisements about hygienic products and practices meant for women and men of the urban middling classes, who lived primarily in apartments in Moscow and St. Petersburg. Russians did not have the type of publications or professional societies devoted exclusively to the modern home and its interior design, as existed in England, France or Germany. Russians were surrounded, however, by an increasing number of women's and lifestyle publications as well as prescriptive texts that elevated the domestic to a place of importance in the struggle to become participants in the modern, urban landscape of consumer and civil society at the turn of the twentieth century. Markers of the present, from the mundane to the extraordinary, could be found everywhere in Russia's capital cities. Time, whether past or present, was embedded in—and embodied by—household objects themselves: knickknacks peppering the shelves of kitchens; chairs and sofas spread across the living rooms; and the pillows laying in the sleeping quarters. Russians were trying to come to terms with a present that seemed to be speeding ahead at an unknown pace, ushering in a modern era full of both hope for health and progress and despair about the filth and squalor, contradictions so characteristic of industrializing times. The home, its interior rooms and corridors—whether real or imagined—reflected the promises and the fears of the now, of the present moment in a modern age. Yet, the present, in its modern formulation could not be disentangled from the past and always contained seeds of the future.

Chapter 3 involves a close analysis of nostalgic texts and images found in magazines, journals, memoirs and diaries written at the turn of the century in order to understand how domestic space was represented through modern temporal narratives. Here the focus is on memoirs of childhood, nostalgic journalistic portraits of estate life and artistic representations of waning peasant traditional crafts. These texts include early twentieth-century lifestyle magazines—such as *Stolitsa i usadba* and *Starye gody*—and memoirs written both by members of the emerging middle classes—merchants and others—and by members of the tsarist intelligentsia. Included here is a discussion about the embracing of peasant traditional domestic handicrafts by members of the merchant and artistic segments of society and the creation of the nostalgic Style Moderne evidenced in magazines, such as *Mir iskusstva*, as well as many visual and performing arts. Nostalgia, with its embracing of movement, change and rupture, reflected the modern circumstances of urbanization, mass production, political upheaval and industrial change. This historical consciousness transitioned from an earlier, pre-emancipation, emphasis on the pastoral timelessness of life on the estate to an emphasis on the permanence of the past along with open, endless vistas in the future.

The final area of inquiry, Chapter 4, involves visions of the future during the early years of the Soviet regime and its experiments in—and ideas about—utopian, communal living arrangements. The early years of Soviet rule included the proliferation of women's magazines, from the popular *Rabotnitsa* to the continued run of tsarist-era journals such as *Zhurnal dlia khoziaek*. Each, in its own way, created and defended revolutionary ideas about the future of communal domestic life. Communalism in the 1920s, however, with its future-oriented aspirations, was not the only vision of Soviet domestic space. At the same time that many embraced utopian desires for a communal future, in 1922 a Society for the Study of the Russian Estate emerged. This group, developed under the leadership of a group of scholars at Moscow State University, proposed the creation of an academic field of study, "estate studies," harkening back to a tsarist and Russian past. *Modernity, Domesticity and Temporality in Russia* considers these Russian nostalgic impulses alongside the Soviet utopian ones.

The final, concluding chapter comments on the post-Soviet embrace of a bifurcated domestic longing, which at once embraces the tsarist-era; Soviet times and desires for its materiality; and something else altogether. In the urban—and soon suburban—landscape of Moscow and St. Petersburg, writers and readers began to reach into the past and emulate, or dream of, grand estates with spacious drawing rooms, while others built museums of Soviet culture and quickly and quietly resurrected Soviet icons, whether children's toys or commonplace lampshades. This look at the current-day Moscow, albeit brief and impressionistic, will bring the book full circle to the nostalgic longings of a century ago, but inhabited by a timelessness of present day.

This book makes three overlapping historiographical and theoretical contributions. First of all, it uses the nexus of time and space to understand the regional nature of modernity. One of the key tropes of Russian historical inquiry hinges on the question of Russia's place within—or more often outside of—"normal" European patterns of modern development. At no moment was this question more crucial than the turn of the twentieth century, when Russia was industrializing and experimenting with a liberal political culture. *Modernity, Temporality and Domesticity in Russia* grounds the discussion of Russian modernity in an exploration of representations of domestic interiors, both textual and visual. The core feature of this modernity, namely the new definitions of time, felt so vividly in the public realm of mass politics and mass consumption, had its counterpart in the home. The domestic interior in the early years of the twentieth century took on new cultural meanings across Europe and Russia and became an area of contest over new ideas, including ideas about efficiency in the emergent bourgeois consumer culture of the now, a longing for a Russian national past and dreams of a utopian future. Advice about domestic interior design, memories of childhood homes and discussions of the shared spaces of tomorrow, taken together, reflect the ways in which Russians embraced historical time awareness on their own terms and simultaneously with their counterparts to the west. This study looks at the ways in which modern notions of time underpinned textual and visual representations of domestic spaces—the gentry estate, the urban apartment and the communal apartment— in the years leading up to, and just after, the Bolshevik Revolution. Modern time thus includes an emphasis on the overlapping of eras, as past, present and future all merge. Nostalgia is a key aspect of this merging and fluidity. *Modernity, Domesticity and Temporality* shows us that in Russia, as elsewhere in Europe, there was a burst of nostalgic sentiment in publications about home life in the 1910s. These ideas, however, did not disappear with the revolutionary—or the post-revolutionary—impulses of later years.

This book also makes an intervention into the scholarship on Russian intimate life and domesticity per se. By using temporality as the main conceptual lens, this book finds that even as readers and writers focused longingly backwards on waning estate life, they also embraced present-day and future-oriented desires steeped in bourgeois domestic aesthetics attached to modern, hygienic practices in urban apartments. The proliferation of actual apartments, combined with the whirlwind effect of the publication of prescriptive tracts and autobiographical reflections instructing newly urban Russians how to decorate and set up their homes, relied on a temporality that focused not on the past but on the present and its aspirations for scientific, efficient and hygienic homes.

Finally, *Modernity, Domesticity and Temporality* contributes to studies of Bolshevik utopian dreams in the early years of revolution. While fin de siècle middling classes reveled in their desire for bourgeois domestic norms in the everyday of their own times, post-revolutionary writers rejected nineteenth-century norms of domesticity and created a revolutionary, utopian vision of space and of time, which looked to a future point when bourgeois arrangements would dissipate and communalism would win the day. Many intellectuals dreamt and wrote about the creation of new, communal—and future-oriented—spaces of domestic life: collective cafeterias, laundries and communal apartments. Although scholars have explored, at some length, artistic utopian dreams, few have understood those images and ideologies as part of an ongoing discussion of time and space per se. Using this dual lens of time and space, *Modernity, Domesticity and Temporality in Russia: Time at Home* permits us to understand the revolutionary domestic experiment as part of a longer story about the emergence of modern historical time. In particular, even as some Bolshevik writers articulated their utopian desires, other members of educated classes joined together to celebrate the eighteenth-century estate. They celebrated the past even as the future was upon them.

1

Russian Modernity through Time and Space

Theories of time: Time waits for no one and yet we are still waiting

Scholars have begun to write about "the temporal turn," one a long time coming and not yet complete. Historians, sociologists, cultural geographers, art historians and so on have approached the historically contextual nature of time and temporality in fits and starts. Scholars have begun to acknowledge the ways in which temporal narratives, such as spatial ones, emerge within fields of power and hierarchy. The early modernists, for instance, contest that modernists imagine a linear march toward progress as centuries move along; creating value judgments about what is modern and not yet so. Modernists claim a certain hegemony, created through Enlightenment-tainted glasses, resides in nations in the West. Yet, because of the long-standing nature of this scholarship and yet its nascent status as a yet-to-emerge field, there is room for maneuver. There is room still for discussions that question these hierarchies and hegemonies from the start. This is precisely the work to be done here, putting Russia and then the Soviet Union at the center of inquiry, a place always and at once modern and unmodern, enlightened and untouched by the enlightenment, intent on swift-paced progress and stuck in the past.

Philosophers and scholars have discussed the meaning of time, whether the rise and fall of the sun, the ticking of a mechanical clock or the impulse to glance backwards toward the closing door and its manifestations through space. Virginia Woolf, in *To the Lighthouse*, evokes the tenuous and contextual nature of time.

> With her foot on the threshold she waited a moment longer in a scene which was vanishing even as she looked, and then, as she moved and took Minta's arm and left the room, it changed, it shaped itself differently; it had become, she knew, giving one last look at it over her shoulder, already the past.[1]

Here Woolf juxtaposes measurable so-called "objective" time ("a moment longer") with an elusive glance "over her shoulder" and "already in the past." She does so again, as she presents mechanical time and personal time side by side in the following sequence in *Mrs. Dalloway* (1925):

> For having lived in Westminster – how many years now? over twenty – one feels even in the midst of the traffic, or waking at night, Clarissa was positive, a particular hush, or solemnity; an indescribable pause; a suspense (but that might be her heart, affected, they said, by influenza) before Big Ben strikes. There! Out it boomed. First a warning, musical; then the hour, irrevocable. The leaden circles dissolved in the air.[2]

The chiming of Big Ben lies at the center of Virginia Woolf's story set in a single day. In true modernist fashion, the characters thought to themselves, operating according to the logic of personal time, even as Big Ben chimes in juxtaposition. This passage captures a basic tension in *Mrs. Dalloway* and in conceptions of time more broadly. The free flow of Clarissa's thoughts was interrupted or constrained by the predictable chiming of the clock, which marked minutes and hours of the day. This duality, or tension, between mechanical, clock time and more free-flowing personal time reflected some of the tensions within modern time itself. Here Woolf introduces her readers to the concept of private, interior, intimate time and public, civic time, each of which is evoked in the Russian conceptions of time in the early twentieth century, on both sides of the revolutionary divide. Both, too, in various forms, existed well before Virginia Woolf immortalized them in her beautiful prose.

Time, it hardly bears saying, is at the center of history, historical thinking and thus the conceiving of history itself. William Sewell, in his seminal work *The Logics of History*, explained how all of historical work is the study of time. He wrote that historians are conditioned "to think about the temporalities of social life."[3] Historians, Sewell instructed, are the "theoreticians of temporality." In describing the historian's craft, thusly, Sewell wrote: "I think we believe that time is fateful." This notion of fate itself is contested. Sewell emphasized the irreversibility of time, necessitating a sense that the past is always the past. Time is irreversible, and therefore "an action, once taken, or an event, once experienced, cannot be obliterated. It is lodged in the memory of those whom it affected and therefore irrevocably altered the situation in which it occurs."[4] And yet, even this contention is contingent, as Sewell himself articulated: "historical temporality is lumpy, uneven, unpredictable, and discontinuous." And too, "social temporality is extremely complex."

Ultimately all historical stories involve a kind of continuity and change, where "time is *heterogenous.*" Historians focus on "historical contextualization"—a concern with chronology, sequence and the broader dynamics at play in any particular moment.[5] And yet, this very contextualization with its chronological contingency presumes a certain linearity of time. And it is precisely this notion of linearity that was questioned by historians of earlier eras and of nations touched by European imperial ambitions. Why is time "modern" or "more complex" at any particular moment? Is there a notion of time that is quintessentially modern? Scholars tend to agree that temporality itself is a mark of the modern moment and central to the modern experience, a uniformity of time.

Why, though, are some societies considered "modern" and others "traditional"? And where is Russia in all of these conceptual imaginings? The Enlightenment itself projects a linear march toward progress that often begins with Paris, and perhaps 1789, as the center and slowly moves outward from there. Scholars of modernity whose geographic expertise begins in the so-called periphery, in old-fashioned speak, the second or third worlds, have made a multitude of arguments about what constitutes the modern, what its markers are and how its central components ultimately are on a progressive path from darkness to light. Yet, scholars both of Europe and other regions around the globe, including Russia and then the Soviet Union, question the notion of a singular path to, or toward, modernity. Rather, many argue for models that account for "multiple modernities" or "alternative modernities." Simply put, the multiplicity of definitions of what is modern challenges the idea that the mythological West is always at the center of definition. The study of the "shapes of time," too, serves to "unsettle" narratives of modern progress. Once the lens incorporates "the multiple ways in which modern subjects, both Western and non-Western, have conceived and experienced time, it serves to highlight the multiple times, or 'pluritemporalities', of modern life." This multiple approach tends to challenge the singular path to modernity thesis with its emphasis on linear, progressive temporal rhythms.

None of this undermines the profound change in time and temporal narratives over the course of the nineteenth century. These changes associated with the nineteenth century might include the standardization of time symbolized by Greenwich Mean Time as the international standard and the basis for a global system of time, mechanization and standardization of clock time over the course of the nineteenth century, which includes the emphasis on efficiency and streamlining on the shop floor in factories.[6]

Just as citizens across the globe lived in multiple modern frames, so did they in temporal ones. "Transferring the paradigm of multiple modernities to temporality, it is readily apparent that individuals live within a plurality of social times." Within modern life, this multiplicity might include "the time of seasons, governments, school timetables, churches, clocks, instant messaging, pop concerts, political referendums, holidays, veterinary visits, reproduction and birthdays." And, too, these measures or markers of time coexist with the more mechanical nature of temporal measurements. For example, as scholar of time, A.R.P. Fryxell, notes in a recent exchange in the journal *Past and Present*:

> Thus, while a young woman in 1924 might observe hours and minutes according to her wristwatch, frequent the cinema, and feel as if the events of 1914–18 had irrevocably transformed her world, she might also subscribe to forms of temporality ostensibly antithetical to standard time or historical chronology. She might believe in reincarnation, attend seances to communicate with departed loved ones, and profess herself to be a devout follower of spiritualism. Modern time cannot be reduced to a single framework or methodology.[7]

In this example, as with the opening Woolf sequences, differing temporal regimes coexist alongside one another.

Scholars too have asked questions about the nature of Russian and Soviet modernity, and to a lesser degree, about Russian time regimes. At the turn of the century, when this story begins, Russia, of course, was in a tremendous transitionary moment, and especially regarding processes that echo those that took shape in Germany, France and England decades, if not centuries, earlier. Russia, therefore, had a particular place in this debate about the nature or multiplicity of moderns and its temporal position vis-à-vis its European neighbors. Scholars of Russia have questioned the appropriateness of claiming modernity's hold on the Russian imagination, and especially in relationship to categories born in lands to the west, at the end of the old regime. Yet, change was afoot. This was undeniable. Russia at this late nineteenth-century moment experienced tremendous transformation, from countryside to city, from autocracy to tentative civic and political participation, and so on. The social hierarchies were toppling as aristocratic elites were fighting for their way of life as peasants abandoned estates and villagers made their way to the city. And, too, new elites emerged, born and bred through education and money, challenging traditional hierarchies of power and control. The eighteenth- and nineteenth-century way of life felt, no doubt, under siege, as modern concepts flooded the Russian urban landscape. Russia, albeit on its own path, was becoming modern.

Although certainly categories are never transferable wholesale, scholars of Russia and of the Soviet experiment have reached a tentative consensus about the applicability of modern frameworks to the Soviet years. Michael David-Fox describes some of the scholarly trends regarding Russia's place within the grand narrative of modernity's ascendency. David-Fox posits that there are two distinct ways of conceptualizing the Soviet path to modernity: "exceptionalism and commonality."[8] Scholars who embrace the idea of Soviet exceptionalism might emphasize the degree to which the Soviet modernity project was fundamentally unlike anywhere else because its main focus was to confront Russian age-old backwardness, a temporally motivated framing. By contrast, other scholars, including very prominently David Hoffman, emphasize the ways in which the Soviet experience was—in significant ways—on course with the West. David Hoffman,[9] in his cultural history on the heyday of Stalinist values, emphasizes the degree to which the notion of remaking a society at its very core was part and parcel of European modernity and not unique to a revolutionary state. If, indeed, the commonalities thesis holds sway, the issue of continuity in the embrace of modern temporal narratives becomes all the more important. Modern temporal narratives found in Soviet discourses, domestic and civic and otherwise, whether those that emphasize the large-scale epochal change or the smaller-scale modern daily time routines, had resonances both in the fin de siècle and in the postwar moment.

Hoffman does indeed attempt to imagine Russia on the "normal path" with other nations to the west. He highlights, in particular, how he defined modernity in terms of two features common to all modern political systems—"social internationalism and mass politics." This formulation, he assures, is not new: Anthony Giddens, he writes, "identifies a key aspect of modernity as trust in expert systems, which established rational procedures and norms to replace traditional ways." Zygmunt Bauman, likewise, "sees as a fundamental characteristic of modernity the impulse to manage society through the application of bureaucratic procedures and categories."[10] Enlightenment thinkers too contributed to an emphasis on "social interventionism with their belief that society could be reshaped through [...] [the creation of] a rational social order." Yet, as Hoffman instructs, social transformation involved not only "a scientific understanding of society, but also a means to change people's thinking and behavior. It necessitated the inculcation of new cultural norms and values that could make everyday life orderly and productive. Norms of efficiency, hygiene, sobriety, and literacy."[11] There was also an ingrained impulse to refashion traditional values through intervention. This intervention included, to some

extent, as this book will show, the remaking of daily habits and approaches to the
fundamental rhythms of life, including temporal narratives. All of these features,
Hoffman argues, were common to the Soviet experience and experiment.

The question of *when* precisely modernity took hold remains an open one.
Although the era of so-called mass politics, industrialization and urbanization
at the fin de siècle no doubt marked a key moment, scholars of earlier eras
posit an alternative entry point and differing criteria. Turning time backwards
a century or two, there is also scholarship on Russia's so-called leap to the
modern in the eighteenth century. Luba Golburt, in her study of eighteenth-
century Russia, describes the role that eighteenth-century literary culture
played in inspiring new perspectives on modern time. The emergence of
secular literature, Westernization, modernized vernacular culture, including
the spread of universities and the periodical press and so forth, all pointed
to new understandings of Russia's place within Europe as well as the tenor
of Russians' daily lives in the modern world. From this perspective, "the
eighteenth century stands as the originary moment of Russian modernity,
both historically and literarily."[12] She highlights "how the circumstances of
the eighteenth century were transformed from a meaningful present into
a seemingly meaningless past."[13] Time, and eighteenth-century temporal
rhythms, Golburt highlights, were circular in nature. The past played a major
role in conceptualizing and reconceptualizing the present moment. She writes
how the transformation of presents into pasts proceeds neither uniformly nor
linearly. Bits of the past are necessarily forgotten, recalled and often invented
altogether. She explores how subsequent centuries imagined the eighteenth
century in memory as a duality: on the one hand it is modern and central, on
the other hand it is "pronounced dead."[14] Temporality, therefore, is a layered
phenomenon, where past eras layer on top of one another to define and
understand the present moment.

Golburt's analysis is self-consciously about time. She writes about the
transition from the eighteenth-century to the early nineteenth-century
temporal imaginary and explains that many believed that time moved "faster"
once the nineteenth century arrived: "Historical time in the early nineteenth
century appeared to move faster. It was also, compared to the eighteenth
century, radically decentered, as the domain of historical knowledge grew."[15]
These changes correspond to one of the major revolutions in Europe and to
"the rise of historicism and epochal consciousness." Golburt writes that as this
historicist turn became the "dominant interpretive framework," which posited
that the "present no longer was conceived of as repeating the past in a cyclical

pattern," the particulars of the past mattered and were distinct, while the present itself inevitably was "prefigured by" the past.[16]

Golburt also provides a historiographical view on the debates around modernity's rise in Russia. There are two alternative accounts of Russian modernity in the eighteenth century, she contends. First of all, there is the story about how Peter the Great's reforms ushered in the modern moment from above and generally by decree. A second alternative includes an emphasis on the maturing social relations and intellectual culture that "finally seems to take root and gain full legitimacy in Russia" by the early decades of the nineteenth century.[17] The simple positing of alternatives, of course, attests to the contingent nature of modernity itself, its definitions and its meanings. Perhaps too, modernity was born when the past was put on full display in a conscious fashion. In the early twentieth century, there was an impulse to reify the past in hopes of defining the present. The eighteenth century, Golburt explains, came into fashion.[18] The past integrated into the present and in the early twentieth century there appeared the "Historical Art Exhibit of Russian Portraits" organized by the art critic, Diaghilev, and his World of Art Association, which had a particularly prominent place from the eighteenth century. This exhibit also had an emphasis on domestic interiors and the creation of a kind of "authenticity" through the home, one that included both old and new aesthetics. This meant that newly urbanized Russians struggled to embrace a modern present, which seemingly required significant distance from the always-encroaching past of the village.

Early twentieth-century philosophers and their interpreters emphasize these relationships among the past, present and future. Martin Heidegger wrote his famous, albeit somewhat impenetrable, *Being in Time* in 1927, where he engaged the conceptual relationship among past, present and future. As one scholar described Heidegger's ideas on time: "We can only understand the future in contrast to the present [...] and our past [...] each temporal dimension must be understood from another."[19] This, of course, means that the past is never quite past and the present itself is necessarily imbued with echoes from the past and promises for the future. Heidegger, in his masterpiece, presents his readers with a multitude of understandings of time and most centrally with the idea that past, present and future are layered temporal narratives that are necessarily intertwined. For Heidegger, temporality is "neither staccato nor fluvial," rather it has "more connectedness and stretch" than a "staccato of disconnected Nows" might have.[20] Temporal rhythms are not fluid as they are not forward moving; they do not flow from past to present and then to the future. The starting point, instead, is the future, from which everything else flows. Time "comes out of the future, and then it goes into the past and comes around into the present." The past would then "consist of formerly present-at-hand Nows" that have occurred, and the future would consist of soon to be "present-at-hand Nows that will occur."[21] The flow of time is not linear.

Henri Bergson, who wrote on time and memory and famously emphasized "duration" as key to understanding modern temporal rhythms, found fame and a wide audience in his life time at the fin de siècle in Paris. Like many across Europe, young Moscow University students were engaged in a host of ideas at the university in the aftermath of the 1905 revolution, including discussions about time, duration and Bergson. Bergson's ideas appealed, in part, because they resonated with the "deep intuitivism of Russian Orthodoxy."[22] Many turned to him in reaction to Marx and his materialism. Bergson stressed the "limitations of pure, rational thought in apprehending the true nature of reality." The attachment to Bergson was, for some Russians, a neoromantic reaction to nineteenth-century rationalism that best explains the popularity of Bergson's ideas within the context of Russian modernism. Bergson was against mechanistic determinism.[23] "In opposition to the nineteenth-century conception of time as a measurable, quantitative entity, progressing linearly," Bergson conceived of a second kind of time that science could not measure, what he called "real time" or duration. This is the time of one's inner life, always in flux, changing, and therefore impossible to analyze mathematically or scientifically. Bergson defines pure duration as "the form which the succession of our conscious states assumes when our ego lets itself live, when it refrains from separating its present state from its former states [...] both the past and the present states [form] an organic whole, as happens, when we recall the notes of a tune, melting so to speak, into one another." Bergson's theories of time would have seemed familiar to young Russians in the early years of the twentieth century: "On the basis of the Orthodox belief in the intuitive grasp of reality and participation in the divine as accomplished through the veneration of icons, life is seen as organic movement by which one is constantly striving to become closer to the divine [...] the idea of life as movement."[24] Bergson's idea of "duration as 'real time' as opposed to the artificial chronological time of the clock" and his emphasis on the flow of time rather than it being divided into small bits, such as hours and minutes, likely resonated with intellectuals steeped in the writings of nineteenth-century thinkers, from the Slavophile Aleksey Khomyakov to Lev Tolstoy.[25]

In addition to the question of the connectedness of various frames—yesterday, today and tomorrow, and their flow—philosophers of time contemplate how and whether time is best understood as progressive and linear, or rather, made up of a layering of moments into a temporal pastiche. Jose Palti,[26] whose own area of research includes Latin America, wrestles with questions about time, modernity and historical consciousness. He emphasizes how modern time was born out of a clash between these two contradictory notions of historical time: one reflective of modernity (objective) that puts faith in progress and linearity, and the other a reflection of modernism (subjective) that emphasizes perpetual transformation and discontinuity. Either way, what is most essential, Palti tells us, is that "time irreversibility is a key aspect of modern historical time": time can move forward, rupture or layer in a particular moment, but it cannot flow backwards.[27] Within this temporal understanding, a revolution waged, a shop opened or a breakfast eaten can never be undone. And, moreover, each of these actions or events alters the course of the future and becomes part of a temporal landscape that must be understood in a particular contextual frame. Assumptions that seem so commonplace within our own day, however, have a point of origin in the past. This belief in the irreversibility of time and the very modern consciousness of temporality itself was born around the fin de siècle. And yet, this emphasis on irreversibility meant, for many, longing for the place where they could not return, whether a physical location or a childhood memory.

Another way of opening up the study of time is the move from a vocabulary of "time" to one of "temporalities." Methodologically, too, the turn to temporality from time makes possible an understanding of the multitude of ways in which societies have defined and understood time. Theorists of time argue that the term "time" can be used "to refer to universal time, clock time, or objective time," while "temporality" is itself a condition of modernity. "Temporality" is time insofar as it "manifests itself in human existence." The very consciousness of temporal contingency and meanings captures something of the modern spirit.[28] The move from time to temporality unhinges time itself from a concrete, singular definition (much like the move from the study of women to the study of gender per se).

The fin de siècle, when *Modernity, Domesticity and Temporality in Russia* begins, had a particularly pernicious and central role to play in the history of the emergence of modern time, depending upon one's perspective. Some argue that during the 1890s, across much of Europe and in the United States, railroad companies and governments created standard time zones and coordinated ideas about time.[29] Clocks, those mechanized measurements of time passing, themselves detached time from nature and externally imposed a sense of time; "time emerged as an entity disassociated from the natural world [...] [and] from the rhythms of the sun and our bodies."[30] The relationship between past and present became complicated by an insistence on the hegemony of the clock and the calendar as ultimate authorities on authentic time, and the power brokers in understanding the meaning of the now and the speed of transaction, movement and even development of self.[31] Clocks began to order the everyday in more intimate ways. Against the backdrop of these standardization and modernization efforts—industrial drive, urbanization, political liberalization—Palti writes that in its modern concept, historical progress, "unlike in the Christian eschatology, is not the result of a focused supernatural intervention but, essentially and necessarily, a human task (and, in consequence, an infinite and endless one)."[32] In other words, notions of so-called temporal precision and mechanically validated accuracy became paramount as individuals began to rely on the ticking of the clock or the passing of days, weeks, months as measured "objectively" in order to define their daily lives in the now and derive meaning beyond that.[33] By the late nineteenth century, thus, the now, the present, was being understood in increasingly standardized and unified ways. In 1888, for example, Russia set its clocks to unified, if multi-zoned, time.[34] Moreover, at 10:00 a.m. Paris time on July 13, 1913, the Eiffel Tower sent out its very first signal that was transmitted around the world. In unprecedented ways, time was imagined as uniform and created a proximity of space, closing the distance between otherwise distant lands and times.[35] Notions of the present, in other words, were imagined as the culmination of the "simultaneity of distant events"[36] into a near whole. Modern philosophers, artists, editors, and aspiring members of an increasingly urbanized and educated elite imagined that events across space could occur simultaneously.

These notions of simultaneous time included an emphasis on two, often seemingly contradictory, temporal narratives: progressive linearity and multilayered pastiche. As Bergson wrote of flow and duration, there emerged too at the turn of the century a temporal narrative of modernity, which emphasized historical time as progressive, temporally irreversible and linear. While a belief in linearity was not new, per se, its coupling with an emphasis on irreversibility was distinctly modern. Time, while moving along a straight, progressive path to an improved future, could not be reversed. Reinhart Koselleck, a well-known German historian and author of *Futures Past*, discusses both modern temporal orders: linear and pastiche. An embracing of irreversible linear time, he suggests, reflects a late nineteenth-century belief in progress and science and ontological knowability, and arises alongside processes of modernization, such as waves of industrial change, urban migration, and technological innovation and advancement. This emphasis on progress, the march forward, "the endless becoming," to use Palti's phrase,[37] and the perfectibility of the human experience all contribute to the emphasis on progressive linearity in movement. This emphasis on linearity emerges within numerous fields, from the everyday and home life to urbanization and the factory. There was the belief that the structure of history and "the uninterrupted forward movement of clocks, the procession of days, seasons and years, and simple common sense tell us that time is irreversible and moves forward at a steady rate."[38] This had implications for how one went about one's day, whether at home or at work or on the streets.

Linear progress is but one aspect of, and one perspective on, modern temporality. Modern ideas about time, and especially historical time, include nonlinear modes of understanding and modernism's clash of temporalities and the mixing of aesthetics and actions from various eras. In the case of modernism, time was not always, or simply, reliant on a progressive movement forward in a straight line. The very fragmented pastiche, with its mingling, clashing of time frames, marked the modern age and was heightened in the last decade of the nineteenth century and first decades of the twentieth century. In this respect, modern nonlinear time "is less of a retrospective notion because it has risen from the present, which is opening out toward the future." The future "is thought to be open and without boundaries."[39] And yet, as we know from nostalgic portraits, modern temporal orders also incorporate the past. Thus, the modern concept of temporal progress found its antithesis in artists and writers who embraced the concept of the "heterogeneity of time." This emphasis on the fluidity of eras and the layering of time was essential to the modernist impulse. In the years immediately preceding the First World War, sociologists, anthropologists, psychologists, psychiatrists and physicists, to name but a few, found themselves embracing new ideas about time and its relativity. Durkheim and others, for example, played with the idea that concepts of time are "closely connected with social organization" and explored the relative meaning of time across cultures.[40] Time was imagined as a "flux" or a "stream," and not the "sum of discrete units."[41] This metaphor of fluidity includes the overlapping of time, as past, present and future all merge. In these works of art, characters' thoughts about past and future merged along with "current perceptions" to create a modern sense of time.[42] Such layered notions of time inspired many artists and writers in the modernist movements across Europe. Modernist fin de siècle thinkers, who traded in disparate fields of knowledge, challenged ideas about the teleological and unidirectional movement of time, and instead emphasized time that relied on reversals, movements in "irregular rhythms" or moments when time "came to a dead stop."[43]

Theorists began to posit how time, and especially present time, manifested through space. Precisely at this moment across Europe, as historian of European temporality, Stephen Kern, writes: "And so with time: we cannot consider movement a sum of stoppages nor time a sum of temporal atoms without distorting their essentially fluid nature."[44] It was precisely this fluidity that caused the sense of constant alarm and fear. The very idea that time is measured through duration and is malleable and can be stretched or saved or repurposed led to the emphasis on the always proximate past, spilling over, stretching into today. This time/space nexus included the ideas of scientists such as Albert Einstein. Einstein understood that time "is not independent of, but is influenced by the site of its measurement, and that site is always relevant to other sites." Einstein believed that "there is no objective time"; it must be measured by its position and its place.[45] Simultaneity, like the idea of duration, emerged as a prominent concept among philosophers of temporality and spatiality: simultaneity relied on the intermingling of time and space, as it reflected the modern emphasis on temporal uniformity and the standardization of time across space. To combat the fluid, encroaching past, thus, moderns tried to ward off the particular dangers that it posed and to keep it free from the present moment, whether dirt, chaos or inefficiency. The home was one place where some believed time narratives could be controlled. It was itself one space where this was particularly important and where this seemed possible. Efficient and hygienic practices of cleanliness in the home were meant to combat the shadow of the past and its expandable duration.

At the fin de siècle there was no turning back. And yet, many Russians glanced backwards, if only as a means to grapple with the present. This is the context in which nostalgia found its way into the pages of magazines and memoirs written in the last years of the Russian tsarist regime, a time of rapid industrial growth, urban migration and tentative political transformation. Expressions of nostalgia for an imagined past mixed with a rapidly changing environment, where peasants became landlords and intelligentsia families fled. As a phenomenon of the late nineteenth and early twentieth centuries, nostalgia exposes not the past but rather a fractured and modern present. In other words, despite the glancing backwards, the portraits of gentry estates created in the self-writings and journals of this era are both reflective and constitutive of Russians' modern notions of time and space, and "coeval with modernity itself."[46] Nostalgia, as a sentiment, requires a sense of historicity, an investment in the movement of time and the flow of human activity and its environment. In the case of late tsarist Russia, nostalgia inspired writers to show their readers how time embodies space, and especially domestic space. This monograph explores these dynamics over the course of the first several decades of the twentieth century. While the scholarship is nascent, there have been a handful of histories that have put time and temporal narratives at the center of inquiry. These are instructive for understanding the dynamics within the Russian-turned-Soviet case.

Nostalgia is one way in which temporal narratives are layered (then, now and later) and where time and space meet. Nostalgia is a longing or desire for the past, often manifest through place or space (to be nostalgic for somewhere). But nostalgia is also the "flip side" of modernity and therefore part and parcel of it. Svetlana Boym in her monograph *The Future of Nostalgia* presents two distinct understandings of nostalgia. Each of which, she contends, has a place in history and draws together temporal and spatial narratives: restorative nostalgia and reflective nostalgia. Restorative nostalgia stresses nostos and attempts a transhistorical reconstruction of the lost home. It thinks of itself not as nostalgia per se, but as "truth and tradition." Restorative nostalgia proports to "protect the absolute truth" and is at the core of recent nationalist reimaginings. Reflective nostalgia, on the other hand, thrives in algia, the longing itself, and delays the homecoming—"wistfully, ironically, desperately." It "dwells on the ambivalences of human longing and belonging and does not shy away from the contradictions of modernity." It is, in essence, "social memory."[47] In her depictions of nostalgia, Svetlana Boym describes Walter Benjamin's travels to Moscow in the late 1920s and what he found vis-á-vis notions of nostalgia and modernity. In his descriptions of the "incongruent collage of Moscow (in the 1926–27)," Benjamin thought of the past, present and future "as superimposing times, reminiscent of contemporary photographic experiments." Boym highlights how, for Benjamin, "every epoch dreams the next one and in doing so revives the one before it." The present "awakens from the dreams of the past but remains 'swollen' by them." Boym describes how "swelling, awakening, constellation" are each Benjaminian images of the interrelated times. Benjamin, like Nietzsche and other modern nostalgics, rebelled against "the idea of the irreversibility of time," only instead of the "Nietzschean wave of eternal return," he promised "waves of crystalized experience."[48] Boym, thus, like Benjamin, posits modernity not as a teleological march toward progress or transience, but rather as a matter of "superimposition and coexistence of heterogeneous times."[49] How, though, can such abstractions be delineated in particular contexts? Historians and scholars of other disciplines have used temporality as a way to understand and explore certain historical and contemporary problems. They have taken the temporal turn.

Historians on Russian time

The very meaning of modern time, how individuals and cultures approach the seconds, minutes and hours in their daily lives or dream about their pasts, is not an easy subject for historical study or any study, for that matter, in general or in particular. In the recent volume of *Past and Present*,[50] mentioned above, there appears a discussion of temporalities and its newest scholarship. These authors in *Past and Present* contend that much of the commonplace insistence on the singular power of the clock—within the context of the modern turn of the century and beyond—to instill a somewhat uniform sense of authentic time, does not provide a complete picture. These authors contend that the work of scholars such as Reinhart Koselleck had it wrong and created difficulties for those who wished to focus on a particular geographical place at a specified moment. The scholars represented in this volume insist on de-emphasizing the notion of "rupture" between past and present, and reaffirming their distance from what they consider a presentist impulse. They insist that there should be no "litmus test of teleological progress."[51]

Conceptions of time, this group of global scholars agree, are intertwined with points on a map of history, of periodization and of some sense of temporal movement in a linear narrative, which inevitably divides periods among "modern" and "pre-modern" and perhaps "post-modern." How a society approaches the meanings and measures of time reflects, to some extent, its understanding of the modern. And yet, the very notion of modernity is neither singular nor uniform but rather multiple and layered. And so modern time is not necessarily and always a matter of a singular approach to mechanization or accuracy or any one thing. We cannot assume that "standardization" or the "uniformity of time" is *the* marker of modernity.[52] The authors in this 2019 *Past and Present* issue are all intent on debunking the idea that precision and by extension "accuracy" is intrinsically modern. They contend that Koselleck had it wrong. People living in early modern times cared about time and temporality. Moreover, modern time itself is heterogenous (as are all temporal frames). We should not "fetishize" accuracy and its relationship to mechanization and technology. Accuracy is neither the only marker of the modern nor is it absent from the earlier centuries. And, too, the Western European experience of modern time (including mechanization and the fetishization of accuracy) was not the experience of all nations in the "modern era"; there was not just one way to be modern. Rather, there were multiple modernities and multiple temporalities, each of which existed simultaneous to one another. For instance, David Gange in "Time Space and Islands: Why Geographers Drive the Temporal Agenda" reminds us how time played out in unexpected ways in places such as Egypt or Lebanon or India: "They demonstrate how the apparently hegemonic technologies of modern time, from the time zone to the telephone, were reimagined, reformulated or rejected by the diverse communities they had supposedly been 'imposed' on." There was no single standard.[53] In other words, there is no singular "modern moment" to reify. Modernity, thus, can be imagined "as pleated or crumpled time, drawing together past, present and future into constant and unexpected ways." This very idea of "pleated or crumpled time" and its relationship to "temporal multiplicity" or "pluritemporalities" allows historians to focus on a multitude of eras and ways of becoming and being modern.[54]

Scholars tend to agree that the parsing of the meanings of time and time measurement has always been far from straightforward. Penelope J. Cornfield in her history entitled *Time and the Shape of History* insists that time refers to both "the long duration and to continuously unfolding change within that duration." This combination, a "uniquely dynamic process," embraced "immense reaches of the past, the immediate here and now of the fleeting present and the potentially vast expanses of the future."[55] Yet how does the historian study time? The study of temporalities is always bound up in the moment of historical analysis, as with any history.[56] Many historians have put time and the historicizing of the meanings of time at the center of their studies for a variety of reasons, as a way to understand the rhythms of daily life, as a measure of modernity and simply in order to understand the ways in which a nation imagines itself.

Peter Fritzsche, historian of modern Europe, put temporality at the center of his scholarship and asked questions that revolve around the relationship between temporal narratives and revolutionary ones. How, he asks, do perceptions of time change in the "modern era"? An era that he demarcates as beginning with the French Revolution, industrialization and an emphasis on the nation as the main source of group and individual identities. Peter Fritzsche, one of the most prominent scholars on European nostalgia, circles around the French Revolution as the pivotal event in "the West" ushering in modernity and with it a new sense of time. Fritzsche introduces the idea of nostalgic sentiment within the context of political and social upheaval when the perception of "the restless iteration of the new" took over so that "the past no longer served as a faithful guide to the future." The past became an object of curiosity, unpredictable and strange; both contingent and unrepeatable.[57] In the French context (and also in the American) the revolution encouraged individuals to think anew of their own lives and destinies in a "historical fashion." The experience of revolution "conjured up fantastic stories about national origins and tall tales of lost childhood, along with a passion for things in the past."[58] There emerged a sensation of longing for life before the revolutionary upheaval simultaneous with the knowledge that the future was uncertain but the past could not truly be recaptured. Fritzsche describes how by the early nineteenth century in France and elsewhere in "the West," "history would be contemplated from the standpoint of epistemological uncertainty [...] [and] an increasingly strange past came into view and became an object of both public and private lives." The past became "an historical artifact" and was recreated in the present through nostalgic longings expressed in writings, whether diaries, autobiographies or journals, to name a few. For Fritzsche, it is the Revolution itself that changed temporal thinking: "Enlightenment thinkers conceived of the present as the most forward point of a great continuum of progress pushed on and on, after the French Revolution observers were more apt to think of the present as a point of transition, one which moved away from the past."[59] Modernity, he writes "is not simply determined by the imperatives of the present, but also sustains the desire to explore a strange and remote past."[60] This post-revolutionary past, part and parcel of the modern imaginary, he argues, "conjures up fantastic stories about national origins and tall tales of lost childhood, along with a passionate longing for the past." It is the very discovery of history (whether war, revolution or industrialization) that was newly developed around 1800. The French Revolution made the past remote and created a sense of melancholy.[61] This profound notion of loss was a conceit of modernity, namely that "history is the relentless iteration of the new"[62] and that we all must mourn the loss of yesterday. It is worth noting that much of the same can be said of the Russian Revolution as of the French. In February 1918, Vladimir Lenin declared that the Julian calendar was no longer the standard bearer, and the Gregorian calendar became the new norm (although the decree required that the Julian date was to be written in parentheses after the Gregorian one for the first several months of the new day). This combination of a "new time," a changed calendar, as Chapter 4 will demonstrate, and the strengthening of a nostalgic impulse, which Chapters 2 through 4 comment upon, were as true in Russia as they were in France.

Other histories focus less on a formative moment per se in the making of modern time, instead they provide a broad sweep of the temporal story. Vanessa Ogle in her scholarship on world time describes the impact of standard mean time on all corners of the world. She emphasizes that there was an attempt to make time more standardized and uniform from the 1870s to the 1940s around the globe. She explores the question of geographically where the center of temporal gravity resides, which begs the questions: where does the center of time reside, where is the temporal force of gravity and what does *uniform* mean? Ogle also points out how the emphasis on standardized mean time impacted the many manifestations of time: clock time, calendar time and social time. Ultimately, it meant standardization and the loss of more flexible social time.[63] Once time was imagined uniform and could be somehow objectively measured, its meanings and uses transformed and became much more rigid.

Similarly, in his monograph the *History of the Hour*, Gerhard Dehrn van Rossun, describes how definitions of time transformed over the longue durée. His starting point is the dramatic transformation from measuring time through "movements of the sky" in the late Middle Ages as "an absolute frame of reference" to the epoch of mechanized time, when the clock became a prerequisite for the "handling of everyday time." He insists that the clock became "the symbol of the process of European modernization."[64] By the fifteenth century "the use of everyday time and the possession and use of clocks" were considered indicative of modernity.[65] Dehrn van Rossun posits that the clock marked a transition from "pre-industrial" to "industrial" time, a demarcation that is contested by others who insist on the late nineteenth century as the major point of transition. Part of the argument is that the "factory of the nineteenth century adapted practical and symbolic elements of the time organization of the late medieval city, with the difference that clock time, in the minds of the affected, had become largely alienated time dominated by the powerful."[66] The clock, this book argues, had a significant amount of power. This seems to be a common theme in the historiography, the power of technology and the clock in regularizing routines and behaviors. Although, context matters.

Temporal norms reflect hierarchies of power and class and culture. Michael Manchard explores time and the racial and colonial order of things in his article "Afro-Modernity: Temporality, Politics and the African Diaspora."[67] The past in diasporic narratives, he explains, is erased in order to put society on the path of modernity and progress. In order to move forward, the past must be captured and recast for colonial purposes and to keep the hierarchies intact. What Manchard coins as "racial time" is linked to hierarchies and ultimately subordination and "backwardness" within colonial hierarchies. Power and violence too were intrinsic to the use of mechanized time in particular contexts. The political, social and economic powers of the clock were also implicated in the institution of slavery. In the award-winning monograph, *Mastered By the Clock: Time, Slavery and Freedom in the American South*, Mark Smith shows how, when and why clock time came to the American South in the context of slavery and the early nineteenth century. This moment, he contends, emerged as the "birth of time discipline and clock-regulated work," which were always imagined "intimately tied up with the emergence of capitalism," and in this case overt violence.[68] His book depicts how in this transition era, and in general, differing ideas of time coexisted, from natural time to mechanical time, or conceived of differently, natural time (task orientation) versus time discipline (clock time). Smith argues how slave masters attempted to discipline their slaves using the clock; although ultimately, Smith highlights, time obedience transcended external mechanisms from the outside and became more akin to internalized industrial time discipline (slaves had no time pieces of their own). This notion of internalized time resonates with revolutionary impulses to internalize efficiency and speed.[69]

Speed, or time and space compression, emerges as a key temporal trope, both in terms of the literal speed with which one accomplishes an individual task and as it relates to the development of nations. Backwardness is a way of conceiving of the "development" of nations that is very familiar to historians of Russia, the Soviet Union and socialist countries of the East. Maria Todorova, in her article "The Trap of Backwardness: Modernity, Temporality and the Study of Eastern European Nationalism,"[70] articulates precisely this temporal dynamic. She contends that the notion of temporal lag is ubiquitous, especially in the context of linear, progressive temporal frames. It is how nationalism is understood. "Visions of the future are predicated on this sense of belated arrival."[71] Russian and Soviet scholars, and indeed historical actors in the nineteenth century themselves, confronted narratives of backwardness and the lagging development vis-á-vis a mythical "West" for decades, if not centuries.

While the scholarship is sporadic, there are several studies explicitly on Russian and Soviet revolutionary time and more still that rely centrally on long-standing historiographic tropes of Russian backwardness vis-á-vis the West that presumed linear historical progression over time. Russian and Soviet time, thus, while deeply embedded in cultural reference frames—from the speed of the industrial drive at the fin de siècle to the perpetual problem of slowly lagging behind the West—have long been embedded in the grand narratives of Russian and Soviet History. The reasons for this so-called lag have included its challenging geography, its majority peasant population, its Russian Orthodoxy, the longevity of serfdom and its tenacious commitment to monarchy. In the eyes of some scholars and Russians themselves, these qualities have meant that Russia is not only seen as other to the West but also *behind* in the arc of European progress and forward movement.[72] Many scholars have addressed the question of "the peasant problem" and how even when rural people moved to the cites to find work in factories and elsewhere at the turn of the century, they remained, at least partly, backwards peasants. This process was, thus, unlike the urbanization that took place to the west. Peasants who made it to the big city to work at the end of the nineteenth century, but who did not share the "vision" or "agenda" of the existing workers, were labeled "backward."[73] The idea of Russia as a backward nation or as a nation on a different temporal development trajectory than those to the west, held sway among the revolutionary ideologues themselves, including Lenin, Trotsky and Bukharin. Historians and historical actors imagined Russia and then the Soviet Union in a perpetual game of "catch up."[74] Stephen Marks writes that "Tsar Nicholas II had to contend with a society that was changing so fast he could not keep pace. Russia was a rural impoverished nation undergoing industrialization and urbanization at the same time that its political system remained rigidly autocratic. The tsar and his court were reactionary and unimaginative."[75] Thus, backwards. The tropes of Russian backwardness and attempts to "catch up" have long been part and parcel of both scholarly discussions and national self-definition.

Another window into the study of time at the fin de siècle, in particular, is material culture and ruins, and how elite Russians in the early twentieth century understood their present through collecting material objects from the past.[76] Andres Schönle describes the role that ruins played in Russians' understanding of their past. Ruins, he writes, evoke "layers of the past" without a pretense to represent any one in particular. "Modernity fabricates ruins in order to dramatize its difference from the past. Ruins can function as signatures of historical breaks, but such breaks paradoxically rest on the continuous presence of the past within the present."[77] Ruins "articulate overlapping temporalities" and resonate too with nostalgic impulses: "As residues of the past that have been rejected or are by-products of economic progress, ruins can become the site of a critique of the ideology of progress, of the ever-more stringent, forward movement of history."[78] The romance with the gentry estate described in Chapter 3 of this book echoes this engagement with the past and its layers of history manifested through elite domestic spaces.[79]

Mark Steinberg, in his many works on the cultural and social world of the fin de siècle, highlights in particular the proletarian imaginary and ultimately its relationship to temporal narratives.[80] "Modernity," Steinberg writes, was always "an elusive category," which included a kind of ambiguity. "Only in part can modernity be defined by the processes and values of rationalistic and scientific modernization." Steinberg continues to describe how postmodernists moved beyond this kind of dichotomy and "recognize[d] multiple worlds of modernity" and thus temporality: "the pervasiveness of disjuncture and difference [...] [including] the varied rhythms of time, in which hybrid temporalities are marked not only by acceleration, newness, and innovation but also by continuity, repetition, and revival; and the variety of modernities over time and space." This encompassed "a new experience of time that simultaneously included faith in rapid progress, nostalgia and an intensified vision of a coming end time." Steinberg here alludes to the narrative of Russian backwardness vis-à-vis temporality. Russians, he explains, had a particular relationship to modern time: they "shared deeply in these European experiences and visions of modernity, which were intensified by Russia's notorious and often obsessively self-aware 'backwardness'; by its lateness to embrace and experience industrialization, urbanization, and the contradictory drives of modern discipline and disorder."[81] Steinberg, thus, provides room for Russia's differing path and its modern trajectory simultaneously.

There is also an emerging scholarship on time in the Soviet context, including the work of Steinberg on utopia. In a series of three articles on the utopian writings of Alexandra Kollontai, Leon Trotsky and Vladimir Mayakovsky, Steinberg argues that their ideas were aligned with many in the Frankfurt School, such as Walter Benjamin, who believed that utopia was not a pipedream but rather "a view of human desire for a radically different world not as an illusory wish but as a deep facet of human experience and consciousness."[82] The emphasis, too, was on temporality per se. Utopia, Steinberg argues, "is this open disruption of the now, for the sake of possibility, not a closed map of the future. It is the leap not yet the landing."[83] In this view, utopia, at the heart of revolutionary Russian thinking, brought an unknown, but full of possibility, future into the present moment.

Another aspect of temporality that was intrinsic to the modern Russian revolutionary moment was speed, or time-space compression. This emphasis on speed could be attributed to not only the process of industrialization and its accompanying mechanization and efficiency, but also to the desire among the Soviet planners to "catch up" with the West, if often using German, American and other know-how at breakneck speed. In his book entitled *Fast Forward: The Aesthetics and Ideology of Speed in Russian Avant-Garde Culture, 1910–1930*, Tim Harte engages with aesthetics and ideology across the revolutionary divide, quoting Filippo Marinetti, the force behind Italian Futurism: "We affirm [...] that the world's magnificence has been enriched by a new beauty: the beauty of speed."[84] As Harte contends, speed, "while an invigorating force in the West, came as more of a shock to early twentieth-century Russia."[85] Speed, of course, as Harte insists, is always part and parcel of temporal definition. The "cognition of speed [...] stems largely from our understanding of time, for only a clock can establish the rate of any given motion through space [...] time is conceivable only as long as bodies or objects move through space."[86] Speed, in this context, meant a fast-paced life and an emphasis on the industrial over the rural, and mechanization in art (cinema) as well as everyday life.

On a more macro-level, in his study of ideology and revolutionary time, *Time & Revolution: Marxism and the Design of Soviet Institutions*, Stephen E. Hanson opens with a discussion of Marx's vision of time. These ideas are worth briefly rehearsing here. Hansen explains that Marx, Lenin and Stalin each rejected, on the one hand, the Western capitalist notion of "time as an abstract, linear grid outside all concrete events [...] which is culturally internalized in the capitalist West." And they also rejected the "purely 'charismatic' conception of time as a force that can transcended through revolutionary will," which is often embraced by anarchists, on the other. They settled instead, Hansen writes, on a notion of time that was based on Marx's "principle that effective revolutionary praxis depends upon utilizing rational time discipline to master time itself."[87] In a sense, this revolutionary notion combined "charismatic and rational time conceptions."[88] And, in the Soviet context, as this story of time and home will show, time discipline itself was meant to be internalized.[89] The factory clock and then other forms of external time keeping, themselves, were increasingly obsolete.

Time, in a revolutionary context, as Hansen suggests, challenges the standard so-called "Western" definition. While there are obvious similarities with notions of efficiency and speed across the revolutionary divide, the ways in which time discipline is to be internalized and collectivized reflects a particular Soviet ideal. And yet, the two concepts of duration and simultaneity held currency in Russia, as they did throughout Europe. Readers and writers imagined time frames malleable and fluid and they feared that the past might bleed into the present, and the present into the future. The threat of intrusion loomed large. The stretch of a moment or duration of a period of seconds, minutes or hours potentially included the residue of the moments that came before, always threatening to flow into the now. It was precisely this malleability that was feared and aimed at undoing: the past could flow into the present.

The spaces of everyday life, the home, served as the stage upon which uniformity and the "now" was created and the past defeated. New tools, whether a potato press or a flour mill, and products of various types helped to make uniform and mechanize the keeping of the apartment and the measuring of time in the home in Russia of the first decades of the twentieth century.

Time inside the home

This book, *Modernity, Domesticity and Temporality in Russia: Time at Home*, explores the nexus of the temporal and the spatial, looking at precisely how temporal narratives were refracted through the home and how these narratives interacted with an ideology of domesticity in these first decades of the twentieth century, framing the revolution. Like temporality, narratives of home and the domestic were animated by concerns regarding Russia's path vis-à-vis an arguably mythical, albeit powerful, "West." In the case of home, it was the modern bourgeois ideal, including ideologies such as the "angel in the house" and the "cult of true womanhood," that haunted tastemakers and aspiring city-dwellers. Historians have long asked themselves the question about whether or how a bourgeois aesthetic or ideology ever penetrated the Russian landscape by the end of the nineteenth and start of the twentieth centuries. Was there, in other words, even without a full-blown capitalist consumer culture, a pattern of so-called middle-class domesticity that the Bolsheviks had to conquer (in theory) in the early years of revolution?[90] How could there have been an overturning of bourgeois, traditional norms with the revolution or the reemergence of bourgeois norms in the 1930s if those norms never made their way onto Russian soil? These are questions that are quite central both to a gender historiography and to scholars' broader understandings of the place of Russian society within European and global frames. Some answers have begun to emerge. I will only touch the surface here.

Some decades ago, historians had begun to comment on how an ideology of domesticity, which emphasized close-knit affective domestic relations, prevalent in Western Europe, had made its way into Russian family life by the second quarter of the nineteenth century.[91] This scholarship offers a direct challenge to historical arguments that hinge on the notion that there were necessarily contentious relations between generations—whether mothers and daughters or Turgenev's fathers and sons—which tore the family apart and undermined its centrality in the moral upbringing of future generations.[92] And, some might suggest, set the stage for revolution. These are, by now, known and contested narratives.

The scholarship on the domestic interior and its ideologies per se in the nineteenth and early twentieth centuries remains relatively sparse. From research on individual gentry families to gentry correspondence and its reflection of emotional domestic attachments,[93] to my work on student masculinity in the early nineteenth century,[94] and David Ransel's study of close filial ties, and "companionate marriages" in the nineteenth century, work on the nineteenth-century home is quite rare, but exists.[95] Despite Russia's differing social and economic circumstances from France or England—including the absence (or "incompleteness") of factors long associated with the rise of a gendered bourgeois self, such as a middle-class and a full-blown industrial revolution—this scholarship contends that ideologies of domestic affection appeared on the Russian landscape among participants in official life and educated society in the early decades of the nineteenth century. Women, according to this logic, belonged to the domestic sphere where peace and tranquility reigned, at least in principle, if not in reality. This continued to be true, to an increased degree, as the century waned.

Barbara Engel, in her monograph on wife abuse at the turn of the century, *Breaking the Ties That Bind*, argues that there emerged a new fin de siècle notion of the ideal domesticity, which centrally included the *khoziaka* in creating tranquil and efficient domestic interiors, and all that entailed. Engel asserts that there appeared a new expectation of gentility within marriage, with modern roles imagined for both husband and wife among the middling and merchant classes. This "cult of domesticity" contributed, to some degree, in the Russian context, to "elevating the domestic sphere and the role of the wife and mother."[96] Engel highlights how, echoing Catriona Kelly's masterful work on prescriptive texts, there was a flourishing of domestic discourses in post-reform Russia.[97] Engel finds, though, in the early twentieth century, despite the fact that the idea of domesticity manifested in a proliferation of prescriptive texts, the role of the *khoziaka* was not imagined as a "measure of virtue" for middle-class Russian women, as it might have been for women living in nations to the west, but the role did matter in practical and emotive terms, and the home was central to the lives of the emerging middle classes in Russian cities.[98]

It is the home itself that is of concern here. Catriona Kelly in her monograph on prescriptive texts affirms the increasing importance of the domestic spaces for the self-definition of the post-reform, nineteenth-century aspiring new-monied classes. While no one, she explains, would have wanted to be associated with the *poshlost* or crassness of the middling classes, there were many newly wealthy urbanites eager to learn the ways of polite society. The "well healed but brutish *meshchanin*" was found in the city, and he desired a well-ordered and respectable home. He was in great need of education in the principles of gentility as he lacked the education and refinement of those who came before him. Despite these deficiencies, he had access to resources and capital, and he was eager to be "educated" to behave in respectable ways at home and on the street.

His home, like the homes of many of the middling classes across Europe, in theory, was supposed to be orderly, efficient and reflect modern values of decency so characteristic of the day.[99] As Kelly describes, along with this desire for refinement came a new literature on the proper way to set up domestic spaces and conduct oneself at home. Chapter 2 of *Modernity, Domesticity and Temporality in Russia* outlines in great detail how these prescriptions manifested at home and in temporal terms. Kelly highlights Mariia Redelin's *The House and Housekeeping: A Guide to Rationale House Management* (1900), which was among the most popular—if aspirational for most—of the age. Redelin recognized the familiar notion of "separate spheres" where domestic duties were to be handled by the women of the house. As this popular prescriptive text insisted: "If the master of the house is successful in his intellectual work, then this is usually because of the quiet and unnoticeable contribution of his wife, the manager of the household, since it is her sphere, the household, which creates the right mood for his work, giving him spiritual and intellectual energy."[100] The well-healed and/or aspiring urbanites at the end of the nineteenth and turn of the twentieth centuries hung on to notions of domestic peace that shared gendered roles and hierarchies with their neighbors in bourgeois Europe. And with this came an insistence on temporal efficacy and cleanliness, which relied on hygienic modern scientific domestic practices. And thus peace reigned.

What is clear from the scholarship, which cannot be fully fleshed out here, is simply that these ideas about the home, like time itself, were in flux in Russia at the turn of the century and echoed many of the values of the middling-class home across Europe and beyond. Not only were many people actually moving into new homes as rural life gave way to urban living, they were also influenced by new domestic ideologies and expectations. These domestic ideologies often migrated east from Europe and transformed when grown in Russian soil, both in bourgeois and revolutionary utopian iterations. Long imagined by scholars to be absent in tsarist Russia, bourgeois domestic aesthetics did emerge in Russia at the end of the old regime, if never perfectly parallel to domesticity in other parts of Europe. Domestic interiors, as represented in portraits and prescriptions, contained nostalgic desires for a time long past, even as some urbanites embraced the hygienic norms of the present. Moreover, during the years of the First World War, the present itself was transforming at a rapid pace as soldiers went off to fight and the home itself became inundated with war imagery and realities. Once the old regime fell and Russian participation in the war ended, Russians looked to the future for a new revolutionary domesticity, which never completely shed its bourgeois—or even gentry—past.

Historians of the early Soviet period have explored questions about home and hearth in the early revolutionary era as well, and some have questioned the degree to which the revolution itself changed anything in this regard. The debate over the question of domestic roles and the meaning of womanhood in the early Soviet period, both in terms of ideology and practice and the interstices between, is heated and ongoing, and there is little need (or opportunity) to rehearse it all here. The most poignant aspects of this historiography in this context relate to whether or how official gendered Soviet discourses propagated traditionally oriented gendered norms replete with a sense of bourgeois refinement, whether in individual or collective contexts. And also whether and how the Soviet ideas both ideologically and practically created a real sense of gendered equality of domestic duties. The consensus, and it is articulated in the work of Susan Reid among others, appears to be a resounding "no." It was always women both immediately before and after the revolution who were primarily responsible for tending to the domestic interior, whether the form was individual and filial or collective and social. The Soviets, in other words, did attempt a sense of collectivity in the home, but it remained deeply gendered with women in charge. This is not to say the revolution brought no change at home. The creation of collective living spaces, even if tinged with the residue of bourgeois gendered habits and hierarchies, reflected revolutionary ideology. Scholars have highlighted how Soviet ideology-makers attempted to transform the nuclear family in order to make room for the state's role in domestic caregiving. Early Soviet ideology emphasized the collective and communal ideals of the everyday, including living arrangements. Domestic interiors were to be constructed as spaces both revolutionary in their communalism and efficient in their modernity. Ultimately, the communal impulse and time regimes were to be internalized by those living there.

Desires for past, present and future were all manifest within the domestic interior, both before and after the revolutionary period. The more intimate, private aspects of modern historical time flourished at the fin de siècle within gentry estates, urban apartments and communal arrangements, as writers and readers struggled to define themselves in new ways and through new modes of temporality, at once embracing of the past and imagining the future. Taking the reader from the proliferation of urban apartments through the nostalgic longings for the waning gentry estate to the utopian visions of communal living, this book traces the intersections of modern time awareness and domestic ideology over about three decades at the start of the twentieth century.

Svetlana Alexievich's entertaining writing based on a series of oral histories, *Secondhand Time: The Last of the Soviets*, sets out to capture the history of the "domestic" or "interior" aspects of socialism, and she explains that those are best captured by looking into a "person's soul," which, she explains, constitutes "a miniature expanse: one person, the individual. It's where everything really happens."[101] As the following chapter on the present time of 1900 and the growth of the urban apartment ideal will show, no matter how determined tastemakers and members of the aspiring middle and working classes were to create spaces of domestic cleanliness and efficiency, the past always loomed large.

2

Present Time, Hygiene and the Urban Apartment

In a 1908 issue of the women's magazine *Zhenshchina*, or *Woman*, there appeared an article celebrating a new domestic interior style. The middle-class readers were meant to emulate the modern, "New Style" of interior design and architecture as a strategy for living in the modern everyday.[1]

> The whole world is moving ahead, everything is changing: we leave behind old habits and ways of doing things and usher in the new. A million ways of living are dying and in their place rises a new generation of ideas and beliefs [...] old ideas and former orders give way to new ideas and orders [...]. This is how we move forward.[2]

This modern aesthetic touted by the editors relied upon an awareness of history and an embrace of historical time.[3] Markers of the present could be found everywhere, from the mundane to the extraordinary. Time, whether past or present, was embedded in—and embodied by—household objects themselves: knickknacks peppering the shelves of kitchens; chairs and sofas spread across the living rooms; and the pillows laying in the sleeping quarters. Readers and writers of popular women's magazines possessed a time consciousness that marked the modern age.[4] Russians were trying to come to terms with a present that seemed to be speeding ahead at an unknown pace, ushering in a modern era full of both hope for health and progress and despair about the accompanying filth and squalor, contradictions so familiar in industrializing times. The celebration of speed, of the railroads, embedded in the value of efficiency and scientific invention, proved integral to these modern conceptions. The very idea of speed invokes a sense of time-space compression as well as efficiency of action. On the brink of the First World War, as technological advances crept into everyday life among urban Russians, from household technologies to railroads, Vladimir Mayakovsky gave a lecture on the power of speed. He wrote:

Telephones, airplanes, express trains, elevators, rotary presses, sidewalks, factory smokestacks, stone monstrosities, soot and smoke—these are the elements of beauty in the new urban environment [...] most significantly the rhythm of life has changed. Everything now has become lightning quick, rapidly flowing like on a film strip.[5]

This love affair with speed and with its adjunct embrace of time-space compression, represented by the shrinking distances between places, was celebrated not only by the mainstream press but also by the pan-European avant-garde, including the futurists themselves, who embraced "the beauty of speed."[6] Speedy efficiency marked aspirations found in the public spaces of street and factory as well as in the domestic interior. The home, its interior rooms and corridors—whether real or imagined—reflected the promises and the fears of the now, of the present moment in a modern age invested in time saving, efficiency and speed. Women, in particular, who were the ones to look after home and hearth, regardless of their factory jobs or other labors, read about, dreamt of and ultimately attempted to organize their lives according to the principles of the everyday. As women became increasingly educated and opportunities opened up for the middle classes to work in new fields and take courses at university, the home remained a space over which women were responsible and had some control; there was no radical restructuring of the gender order in this sense. The fin de siècle, thus, offered more opportunities for professional women and continued to see women tied to the home. This modern present, in a variety of ways, contained seeds of the past and hopes for the future.

Damskii mir, or *Ladies World*, offered its readership, including the elite and aspiring members of the middle classes, advice about how to cope with the demands of creating a domestic interior in the early decades of the twentieth century. Even this elite publication, which began as a "deluxe fashion magazine" and morphed into something serving a wider educated public mostly of society women, had to contend with the dirt and grime of industrial production. Publicist Countess Alexandra Zakharovna Muravieva appealed to her readers to attend to the cleanliness of their domestic spaces, which meant warding off the past and its now unmodern aesthetics.[7] Readers, in their daily lives, were confronted by the residue of the past while simultaneously confronting the troubles of the industrializing present. "In our times, impediments exist everywhere: [from] the congestion of housing and the [related] [...] limited nature of space." What "remains of the past," the article explicated, "are carpets that provide coziness in any room."[8] But what the reader quickly learned was that this coziness itself comes at a price too great: dirt and waste of time. Readers were advised that the old-style chairs collect dust and elegant furniture can be difficult—and time consuming—to clean. In the present, in "our times," as writers frequently expressed, interior arrangements, and domestic aesthetics, were meant to embrace modern-day, scientific standards of efficiency and cleanliness. An efficient and hygienic apartment promised participation in the life of the modern city, both by serving as a refuge from the filth of the city and celebrating modern values of cleanliness, health and "saving time." Russian urbanites, whether those huddled in squalor or the readers of *Damskii mir,* at the fin de siècle lived at a time of increased attention to mechanical time, to uniformity and to science. They understood themselves as "modern" through their attempts to distance themselves from the past, imagined in the form of a rural, unhygienic and undisciplined daily life. Among these strategies was the desire for efficiency and health, both contingent on a temporal consciousness that prioritized longevity and creating time for leisure, however modest, and exploring of the city and all that it had to offer.

There are many ways to see and to live in a time-conscious age. Within the domestic realm, a modern temporal frame could be detected in objects and in gestures. This "New Style" could be found in the most mundane of objects, whether "dishes, furniture, [or] the trifles of home life."[9] Even though for most residents of the capitals in fin de siècle Russia, the very notion of the acquisition of decorative objects was a desire alone, such aspirational sentiments proliferated in publications meant to reach new urban dwellers of a variety of socio-economic circumstances. These publications included a host of magazines aimed specifically at urban (and sometimes rural) women in their multiple roles. The so-called "women's press" began to emerge in the mid-nineteenth century and offered its readership advice and information on a broad range of topics, from practical advice to political opinion. From 1860 to 1905, 230 women became publishers or editors of, most often short-lived, publications.[10] Among the most well-known journals in the first decade or so of the twentieth century were *Damskii mir, Zhenshchina, Soiuz zhenshchin* and *Zhenskii vestnik.* Other publications still had increasingly commercial success and included two rather domestically oriented publications: *Zhurnal dlia zhenshchin* and *Zhurnal dlia khoziaek.* In the context of women and their continued gendered roles within the domestic interior, it is worth pausing on the tremendously varied and all-encompassing publication, *Zhenshchina. Zhenshchina* was uniquely organized into small sub-magazines, each of which was named after and contained information on women's various roles, including "Woman Worker";

"Women Homemaker"; "Woman Mother"; "Women Doctor"; "Woman Wife"; and "Children's World." Each week subscribers would receive about six or so two- to eight-page sections of this magazine. Women's responsibility to organize and inhabit the domestic sphere, to decorate it, to make it efficient and modern, peppered the pages of the magazine each week.[11] Whether as laborers only dreaming of their efficient new flats or as professionals purchasing gadgets for their kitchens, Russian women were surrounded by notions of domestic interiors that reflected contemporary understandings of hygiene and uniformity,[12] concepts fundamental to modernity itself. As conditions in many arenas became unpredictable, the domestic interior was called upon to serve as a refuge from the storm, even as it embodied the many contradictions found in life outside of the front hallway. This became an integral part of urban, modern femininity, even as women continued to occupy roles in the world of work and the public sphere of consumption.[13]

A new temporal order

Life on the ground was shifting at a fast pace during the final decades of Romanov rule. The gentry and its influence waned and the working classes boomed in numbers as peasant migrants left behind their families, whether briefly, seasonally or permanently, to seek work in the city. New members of urban middling classes struggled to define themselves and find their place within a changing urban scene, including reimagining their living spaces. As Catriona Kelly writes of the audiences for the ever-proliferating prescriptive texts in these final decades of the imperial era, "there was now a public that craved refinement, but lacked the immersion in literature, fine art, history and ethics" so characteristic of just a generation or so before.[14] Men and women battled each other over manners and morals and the appropriate behavior, expectations of others and the upbringing of future generations. Manners and taste became a potential avenue for social mobility among city dwellers, if only aspirational at best.

This very uncertainty became the spirit of the age. As the cartoon in Figure 1 shows, even those who were fortunate enough to acquire their own dwelling—to modestly furnish it, put food on the table and live according to the latest hygienic standards with window open and tree in the background—would likely end up miserable, embattled and weeping.[15] The city brought with it many challenges, including setting up one's home according to the standards of the day.

Figure 1 "Humorous Album," *Zhenshchina* 3 (1907): 15. Public domain.

With the intense speed of industrial change by the 1890s and beyond, and all of the challenges it brought, older notions of exclusivity and refinement granted to the aristocracy alone were on the wane. They were challenged by those who had newly acquired wealth, even if they lacked the proper education and refinement. Members of this new public, made up of lesser gentry, townspeople, professionals, elite workers and many others with aspirations for social mobility, "craved refinement," had some money to spend, but lacked the manners of their elite predecessors.[16] There was an ongoing dispute between the dying aristocracy and the emergent middling classes, so much the object of Anton Chekhov's stories, who had cash and lacked the education and instincts. It was precisely these new city dwellers who longed to create modern apartments and live according to acceptable norms. They comprised, in the words of Stephen Lovell, a new "non-aristocratic urban public." They embraced new consumer patterns, leisure activities, professional opportunities, roles in civil society, and brought with them, to the boulevard and the department store, modest spending power and the desire to truly inhabit their new place as the individuals representing a civilized, urban and modern Russia.[17]

Buying power was one avenue for the consolidation of this new middle-class sense of belonging and status. Beginning in the late nineteenth century, Russia experienced, for the first time, the opportunity for mass consumerism, which appeared in tandem with the emergence of a "retail culture," an advertising industry, increased urban leisure pursuits and ultimately the rise of the person of the consumer with at least moderate spending power and the desire—if not means—to fashion herself or himself "modern" and middle class.[18] Goods were now sold in a variety of retail environments, from the smaller more specialized shops to the large-scale, and fancy, department stores. Moscow's Muir & Mirrieless represented the new department store culture. Opening in 1885 on Theatre Square in Moscow, Muir & Mirrieless offered its patrons a modern culture of consumption, replete with elevators, snack bars, bathrooms and polite help.[19] In Moscow, in the 1890s, urbanites also watched as the new Upper Trading Rows on Red Square were constructed in the heart of the city. These rows were meant to indicate Russia's move toward modern consumerism, including technological innovation, efficiency and civility. At the end of the nineteenth century, thus, a kind of aspirational "bourgeoisification of Russian culture was underway—with a consequent emphasis on respectability, middle class ascendency and pleasurable consumption."[20] One aspect of this new active public life was the rise of the availability of popular leisure activities. Leisure grew exponentially in these years, including the expansion of sports such as soccer and ice hockey, bicycling and roller-skating as well as theatergoing or shopping.[21] Opportunities for participation in activities outside of both work and family increased significantly. These pursuits created the desire for more time. Urbanization and industrialization produced new forms of inequality, poverty and outright inhumanity in daily life. Many of these conditions created significant constraints on time at the very moment when an increase in leisure options demanded work be done efficiently to make space for relaxation. Not only did workers find themselves living according to the punch clock, many for the first time, but all of those with insufficient wages and squalid living conditions had little, if any, opportunity to participate in these new leisure arenas. Yet, no doubt, many dreamt of just that and aspired to a longed-for access to a more leisurely existence. The efficient use of labor time and the increased pace of life, at home and at work, could allow for increased "free time" available to enjoy, or dream of, the delights in the city. At the same time, however, demands were placed on women in their new apartments to create healthy and happy environments for their families, as the struggle to win time at home raged as well.

Those who longed to participate in the public arena and take advantage of the growing variety of leisure pursuits had to find the hours or days to do so. Increased pressure was put on families of all classes to create healthy environments at home, attentive both to the dangers of the past and to the challenges of the urban, filthy present. They were to live healthily and efficiently and take advantage of all the city had to offer. There is some consensus among historians that there was a burgeoning "cult of domesticity" in post-reform Russia. There was, as Barbara Engel writes in her account of marital violence, "a far greater concern than there was previously with household management and child rearing." And Catriona Kelly illustrates this gendered domestic ideology through the proliferation of prescriptive tracts.[22]

Overall, Russian cities encountered profound challenges as many rushed in to find work and pursue pleasure. Even though the housing infrastructure was notoriously unequipped to handle increasing populations coming from the countryside, the final decades of the nineteenth century through the revolutions of 1917 were a time of great movement and migration in Russia's urban centers, from Moscow to St. Petersburg to Warsaw and beyond. Peasants left the countryside and moved to the city for at least part of the year to try their hand at new trades. These patterns of migration continued even after a couple of generations of peasant-cum-workers had settled in the city. There was so much growth in industry that peasants could still find work. When they arrived, however, they found that working conditions were abysmal; pay too small; and housing too expensive and scarce.

In terms of housing, what newly arrived folks found was utter squalor and overcrowding on a massive scale. In St. Petersburg alone, population density reached scandalous levels and housing conditions reached unfathomable lows. Although workers in the cities had a greater variety of money-earning options than those who lived in the countryside, since they could not afford public transportation their options were limited, and they remained in slums near the factories.[23] Housing conditions became increasingly dire as urban populations exponentially increased. In one official survey from the time, 10 percent of the St. Petersburg population around the turn of the century lived in a "corner" of an apartment. There were twice as many residents per apartment in St. Petersburg than there were in Berlin, Vienna or Paris.[24] As to the contours of the apartment houses themselves, St. Petersburg witnessed a significant growth in the numbers and size of apartment buildings overall, but still never sufficient. According to the 1881 census, 19 percent of buildings had one story, 42 percent had two stories, 21 percent had three stories and 18 percent had four stories. By the turn of the century, St. Petersburg buildings moved to the limits of what was allowed, six stories.[25]

These conditions, though, were not unique to St. Petersburg. Moscow, too, experienced very heavy waves of newcomers and likewise lacked the infrastructure to deal with them. In 1882 in Moscow, fewer than 5 percent of the city lived in apartment buildings with more than two stories, but by 1915 the city was peppered with four- to five-floored buildings to meet the incredible demands of a growing urban population. In 1912, on average eight and a half persons lived in a single Moscow apartment unit.[26] Yet, despite the obvious need for low-income housing, the new apartment buildings were often designed for better-off clientele in mind. Overall, the housing situation was dire, and space was sparse, to say the least.[27] By the fin de siècle, Moscow was a burgeoning metropolis, complete with a growing intellectual and professional elite. Moscow was a center of European art and had a thriving merchant culture. To quote Joseph Bradley, "the big village had become a metropolis."[28]

Building new residential spaces thus became a priority in the major cities. At the close of the nineteenth century, apartment construction in St. Petersburg was a priority, resulting in an increase in six-story buildings and rows and rows of buildings in a variety of eclectic styles. There were several-hundred construction projects in the city by the turn of the century, some of which followed the new architectural fashion of the Style Moderne.[29] As in St. Petersburg, in Moscow, the increasingly dense population demanded the construction of apartment buildings. The target audience for new construction, in both cities, was always the middle classes. In Moscow the large apartment building emerged as "essentially a product of the new style, whose standards of efficiency, comfort, and technological progress" were a perfect fit for the growing professional and middle class in the central area of Moscow, "the limits of which were expanding with the tram network."[30]

Although well-known architects in Russia recognized the desperate need for additional housing among the cities' most unfortunates, the majority of their projects were only within reach for the middle, upper-middle and elite segments of the population.[31] Even large segments of the urban middle classes, those working in offices or members of the intelligentsia, could not afford to rent apartments that were part of the new construction boom. Advances in building technology as well as science and hygiene meant that those apartments that were built, though, made strides toward conforming to new norms and expectations, even if residency in them was out of reach for most.[32]

Most residents of cities, thus, continued to live in squalor or at least in very tight quarters. This dearth of living space, whether for the bourgeois apartment resident or the worker living in a dormitory or in the corner with his family, meant contending with the daily consequences of urbanization on health and hygiene. In swampy St. Petersburg, where disease had long been a real problem, the shortage of housing only intensified the worsening conditions. Diseases and illnesses spread quickly in the tight residences in the workers' dorms and overcrowded apartments. The spread of cholera and typhoid did not slow down with the rapid creation of some urban infrastructures, such as a water system. The water supply itself was contaminated. The paradoxes of progress and modernity reared their ugly heads as new technologies meant to create healthier and cleaner environments ultimately led to more disease and death. Despite new technologies to filter water, the inadequacy of the infrastructure meant that water remained contaminated. Thus, despite attempts to accommodate change and create new living quarters, disease and death lurked in the shadows. There seemed no escape. Writing on the St. Petersburg urban milieu at the fin de siècle, Mark Steinberg describes an atmosphere full of melancholy, fear, pessimism and, for some, the urge to stare hopelessly into the abyss.[33] Yet, others turned to their homes, or imagined their homes, as refuges.

The combination of conditions in the cities, while by no means unique to Russia, created a series of challenges when it came to living according to modern standards, including the desire to create a hygienic and efficient modern home. Many weighed in to offer advice. There were those in the cities with pen and paper in hand, who offered residents advice on how to live their lives and how, very centrally, to set up their homes, to create a calm and healthy environment, whether in one's imagination or in real time. Although following the advice was out of reach for most, the articles and advertisements in the popular press created an emergent set of expectations about domestic interiors that individuals no doubt desired. To many in the middling elites, the home became a key to distinguish themselves from those above and those below.[34] These new Russian urbanites at the start of the twentieth century, thus, turned to the home as one arena through which to define themselves and to express their modern sensibilities, whether aspirational or real.

In the urban apartment,[35] residents remade themselves, dreaming of bourgeois habits and trying to adopt them as best they could. They expressed these desires in the apartments they set up and the magazines they read. Russians moving to the capitals—whether solo or with family, male or female, impoverished gentry or peasant-turned-worker—knew that the ground was shifting beneath them. While finding their new homes, they were inundated with advice about how to live according to new standards of civility and modernity, replete with attention to hygiene, efficiency and living in the now: "in our times." Editors, writers and readers envisioned a place—an apartment—with dangers and changes lurking in every corner, from dusty curtains to gaudy dressers, to festering bacteria. The present moment contained, thus, a fear of a backward, proximate past, with an emphasis on a present that had its own urban challenges. Authors searched for ways to combat the ill effects of both. Magazines and prescriptive texts proliferated in this era and offered their readers advice on how to live according to modern, hygienic, standards, with particular attention to guiding aspiring middling women in how to set up a home as well as comport themselves both inside and outside of the domestic sphere. These new standards reflected the knowledge that "our times" brought a new modern epoch to Russia, one that never fully detached from yesterday but also contained elements of tomorrow.

The Russian press was exploding in these final decades of the nineteenth century. Mass circulation newspapers were proliferating and lifestyle, political and fashion magazines were on the rise. Although not entirely new to the Russian journalistic scene, the women's magazine also took off in new directions in these years. From the 1880s onwards, with the rise of women's literacy, there was a desire for a more entertaining press for women. Some of these magazines and journals offered their readers a very eclectic mix of literary texts as well as household tips, and advice on how to raise and educate children, especially girls. Advertising was also vital to the financing of a women's periodical.[36] On average, the number of advertisements per women's publication in 1883 had more than doubled over that of 1876 and was ten times that of 1867.[37] In these publications, one would also find ads and notices for "books, cosmetics and toiletries, household wares, medications, and other periodicals."[38] By the start of the twentieth century, many women themselves not only wrote the articles but also edited the publications. Although the impulse behind many of the women's publications, especially between 1905 and 1917 when society was highly politicized, was to create a gendered political consciousness, many of the magazines offered advice on how to run a home or how to rear children. The focus, in many lifestyle and women's publications, was the domestic interior, its aesthetics and its values.[39] The popular magazines contained advice columns, articles and advertisements about how to live appropriately in the now. The audience for these publications were primarily the urban middle classes, who were fearful of falling into lesser circumstances.

The women's and lifestyle magazines suggested a series of cures for urban blight, many of which involved the creation of a modern domestic interior, with particular attention to the ways in which daily time should be spent. This advice both confronted the ailments of the present moment and served as a bulwark against the ways of the past. The solution for the challenges of modernity offered on page after page of women's publications would come in the form of an urge to be more hygienic and more efficient in practices in daily life. Hygiene meant not only a faith in the modern attributes of science and "bacteriology," but also an emphasis on the creation of efficiencies, cleanliness and well-being, all of which combined to create a modern, urban sensibility. The women's magazine stood at the forefront of this effort. Russia, of course, was not alone. The emphasis on health and hygiene and the role that women played as keepers of clean and safe hearths resonated across Europe at this very moment.

In Russia it was the urban apartment, where women (and men), recently arrived residents to the city, were advised by writers and editors and even fellow citizens through letters to the editor, how to decorate their homes and transform themselves, even if in theory alone, into modern, bourgeois urbanites. The middling classes had to distinguish themselves from those above and below, and the home in Russia, as elsewhere in Europe, emerged as the ideal venue for these assertions. The modern urban apartment as it is outlined in the imagination of "tastemakers" who wrote the columns and how-to tracts, had to be bright and efficient, and as far away from the rural, peasant past with the image of dank, dark *izbas* and wooden utensils as was possible. The very "precariousness" of the position of Russia's middling peoples strengthened the impulse to insist upon vigilance in creating a proper home.[40] As historian Wayne Dowler puts it: "Disdain for those below, jealousy of those above—such were the markers of middle-class existence."[41] Writing on the Russian world in 1913, Dowler explains that the dissemination of "middle-class values" was widespread in the mass circulation press and the increasingly literate readership of publications from the "penny press" through the thick journals. The press, though, proved a medium where the workers and more educated members of the middle classes could come together. "It consciously strove to fill the gap between better- and less-educated members of society."[42] In this way, advertisements and columns in the press focused on "self-improvement" as well as fashion, hygiene and so forth as a way to lure readers and provide advice on how to climb the ladder of success. Like many across Europe, then, Russians embraced the "civilizing power of informed consumption" so popular in this era. At the turn of the century, widespread anxiety about the persistence of the past and the potentially corrosive power of modernity itself was met with an embrace of values meant to highlight the civilized, modern urban lifestyle of the day. Despite all of the efforts, "the past in Russia, however, also remained present, and daily mingled with the modern."[43] Indeed, the daily was the modern.

Representations of the modern home, whether textual or visual, proliferated in magazines, advertisements and prescriptive texts at the turn of the twentieth century, these came in the form of furniture advertisements and concrete advice on wall decorations or the placements of beds.[44] Authors of how-to manuals and columns implicated the urban apartment—with its decoration—in the emergence of a modern bourgeois culture of everyday life and its modern temporal frame. Apartments were imbued with meanings that reflected the tensions of the age, whether as places of modern capacities, where technology and efficiency as well as health and hygiene were central, or as refuges from the cares of the outside world and its modern complexities.[45] These capacities included new attitudes toward time, time saving and saving one's life. Columns and advertisements instructed newly arrived urbanites on how to distance themselves from the rural past, avoid the dirt and grime of the urban present, and stave off the inevitable, as yet unknown, diseases of the future.

Time consciousness, both large and small

Abstract ideas such as time and space always have concrete manifestations in the popular imaginary and in everyday existence on the ground. At the fin de siècle, as notions of time were being reimagined in a new, urban, industrializing context, long-standing notions certainly had a role to play in configuring the new. New temporal rhythms emerged from phenomena such as technology's intervention in the creation of mechanisms that reduced human effort inspiring efficiency and closing distances as well as the reemphasis among some on messianic time so integral to orthodox thinking. It is not difficult to imagine how modern time narratives might have reached Russia in a particular way, as cultural narratives do in any particular context. Russia, especially in its capital cities of Moscow and St. Petersburg, at the start of the twentieth century was a cauldron of fast-moving change and a time and place where old and new styles and ideologies battled and mixed. The same was true of temporal narratives. At the risk of simplification, one could find Russian Orthodox ideas about chronos or Kairos, or transcendent time, where communing with god through the icon allowed for all logical, ordered time to stand still, at the same moment that speed and efficiency and measurement marked the modern moment. The past persisted through society's preserving the ruins of estates and the past was ushered away as dust floated in through windows. This layered sense of time marked the years leading up to revolution. At the fin de siècle, Russians and others across Europe acquired this modern time consciousness, which manifested, at least in part, in how spaces were defined and organized.

Time was never uniform. Stephen Kern in his *Culture of Time and Space* argues that Europeans embraced a uniform public time based on current ideas about the simultaneity of events across space and the standardization of daily clock time. This uniformity created an increased awareness and adherence to the clock as a way of structuring and ordering one's day, whether on the job or shopping in a department store. Kern emphasizes how public time governed individuals in their lives outside of the home with a certain set of structures and uniformities. He contrasts this public clock time with private time, which he imagines as less rigid and proscribed. For Kern, the hours spent among family or friends in leisurely pursuits at home flowed more freely and were not watched over as carefully. In the Russian case, there emerged a Russian idea of time that included a uniform private time, where there was the demand for some standardization within the realm of the home, including an emphasis on efficiency and mechanization. Rather than a clear divide between public and private time, modern clock time interfered within the domestic interior via advice literature with its demands for efficiency and uniformity. The distinction between public (objective), ordered time and private (subjective) more amorphous time mapping onto distinct spaces seems not to account for the ways in which within the more orderly notions of efficiency and the fight against the past traveled through doorways and windows into the apartments of the newly arrived and long resident alike.

The struggle to move forward on the street and inside the home into the present included a conversation with the past, and by the late nineteenth century, as philosophers of temporality remind us, the present and past were fundamentally intermingled. In these decades, much ink was spilled over the simultaneity of past and present, and over time consciousness itself. Changing perceptions of "now" altered accounts of "then."[46] Edmund Husserl, fin de siècle German-Jewish philosopher, who influenced Martin Heidegger (and to whom Heidegger originally dedicated his 1927 *Being and Time*), claimed that the present moment contained in itself "residual traces of what had immediately gone before ('retentions') and anticipations of what was immediately to come ('protentions')." The present thus, was imagined as "horizontally thick" because it absorbs the past and the future; it has "three dimensions internal to it."[47] French philosopher, Henri Bergson, similarly, understood the intimate relationship among past, present and future. In *Matter and Memory*, he wrote: "the present [...] is a perception of the past and a determination of the future."[48] All three temporal frames, he imagined, in the modern era, overlapped and collapsed into one. Both of these notions of modern time—the simultaneity and the overlapping and collapsing of frames—manifested themselves in the ways in which Russians thought about temporal change. And all of these narratives could be found within the home and within prescriptions for making the domestic interior modern.

Epochal change: A new day has dawned

At the fin de siècle, Russians were aware that they were living through large-scale transformations. Countless members of peasant villages uprooted themselves and traveled to cities to find work in factories and other places of employment; members of long-time gentry households had to sell or rent their homes and move to cities because of their waning assets, members of burgeoning professions took up residence among urban populations in order to practice as doctors, lawyers, journalists and so forth. Day-to-day life in cities was changing and unpredictable. Movement and relocation were ubiquitous, whether temporary, seasonal or permanent.[49] With these changes came an understanding among educated society and beyond that Russia was entering—or had entered—into a new phase of history, a new historical epoch. Russians were living "in our times," distinct from the past and not yet part of certain future. There were endless texts available to ensure that they made it there. And the home sat on the fault lines between the past and the future, emerging as a space for the defining of one's modern sensibilities in the present moment. There was a consensus building that a new day was dawning, as signs of a new era settled in. Magazine articles, advice literature and the growing number of advertisements found in the popular press all reveal this emerging phenomenon at being "in our times." Russians reading prescriptive texts were constantly reminded of the significance of the epoch in which they lived, the privileged place of the present and its continued linkages with the past. Russians, thus, were inundated with time awareness in the broadest sense, with the knowledge that they were living in a profound epoch of change, where the ground was shifting beneath them at incredible speed. Yet, as modern contours of historical time dictate, the past itself did not recede, not completely, older notions of temporal rhythm remained, even as the present sped toward the future. The past, while stridently present, had to be combatted in order to foster a modern, urban sensibility.

The past was palpable everywhere in Russian cities, from the newly arrived peasant who brought with him traditional habits and beliefs, to the infrastructures buckling from the pressure of population growth. Newly minted city dwellers, thus, had anxieties about how to create a modern present while surrounded by signs of a past, of rural life and its crumbling elements. The fact that "the past in Russia [...] remained present, and daily mingled with the modern," meant that the very definition of the "now" incorporated elements of and anxieties about the "then."[50] As such, the past and present were never severed from one another but always intertwined; as one article put it from a popular women's magazine from 1908: "in each fading style there was once in its own time a 'new style' within."[51]

"In our times," this "new style" of interior decoration and design—according to the author of a prescriptive piece in a woman's magazine—was never to "resemble one that was used by our grandmothers."[52] One expert writing in *Zhenshchina* reported: in order to describe the modern kitchen "we must stand at the height of our unsettling, feverish, progressive century."[53] Invoking the kitchen was no accident. Authors and advertisers advised that the shedding of the past and the staving off of the worst aspects of the present were only possible in the face of the creation of a modern, clean and hygienic domestic interior. These modern expectations included the embracing of a temporal sense of present time, as women were advised to create contemporary kitchens, bedrooms and hallways, to name a few, that are contemporary—tasteful, clean and efficient. They affirmed that Russia had entered into a new age, a modern epoch. Yet, the past lingered, as it was a constituent element in how Russians understood present time and their place within it.

The speed of change increased at the fin de siècle, and thus a distance from the past might be greater if reminders were not to be found on each and every corner. Even within the home, old time hung on. In a 1908 issue of *Zhenshchina* there appeared a meditation on the old times versus the new times vis-à-vis the creation of the domestic interior:

> In former good old times, there were not so many different trends in art, and fashion did not change so quickly. This was when all household furnishings remained and were inherited from generation to generation, and together with them was inherited a love or belief in the silent witness of life of a whole generation.[54]

But present life moved much more quickly. This somewhat sentimental vision of a past connecting generation to generation through the passing down of household objects was contrasted to the quick pace of present-day life in the city in the very same article in *Woman*. The romance with speed and time saving is obvious:

> In our modern day we are presented with differing demands. One may frequently change one's residency, and a modern person of middling means likely approaches the question of household furnishings indifferently: he has no time to be sentimental; the battle for existence takes too much of his time; he mostly does not consider or speak of such matters. After all, he will not inherit very precious things and if he does acquire such objects while at the market or some such, those objects are likely made in the factory.[55]

And this sense of loss is tempered here: "there is no real need to be upset about the loss; as a matter of fact, such things can be made by factories and distributed to the masses." This is a compromise in the present, to recreate the past in the guise of the efficient factory-driven present. The article goes on to sing the praises of "artistic-factory made goods!"[56] There is the sense that the modern world allows for the industrial production of artistic aesthetics in the form of household furnishings. The loss of the past, this article advocates, need not be mourned; after all, its residual content remains embedded in a modern form, found in the home in our everyday lives.

Modern time awareness, thus, manifested itself in the material, mundane, everyday aspects of life. Fin de siècle shifts included also a heightened awareness of daily, micro-time, including an accounting of the minutes in an hour and the hours in a day. Time was a commodity imagined to be counted, saved and enjoyed, whenever possible. One had to strive to save time, to create time and—in terms of life span—to extend time on earth. Advice in popular magazines, especially aimed at women and the home, abound on just how to structure daily time and create more opportunities for stepping out and enjoying the city. The growing popular press, especially those publications aimed at women in the domestic sphere, demanded that its readers value efficiency, uniformity and hygienic practices as the backbone of a healthy home life. These values led to longing for the creation of a modern, hygienic and efficient home. This urban domestic space was the object of endless practical advice and literary caprice.

At the peak of his literary career, Russian writer and satirist Maxim Gorky wrote "How to Organize Your Home," a humorous short story describing a newlywed couple's attempts at designing their apartment in St. Petersburg. In these brief pages, husband and wife argue about how to proceed with their nesting and organizing their new domestic space. They debate which objects must be purchased and which are unnecessary. Their plight and disagreements reflect larger processes and preoccupations within Russian society at the turn of the twentieth century, including an enthusiasm for their home and its interior. With an increasing number of Russians moving to urban centers, there was a proliferation of new domestic spaces to decorate and an expanded number of writers, whether journalists or novelists, eager to put in their own two cents, tongue in cheek or not. Whether readers could actually manage to create such a home or if they simply dreamt of its becoming, Russians looked to their homes as reflective of their own role in the modern world. The domestic interior became implicated in the larger project of creating a forward-looking society, one that organized and imagined itself in modern temporal terms. Gorky's husband and wife team, like many of their real-life counterparts, felt they were badly in need of advice on how to proceed and carry out their daily routines. This story—itself a satire of middle-class, urban, consumer desires—raises questions about the degree to which setting up one's home reflected upon one's moral character and social standing. The main female character, the wife, is eager to purchase the items considered respectable for a new efficient and bourgeois aesthetic, a goal, at least in Gorky's estimation, that was for sale.

Scholars of design, architecture and social history have been discussing the role of the home—or more specifically, the apartment in Gorky's case—in the creation of modern subjectivities and the aesthetics of the European domestic interior for decades.[57] Advice, more often than not assumed to be for women readers, on how to manage private space and also individual daily time could be found on page after page of magazines and prescriptive manuals alike. Women's magazines played a central role in disseminating this advice to a growing reading public.

There is a rich scholarship on the role of the magazine, especially the domestic lifestyle magazine, in the formation of modern subjecthood and of modern civil society and publicity, not just in Russia but throughout Europe and the United States. Some have emphasized the ways in which the women's magazines contained or shaped, in some way, "a person's individuality."[58] For many women, whose sense of self was defined in relation to the domestic interior in these decades in Russia and across Europe, "the personally decorated interior [was imagined] a more profound subjective space than had previously been envisaged."[59] Thus, editors, columnists and readers all developed "representational strategies," which were attentive to the psychological processes of the reader. Thus, the women's magazine that concentrated on the domestic realm had a particularly profound role to play in the formation of a gendered modern subjecthood. Writing about France at the fin de siècle, Francesca Berry explains that the woman's magazine and the domestic interior "are mutually constitutive sites for the staging of feminine subjectivities, and therefore must be taken very seriously."[60] Writing on Germany, Jeremy Aynsley likewise highlights how "periodical publications could both reflect and help to actively construct attitudes towards the interior in early nineteenth-century Europe."[61] The home, writes one scholar, "was imagined, in nineteenth-century domestic discourse to provide a powerfully influential space for the development of character and identity."[62] The apartment in Russia's cities at the fin de siècle was no exception.

By the end of the nineteenth and start of the twentieth centuries, the range of Russian publications available to—and aimed at—women seemed ever expanding. These included an increasing number of politicized texts and ones promoting women's education as well as fashion magazines, magazines with childcare advice and others that focused on the domestic realm in each of its dimensions, including weekly menus, advice on furniture purchases and how to wear a corset. This final category of publications highlighting the importance of the home for the creating and maintaining of respectable culture included magazines emphasizing women as mothers and as wives as well as journals focused on the clean and tidy set up of the domestic interior, whether in the city or in the countryside at the dacha. Aimed primarily at the burgeoning middle classes, these magazines tended to have runs of several years and an eclectic range of subjects, from fashion to housekeeping, including an emphasis on cleanliness, efficiency and hygiene, to leisure pursuits. In these three publications— *Zhurnal dlia khoziaek* (Journal for Homemakers; 1912–1926, with a hiatus during the civil war), *Zhurnal dlia zhenshchin* (Journal for Women; 1914–1926, with a hiatus during the civil war), and *Zhenshchina* (Woman; 1907–1909 and 1913–1916)— as well as more minor ones focused exclusively on housekeeping, hygiene stood at the center of advice discourses.

It is worth pausing on one magazine in particular: *Zhenshchina*. Its various sections—including "woman-homemaker"; "woman-doctor"; "woman-wife"; "woman-worker"; "household animals"; and "latest fashions"—each reflected the multitude of roles that women were expected to play. Hygiene emerged as one of the popular themes of advice offered to its readers. A clean and scientifically healthy home environment and daily rituals offered solutions to the troubles of both the past and the present by not only using new knowledge to leave the past behind but also combatting the ills of industrial life to prolong life in the now.[63] The magazine did, though, transform by the end of the first decade of the twentieth century and was much changed when it reappeared in 1913 to 1916. Amidst the war after 1914, in particular, the articles focused less on the details of interior design and more on the plight of nurses and other women involved in the war effort. Yet, in its original form, *Zhenshchina* played a central role in advising newly urban women on how to cope with the challenges of city life, both professionally and personally.

Each of these publications, regardless of their intended audience, offered their readership clear messages about the importance of the domestic interior for the assertion of one's place in the modern present. Readers of these publications, no doubt mostly city women aspiring to a new socio-economic standing, learned that participating in the now required an investment in today's scientific standards of hygiene and efficiency at home. Hygiene and practices of cleanliness and health served as a solution to both macro- and micro-level temporal demands. On the one hand, hygienic practices reflected modern notions of science and an emphasis on the ability to expand life spans, time on earth, by combatting diseases and unsanitary conditions that cause illness. On the other hand, hygiene demands engaged in daily ritual and routine and led, in many instances, to the more efficient use of time, as time became a quantity to save and organize as never before. By way of illustration, in a 1908 *Zhenshchina* piece on the "General Hygiene of Dwellings," the columnist overtly connects hygiene and time, in its macro and micro guises. "It is common knowledge that the character of one's dwelling is of the utmost importance to one's health."[64] He continues to explain that a "stuffy apartment, dry and poorly ventilated, with untidy rooms" would ultimately lead to a variety of "human scourges, such as scrofula and tuberculosis, not to mention the general weakening of the body and the acquiring of anemia." And, even if you are lucky and not put at death's door, the neglect of cleanliness results in the creation of "an environment with very poor hygienic conditions."[65] And, if you are ill, there is a very large role to be played by "social hygiene" to be able to recover and not put others in danger of infection.

Hygiene, thus, emerged as an essential solution to modernity's woes. Writers of popular prescriptive texts emphasized that hygienic practices at home would be key to solving society's large-scale problems, by bringing the individual and society as a whole from the dark, dirty past and into the light of the clean and bright present day. In this sense, hygiene could work to ward off the haunting of the past and move Russian society firmly into the modern moment, while combatting the challenges of epochal change, such as industrialization.

Likewise, hygienic practices helped to solve the difficulties of smaller-scale daily time. A hygienic home was a more efficient home, thus preserving time and saving time according to the clock. In an era of increased leisure pursuits, the endless need for income and work, and burgeoning consumption, time was—newly—of the essence. The city contained endless routes to gratification and satisfaction, if only there was enough money and—more universally—enough time. City dwellers longed for the time to explore their new environments.

New fields of hygiene science emerged as Russian bodies were being crowded into urban spaces. In the 1880s, Russia saw the early institutionalization of bacteriology.[66] It had a significant impact on science and civil society, as the "public culture of science" emerged at the fin de siècle.[67] It had immediate repercussions for families attempting to cope with the hygiene challenges created by the move to the city. The language of contagion and "degeneration" was rife within publications and discussions about Russia's intense industrial drive.[68] The home was a potential repository for many of these dangers and thus advice on cleanliness proliferated. Not all residents of the major cities lived in crowded squalor. By the start of the twentieth century, both cities housed diverse populations too large to comfortably accommodate needs with existing resources, thus creating dramatic challenges for the privileged and struggling alike.[69] The Cult of Hygiene emerged as a cure for all urbanites, as good, modern, hygienic habits contained the potential to distance oneself from the past while warding off new difficulties resulting from the industrializing present.

The fear of being stuck in the past echoed in multiple prescriptive discourses about urban living, whether intended for the well off or the struggling. There were signs of potential dangers all around, including the peasants themselves, who for many embodied the rural past. The physical closeness of urban living quarters reeked of the past; it suggested the proximity of the old ways and the seeping of the past into the present. Urban apartments, thus, embodied the dangers of the modern present: as time progressed forward, the past lingered and impinged on movement forward in the now. At the same time, new urban problems associated with modernization emerged: spitting factories, disease, overcrowding and filthy streets, to name a few. All of these changes were memorialized in the literature of the day. Russians, like their European and American counterparts, oversaw the intensification of a hygiene regime, which ruled apartments across the empire, but nowhere more enthusiastically than the two Russian capitals. The kitchen, by the early years of the twentieth century, became a space for the prototypical Russian homemaker to prove her bourgeois credentials.

Efficiency, or the desire to create a daily, ordered time-saving routine, haunted many across Europe in the first decades of the twentieth century. In an age of both increased opportunities for leisure activities and elevated notions of "domestic science," the value of efficiency in the home took on heightened significance. Domestic science and scientific household management required that time should not be wasted, either the minutes in each hour or the years in a lifetime. Often the most mundane tasks, which could be effectively performed with gadgets, became the most meaningful, as housekeeping began to require efficient means to set up and maintain domestic interiors. Such domestic advice that included more gadgets and scientific elements increasingly embodied a modern ideal.

Both efficiency and its cousin, rationality,[70] were means of distinguishing—in the Russian imagination—between the urban life of the present and the rural life of the past. Mechanization, and its resulting time-saving measures, marked the transition to the modern city. Labor tasks became more mechanized in the factory and overall expectations were more routinized at home and at work. Writers of prescriptive texts urged Russians to distance themselves from the rural life, where it was imagined that peasants had little regard for the contours of time and no control over how they spent their days. In the city, time became a matter of individual and collective discipline, regulation, regularization and science: even sunlight in the home was to be regulated and parsed out according to scientific theories.

Columnists in magazines meant for homemakers and authors of prescriptive texts highlighted how to place rooms in an apartment in order to maximize sunlight, which might be the key factor in deciding whether to rent a certain space or not. Mariia Redelin in her now classic tract emphasized sunlight as an essential factor of healthy, modern living. "The air and light are the first conditions of physical life. Thus, before an apartment is chosen, you must search for one that would not be located in a densely built-up area of the city. Better to find a place to live that is in the sunny side of town."[71] Prescriptive manuals made clear that modernization and the creation of an urban apartment necessarily included sunlight and a healthful domestic interior design.

The urge toward efficiency and hygiene was aided by the burst of consumer products newly available and advertised within cities. Whether living in St. Petersburg or in Moscow, urban Russians, such as Gorky's hero and heroine, were surrounded by signs of the modern present, in advertisements for mechanized cookware, columns in journals on modern interior design and in shop windows selling hygienic soaps. Regardless, though, of one's actual access to these kinds of products, consumers of advertisements that peppered publications developed an aspirational set of norms. Russian homemakers were expected to have a whole array of gadgets to create a functioning and blissful home. Among the products advertised and expectations created were domestic time-saving products and soaps and hygienic products, all geared toward efficiency and cleanliness within the domestic interior. Advertisements for soap, for instance, recommended daily usage and guaranteed that a doctor had made the soap with modern methods in a laboratory.

Even if most Russians could merely window shop, these norms began to emerge and impact city dwellers across socio-economic scales, creating desires and expectations that reflected the growth of a modern, consumer-oriented society. These new expectations of home life were manifest in the everyday objects, and in small gestures, and reflected modern notions of time, of the present with an emphasis on efficiency and its embrace of clock time and hygiene and its embrace of life time.

Many noted the interrelationship between the mundane objects and gestures of daily time and efficiency. In the very first issue of one particularly practically minded column in *Dom i khoziastvo: vestnik prakticheskogo* (Home and Home Economy: Journal for Practical Housekeeping), a 1904 publication that was clearly meant for newly urban apartment dwellers, the connection between the overall sense of temporal shift and the prescriptions for daily time routines emerged: "Although, for the vast majority of our apartment dwellers still in our times, the old system of heating individual stoves prevails, there are central heating systems that have appeared in recent years that are more efficient."[72] The contrast between old and new was felt in one's bones. The creation of modern heating systems did not keep pace with the demands of the modern present: the past continued to blow cool, perhaps dirty, air around the cities. Likewise, when Russians moved into new apartments, they were advised to literally flush out the old air of the past. "In all newly constructed buildings [...] [all aspects of the ventilation system] remain clogged with polluted detritus." The first task, then, of new apartment dwellers, must be a "thorough cleaning" of all old ventilator systems in order to get rid of all of the past, accumulated waste.[73] The past must be flushed out in order for the present to emerge. On page two of this first issue appeared "several general observations about the internal, technical-hygienic workings of our residencies," which focused in great part on the technical aspects of setting up a home.[74]

In our times ["v nashe vremia"], an understanding about the laws of hygiene has already entered into society's consciousness today. It is not really necessary to remind our residence of hygienic practices in general, but the creation of the water supply, heating and ventilation demands certain attention.[75]

Hygienic practices, manifest through mundane technologies, whether ventilation or plumbing, delineated the past from the present and helped to create an efficient and clean modern present. Contemporary times meant an emphasis on health and a well-ventilated household. Moreover, men and women who lived in urban spaces were advised to save daily time, by using new technologies that created efficiencies.

This commitment to hygienic practices and time-saving strategies throughout the home, though, never excluded an emphasis on taste and aesthetics. In an 1894 issue of *Sem'ianin* (Family Man), in an article entitled "Household/Economy in the General Meaning of the Word," we learn that aesthetics, cleanliness and efficiency matter—and reflect upon one another—when it comes to one's apartment and its decoration.

> A room with the simplest furniture has the prettiest and coziest appearance, since only on the doors and the windows have hanging curtains [...]. The curtains, especially in tulle or muslin (curtains), are only attractive when they are long enough and lie with lush longitudinal folds. On every fourth, there is a new longitudinal fold, but the fold must be deep [...] if the curtains hang in such a way that the curtains are able to move apart, it is much more convenient since then it is good for health, since it would then allow a fully sufficient amount of light into the room.[76]

Sufficient light, clean air and properly functional plumbing served as the technological developments of the age and the everyday means of regulating time and health. This interrelationship marked Russian modernity and ushered in a new time-space complex as the apartment emerged as the stage upon which present-day concerns and norms of behavior were played out. Each room had its very own role to play.

All the rooms in the house

The home in general, and most likely the apartment in particular, served as the stage upon which newcomers to the cities could prove themselves modern and live within the guidelines of today. There appeared a number of household manuals aimed at how-to advice on setting up the domestic interior in all of its detail. *Home and Homemaking* by Mariia Redelin was among those texts. Readers of this text encountered in excruciating detail the expectations of how to create a perfect domestic interior. Each room had its own role to play in this unfolding drama. Aimed at aspiring, or already privileged, families who had time and money to purchase gadgets galore, Redelin emphasizes the fundamental requirements of a modern apartment: proper ventilation of air and appropriate exposure to light. These two factors, according to Redelin, had a substantial impact on health, hygiene and general enjoyment of the everyday. She advised that it is best to search for an apartment that has "wide and tall windows," especially in the common room; where light is not blocked by nearby tall buildings at all hours of the day.[77] Each of these rules revolved, in some fashion, around time consciousness, sometimes in a straightforward way and other times more tangentially. The calendar, the clock and the life cycle hovered in the background. In Redelin's advice about the importance of light, she mentioned the significance of the time of the year (during the summer months) and the time of the day (open window in the morning and afternoon, but close at night to maintain warmth in the winter months).[78] She advised her readers to find an apartment where the windows easily open and are routinely opened depending on the time of day and the month of the year. Redelin cautions that light becomes particularly important in "the rooms where children will sleep at night and where they play in the day."[79] Children, as the future of Russia, were imagined as the most vulnerable to the attention of shifting temporal frames, whether day and night or seasons of the year. Although her text assumes a significant amount of economic flexibility in purchasing gadgets and time to spare, her ideas reflect larger patterns and norms found across women's magazines and household management texts. One similar example is P.P. Andreev's 1893 St. Petersburg *Domovedenie. Rukovodstvo dlia khoziaek doma, domashnikh uchitelnits i guvernantok*, which also emphasized what items should be in each home. The difference perhaps is that while Redelin's list is long and assumes significant resources, Andreev's provides a pared-down list of "only twenty-nine items, of which the vast majority are multi-functional."[80]

Just as authors of advice literature stressed the need for appropriate light and air, they cautioned their readers about the dangers of proximity to others and overcrowding. This could mean protection against the spread of dirt and grime caused by inadequate living spaces in the cities, or the dangers lurking due to the proximity of bodies and their waste, natural and otherwise, one to the other. Part of what is described in these sections of Redelin's encyclopedic advice manual is how to cope with the "downside" of the modern city: dirt, grime, smells, etc. Redelin highlighted the dangers embedded in the "the unclean streets, the slop pits, the dumped garbage of warriors and factories" and how all of these conditions negatively influenced city dwellers and impacts the quality of the air that makes its way into the apartments.[81] One family most certainly will have to contend with the detritus from another. The lack of physical distance between apartment buildings and individual apartments had an important role to play. The relationship with the apartments on the lower floors "can have an influence on the air in your apartment." There was also a particular fear of the basement; if it was damp it raised the level of fear regarding health concerns and discomfort.[82]

The connection between health, modernity, efficiency and homemaking emerged as a key theme in a number of prescriptive texts, some of which were aimed at more modest audiences than Redelin's. In Andreev's *Domovedenie*, the reader immediately confronts these overlapping emphases: the study of homemaking must be understood in intimate connection with hygiene—the science of preserving health and warning against diseases. Thus, hygiene ensures that one's body is preserved in cleanliness, through washing and the ability to frequently change the linens, learning housekeeping to know the correct soap to use to wash our bodies and the linens, how to scrub, starch, blue and iron the linens, while at the same time being familiar with the composition of the soap, the starch and the bluing.[83]

The same values of cleanliness, efficiency and beauty were articulated in the advertisements and columns in women's magazines of the day. Readers of the glossy, fashionable magazine *Damskii mir*, in 1912, would have encountered advice on how to create a modern social space, whether a dining or living room, within their apartments.[84] In an article entitled "The Decorating of the Apartment," the author focuses on the dining room, or *stolovaia*. The dining room must be tasteful and minimalist in its presentation. Simplicity is at a premium in creating what is acceptable or expected: "Good taste demands that you do not overload a room with too many ornamentations. The walls of a dining room may have pictures, but it is not an obligation; these pictures might be of fruit or fish. No matter."[85] Likewise, the china must be made of a "good quality antique or from a contemporary factory, but never from a cheap rynok/marketplace." Aesthetics were king: "If there are not enough antiques/old things, then it is better to leave shelves empty than to put on the shelves anti-artistic pieces."[86] The past, in the form of antiques, emerged static and aestheticized, much like the nostalgic descriptions of waning estate life in the previous chapter. The past, frozen in time through aestheticization, was unthreatening and even desirable.

Although texts such as those found in *Damskii mir* and Andreev's or Redelin's provided guidance for the overall domestic environment, these authors also offered advice on individual rooms, whether a bedroom, a kitchen or a closet. While many rooms in the house were highlighted in these journals and magazines, the kitchen—with its potential for embracing new standards of efficiency, hygiene and science—was highlighted most of all.

The kitchen

The kitchen, whether a small, modest space within a tiny apartment or a fully stocked large room or two, occupied a central role in the house and embodied the hopes and the demands of modern times in the domicile of the well-off. It was, of course, a gendered space. Women were inundated with instructions on how to manage the kitchen and create an up-to-date environment for themselves and their families. Sometimes they had hired help, but mostly women were on their own. One 1908 piece included the instructions that "in not bad and modest apartments, always assign a not so big room as the kitchen. In the room there must be an oven, an ordinary stove, made from simple brick and tile."[87] The author continued to explain that every once in a while the stove needed to be cleaned so the flame could be regulated. There was a long full list of items that each kitchen, however modest, must have.[88] Whether modest or fancy, a kitchen had to meet a set of stringent requirements to be efficient and hygienic, and hence, modern. In the above-pictured well-stocked kitchen, the number of gadgets appears numerous, but even the most modest set-ups were expected to meet the requirements of the day. The image of the homemaker—who cleaned and cooked and made use of modern gadgetry in her kitchen—emerged as a symbol of the now with seeds of the soon-to-be: the urban, efficient homemaker. Several journals had columns or sections expressly reserved for homemakers and their kitchen responsibilities. Homemakers, these columns dictated, were required to consult scientific experts and learn about up-to-date domestic technology.

The stakes in organizing the home were high, and thus the power granted to women was significant. The apartment had multiple roles to play in the modern domestic drama: it was simultaneously to provide a cozy refuge from the dirt and grime of the industrial present and to embrace the future through the emergence of new scientific principles for the home. The kitchen sat at the center of those demands. *Zhenshchina* reserved several sections for instructing women on how to govern the kitchen, including what food items, dishes and equipment were considered necessary. There were also sections on the home table, the home garden and the woman-homemaker, and often weekly menus were provided. The magazine's tone and target audience were those women who were both politically conscious and "family oriented [and] middle-class."[89] When the publication first appeared, the editor, a woman, intended to use the magazine to "promote family strength through knowledge."[90] Although the representations of domestic life focused on a number of themes, including childrearing, women's roles inside and outside the household, and the well-being of the family, the kitchen emerged as a key space within which to demonstrate a woman's—and her family's—place within the emergent modern society. The kitchen was a key venue for enacting middle-class modernity.

Household journals and women's magazines had a clear and consistent focus on advising their readers to purchase the necessary kitchen gadgets needed to create not only efficient but also clean and hygienic kitchens, amidst the filth and contamination of the city. Much of the advice—from how to wash silverware to how to approach food preparation—centered on the latest trends in health and cleanliness. Prominent among the objects required for the creation of a hygienic kitchen were particular types of dishes, pots and pans. Authors advised, for instance, that women purchase "cast iron dishes" because of their ease of cleaning.[91] They added that "the bright, sparkling copper and pewter dishes of the past inevitably were more ornate than today's kitchenware," but today's were easier to clean and thus more "hygienic."[92] Women's access to technology and the latest scientific knowledge, not unlike elsewhere in Europe, came in the form of kitchen gadgetry. Gender narratives, thus, stretched to allow women knowledge of science but certainly did not break, as they were still the ones in charge of the feminized domestic realm.

In a series of linked articles entitled "How to Set Up a Modern Kitchen" readers were confronted by this connection among science, technology, cleanliness and the modern:

> In the modern kitchen we find dishes made from many metals: copper, nickel, iron, enamel and clay. Good dishes will have no influence on the flavor of the food. Good dishes should not be too heavy and should clean easily [...] a good pan [...] should not influence the coloring or the taste of the food.[93]

Although—to be fair—the past was not discarded entirely. The author remarked that earthenware "harkens back to the era of our great grandmothers [...] and [therefore] is used in some instances" and is "irreplaceable" in making several dishes, including traditional kashas.[94] The past did not completely recede nor could it be allowed to either join or disrupt the march toward health and longevity.

Like hygiene, efficiency and its reliance on technological advancement and scientific knowledge was valued by the writers and readers, who insisted on the normative kitchen. The kitchen, the site of food preparation and consumption, according to Redelin and other authors and editors, required the most mechanization and technological innovation in order to ensure that time was not wasted, and that food was properly prepared, in a predictable and uniform manner. The kitchen, thus, required the "proliferation of objects," as Kelly writes in her *Refining Russia*.[95] The "gadgets" that Redelin suggests included "a patent doorstop, and a curved tumbler brush for sweeping under fixed furnishings." But the kitchen required more specialized objects than other spaces in the house, this set of utensils included: "cake knife, doughnut pan, enameled pots for boiling water, a cabbage chopper and a coffee funnel."[96] These are but a few examples of the time-saving devices that contributed to the uniformity of preparation techniques in the kitchen. In an early issue of *Zhenshchina*, for instance, there appeared a lengthy description of how to set up and care for the kitchen using scientific knowledge and up-to-date standards. With the enumeration of each machine required for the creation of a modern, well-run kitchen—whether a meat grinder or a "press" to clean potatoes—authors espoused the centrality of efficiency allowed by machinery (albeit very low-tech by today's standards) in setting up a proper apartment. New technologies enabled the more efficient use of time and new knowledge increased the hygienic practices used in the kitchen. The achievement of this modern space, thus, began with the acquisition of things. These new technologies were meant to prevent the homemaker from "a lot of superfluous labor and allowing her the needed time to take care of other necessary tasks in the home."[97] One article in particular insisted: "all serious housewives must possess the correct implements and tools in the kitchen to run a proper household."[98] The modern kitchen, experts insisted, "is more and more made using tools and machines, which were completely unknown in the past."[99] The "nowness" of the kitchen was key.

If not attended to properly the kitchen held the potential for real dangers, not only unhealthy food but also bad air and overall filth. In an article entitled "The Dread of Air," the author—"an expert" —explicates the urgent need for fresh air wafting through the corridors of any home: "Homemakers do not understand what clean air is, how rich it is in oxygen and how important it is for our health and our internal order and external cleanliness."[100] Articles promise that the embracing of these scientific principles by women-homemakers in the kitchen and throughout the apartment will transform their homes and their inhabitants.

Redelin emphasizes the efficiency of the use of space and the efficiencies that proximity can create on a day-to-day basis. In particular, she writes that the dining room should be near the kitchen for efficiency; also, the kitchen should not be too far from anything because "it means the staff/help/servants can work more quickly, and so that the dishes do not have to be prepared too far in advance of when they are served on the table."[101]

The rest of the house

The kitchen was not the only space in the apartment under scrutiny. The other rooms of domestic life, whether social spaces, such as the *gostinaia* (living or guest), or intimate ones, such as the *zhilaia* (living or den) or the *spal'naia* (bedroom), were required to maximize efficiency and hygienic conditions. And women were to attend to these, too. Advice columns stressed the combination of a modern aesthetic sensibility and an investment in science and technology. Whether aimed at the wealthy, the middling or the struggling, these words of wisdom collectively embraced modern conceptions of time, both as a reflection of progress along a linear trajectory and as an embodiment of the temporal values of efficiency, uniformity and cleanliness made possible through science and technology. Advertisements that frequently appeared in *Journal for Homemakers* reflect these two levels of modern temporality: the macro and the micro. On the one hand, a single advert might contain an image of a washing machine with words that remind us of its mechanized technology: "rollers and squeezers," reflecting the advancements—the progress of the age and its distance from the unmechanized past. With a washing machine, women will have more time to enjoy the delights of the city rather than being stuck washing everything by hand. These priorities are expressed in prescriptive texts aimed at women from a diversity of economic and social circumstances. In this instance, we see a woman with a plain dress ready to embrace technology; no doubt she represents the middling everywoman of her time.

The majority of serial publications available on a weekly or biweekly basis were aimed at women of the middling classes. Among the concerns expressed was being smart with money. In a 1913 article entitled "Salary for the Cook," the columnist in *Journal for Homemakers* issues a warning to all homemakers to choose their house help—and especially the cook—very carefully:

And so, I repeat dear homemakers – pay close attention to whether the kitchen set up and the money that you spend on your "table" was created by an experienced, smart and conscientious person, aware of your needs and most importantly, of your economy.[102]

Not all publications prioritized thrift. In Mariia Redelin's popular behavioral manual, which assumes expansive space and endless wealth, demands were placed on heads of households that assumed deep pockets. The so-called "living room," or *zhilaia komnata*, which provided an intimate space for close family to meet each evening, excluded the company of children and their nannies. This very set of assumptions—having nannies and having a separate room, which is neither living nor dining, for the intimate circle—all reflect Redelin's expectations of great wealth. Nonetheless, Redelin's text shares a set of assumptions with its more middling and struggling counterparts. Both look to the organization of the overall domestic geography of the apartment for uniformity, orderliness and efficiency.[103] And it is worth noting that it is not always clear from the magazine columns and prescriptive texts what socio-economic stratum is being targeted by any particular publication. In the section of *Zhenshchina* entitled "Domashnyi stol," or "Home table," there often appears an intimate image of a family dining in a relatively formal looking room while darning formal attire.[104] There are always flowers on the small, cozy table and a white tablecloth. This family likely is of the middle strata, perhaps with upwardly mobile aspirations.

The dining room and bigger living room (*gostinaia*), both meant primarily for entertaining guests—and thus part of the more social or public domain of everyday life—were expected to be aesthetically pleasing and decorated in cozy and tasteful styles and set up to guarantee hygienic practices and the sensible use of space. They were to represent the present through an aesthetic that met the demands of an urban, respectable lifestyle. Redelin stressed the importance of the *gostinaia* in presenting oneself and one's family to the world, perhaps a concern of the privileged but certainly also the upwardly mobile and aspirational, beyond the walls of the domestic: "If the living room served intimate family life, then the *gostinaia* had its primary role as serving society, and so the room must be decorated to reflect this goal."[105] Cleanliness should be achieved by using modern technology and its gadgets; no detail is left unmentioned: every home must have "a brush for sweeping under the cupboard"—with its two attachments to get all of the hard to reach corners—which is pictured and described. Cleaning takes a lot of time and is not a small affair. It was measured in hours. "You need four to four and a half hours to properly clean the furniture" with all of the various solutions that are suggested.[106] There also appears a whole section on "the preservation of furniture" under the homemaker's responsibilities. The very notion of "preservation" implies a staving off of decay caused by the passage of time. "New furniture after one and a half to two years must be polished anew, since without question it is necessary for the furniture's preservation. After the polishing, you must strongly wipe the furniture, again, more or less after three days and then once a week with a soft, dry cloth – do not neglect to do this."[107] Pictured is a carpet sweeper to sweep up dust. The efficient use of each moment—whether to make one's way through the domestic space or to clean up each corner and crevice—is of the utmost importance.

In a lengthy piece in *Zhenshchina*, its middling and aspirational women readers learn in great detail how to care for their furniture, with particular emphasis on the modern, contemporary nature of objects and their care.

> In classical ancient times, all lodgings and seats were made out of stone and metal, which was covered by soft coverings. In our times, the preferred furniture product is carpenter's work, [artisanal] including the types of wood used to make furniture in the first place. The best is walnut, oak and red tree. But, this sort of wood is expensive, and today's industry uses less expensive varieties of wood – pine, alder, etc., which different machines can manipulate [...]. Although this furniture is produced for less money, it is fully respectable furniture, which can satisfy the tastes of the middling everyman.[108]

This quote reveals a number of key and recurring themes. Most notably the article stresses the awareness of the large-scale epochal shift underway at the time as well as the socio-economics of its readership: "the middling everyman." The emphasis on the materials used for furnishing in "ancient" times clearly contrasts to the modern idea, which is not artisanal but factory made and practical; it is, we learn, "simple and solid" and made with "efficiency," both in its manufacturing and in its use. The materials used mean that the owner can "preserve," without wasting much time, the furniture's "shine and freshness." This article also points to the salience of daily time among the magazine's readers and instructs when and how to clean furniture in the apartment according to that very notion of time. Soft furniture with cushions must be cleaned "once a week" in order to knock out the dust, especially if it is plush, preferably with a mallet. Bedcovers must be shaken, turned and put out in the fresh air for one hour each morning. Likewise, once a week, mattresses must be knocked and cleaned with a brush; in the summer, they should be left outside in an open space. All pillows must be washed once per year. In addition to hours and days of the week, advice took into account seasons of the year. In the winter, readers are told, "you can use the snow" in order to clean the furniture.[109] Included in the article are visual examples of furniture and its placement in the various rooms. Redelin insists on the precise placing of certain objects and pieces of furniture, creating a rather uniform sense of how each apartment should be organized to most efficiently make use of time and space. In one instance, readers were shown the image of a "small corner of a living room," thereby encouraging them to set up such furniture efficiently, modestly and similarly. There appears an entire section on where pieces of furniture must be placed in the dining room for the predictability of service and routine. Each piece of furniture is prioritized according to usefulness; the most important decoration in the *stolovaia* is the buffet because its place—"in between two walls, in which the door is found laterally near the corridor or the buffet room"—creates easy access for efficiency's sake. Next to the buffet must stand a samovar serving table.[110] Each proper apartment is meant to have objects placed properly according to expectations of standardization and efficiency.[111]

The bedroom, among the most intimate spaces in the home, held a place of prominence in the prescriptive fantasies articulated by magazine authors.[112] The columnists and readers gave "particular attention to the bedroom," especially given how much time was spent there each night and the potential for health damage, especially if there were neither proper ventilation nor fresh air.[113] The author of one article in particular proclaimed that the bedroom should be "spacious and situated on the sunny side" of the apartment, since during "the course of the day, the bedroom should be thoroughly ventilated" and exposed to maximum sunlight. Moreover, in order to stave off disease and contaminated air, nappies and swaddling clothes should not be dried out/aired out in the bedroom as they do in the countryside and among the poor classes.[114] This was not the countryside of yesterday but the urban apartment of today. In the very same year, another article appeared in *Zhenshchina* about the problem of the bedroom and its placement in the apartment, with the ability for it to be properly ventilated with fresh air and an appropriate amount of sunlight. "Bedroom must be spacious and located on the sunny side of the house." Unfortunately, often the bedroom is given the smallest and darkest room, whilst the living room is given the biggest and brightest. This is just wrong, the authors explain. "Over the course of the day, the bedroom should be thoroughly ventilated."[115] The decoration and set up of one's apartment depended, in great part, upon the time of day and month of the year. The efficient use of space in the bedroom, as in all rooms, was of the utmost importance. Perhaps the most emblematic of items in regard to efficient use of space was the reclining bed-chair found in Redelin's book.[116] Much like a current-day New York City apartment, the reclining chair allowed for the maximizing of floor space for more than one usage.

Columnists writing on the decoration of the bedroom relied upon the science of hygiene and the mores of the day. No one slept in too close proximity to one another, and everyone slept on an individual bed. "You must arrange your home so as to avoid sleeping too many people in a single bedroom." Today's apartment residents could not, after all, live like peasants, who crowded into bedrooms and slept on straw. The requirements were quite exact: "In general, each adult person must have more or less 24 square feet and each child 16 square feet. Thus, in a room with 10 ft. long and 10 ft. wide, you should sleep no more than 4 adults or 6 children."[117] Such recommendations were not frivolous and were underpinned by scientific, so-called expert advice. The growth of bacteria, "Dr. Nussbaum"—a frequent scientist contributor to the magazine—argued, was one of the most troubling aspects of an unkempt, overcrowded home.[118] Dr. Nussbaum wrote that to overcome this hygiene issue "sunlight does provide the best free disinfectant method. It is key for daily use. Sunlight, exposure to the sun is essential in the curtailing of diseases and curtailing the spread of epidemics (spread of bacteria)."[119] Exposure to sunlight also marked the passage of time and the cycle of the day. Women were also advised that they must pay attention not only to "the whiteness of linens" but also to how thoroughly and properly they were washed. Such attention was imaged to reflect the "modern" aspect of housekeeping and incorporate scientific advice. Experts, such as Dr. Nussbaum, advised that even though "in times past, there was the custom of placing in the sun – clothes, linens and beds, especially among the sick and dying," the custom does not conform to current standards. In more recent times, we learn, the achievement of whiteness in linens requires using "a chlorine solution."[120] Technology also provided an avenue to a technologically up-to-date bedroom. As with the small machines for the kitchen, authors depicted a machine used to clean linens and urged their readership to consider acquiring such a device.[121] These machines were not only efficient but also reflected present-day emphases on science, technology and cleanliness. Technology was encouraged to clean the linens in the bedrooms as well as the dining areas. Readers of *Zhenshchina* were encouraged to use modern technology to more efficiently and effectively clean their linens and create a clean environment.[122]

Such advice flourished in publications aimed at a variety of socio-economic levels. In a more practically minded publication, the following tentative advice was rendered: "The beauty of the bedroom, like all rooms, is its simplicity and its usefulness in all ways."[123] Yet, taste must not rule the day entirely: "Before you decorate your bedroom, it is essential to recall that artistic taste should not interfere with comfort or practical considerations."[124] This balance was managed, in part, through the acquisition of objects. Every bedroom, for instance, should have "a bed and a small chair (*stolik*) and a cabinet near the bed." The bed should be "comfortable and hygienic, and in that sense it is practical to get a bed with a frame made of metal and a grid instead of a mattress and a hair mattress." Aesthetics are part of the calculation, we are reminded, as "metal beds are very elegant."[125] The authors continue to explain that there is a balance of considerations in setting up a modern bedroom: taste, respectability and cleanliness are among the most important. "The most intimate and cozy type of bed is one made from wood." But, the article warns, be sure to "find such a bed that is also hygienic."[126] Comfort, hygiene and style all vied for priority as city folk dreamed of creating modern lives for themselves.

Aesthetic and practical considerations were highlighted in representations of sleeping quarters for adults and the children who resided there. Hygiene and practicalities met: "all furniture, especially in the bedroom, but in all rooms, must be hygienic," and rooms must not be cluttered with superfluous chairs, sofas or desks. "The one luxury that it makes sense to have in a bedroom is a soft chair; one that is for mothers and does not collect dust."[127] One such article contained an illustration of a suite of rooms, in which there was one entitled "bedroom" and one called "sleeping room" that was connected to the "children's room."[128] Setting up the sleeping quarters according to modern dictates had particular significance for the authors. Readers were warned that women must be aware of the "evil/harmful [*vrednyi*] old customs" that were long followed vis-à-vis the set-up of a house, especially the bedroom. "The custom of making the most spacious and light room for the living room and the darkest and most crowded for the bedroom" is one of those old customs. "This is a habit of all people across classes – poor and wealthy [...] an intransigent custom" and sometimes a destructive one, as the following expert surmised: "During dreams a person needs fresh air more than anything [...] because of the kind of breathing we do in our sleep."[129] Simplicity marked the present moment. It did not, of course, hurt that simple designs were often easier—and less time consuming—to clean and keep in a hygienic condition. In addition to considerations of mental health, whether dreams or nightmares, readers were urged to consider practicalities when setting up the bedroom.

The child's quarters

Children and childhood were of the utmost concern to educators, doctors, lawyers and parents, among others, at the turn of the century in Russia. As one 1915 article put it in *Journal for Women*, there are great differences between how children were reared and raised in past times and in contemporary ones. One difference, Ellen Kay, an early advocate for children's education, comments in this Russian article "Upbringing Then and Now: From the Field of Pedagogy," is that the nineteenth century was the "century of the woman" and the twentieth will be the "century of the child."[130]

Although scholars debate the question of when modern childhood was born, there is no doubt that children in Russia at the fin de siècle were an object of great interest and study. Moreover, children and children's spaces provide a particularly enlightening case study for how modern time consciousness manifested within the domestic interior at the fin de siècle. In these years, there was a new emphasis on children in the form of "the cult of childhood."[131] Members of various newly formed professions across the spectrum—educators, psychiatrists, lawyers, doctors, furniture manufacturers and others—began to scrutinize the child, the idea of the child and understand childhood as an important stage of one's life, distinct from adulthood. The level of "civilization" that young people had, marked, for many professionals and thinkers of the age, an indication of society's progress and its movement forward. The successful raising of children, not only within individual families but also among society at large, marked Russia's claim to modernity and stake in the future. Yet, even as children were thought to be the best hope for the future, they also were imagined as not yet adults, still becoming full subjects, and as such, they were thought to be vulnerable. As the key to the future, children had to be shielded from the persistent past and also protected from the ills of modern industrial daily life.

The modern city itself housed and produced hundreds of experts in diverse fields who shared their findings on the best, most modern ways of raising children in an industrialized environment with one another and the broader public. A reflection of this embrace of science and medicine and its role in public life is the 1913 First All Russian Conference of Pediatricians and the 1911 formation of the Aid to Mothers, whose charge was "promoting hygienic care for children in St. Petersburg."[132] The emphasis on the scientific underpinnings of upbringing was found in pamphlets, magazines, newspapers and reports. One typical advertisement in one of the women's publications urged parents to "maintain healthy children!" Another pamphlet around the same time was given out to new mothers to emphasize their "hygienic" responsibilities.[133] In these magazines there were entire sections on children. In the magazine *Zhenshchina* there is a whole section called "children's world," which includes stories for children, morality tales, many drawings and painting of children, and advice on indoor and outdoor games for children.

Many of the articles on childhood included advice from experts with the underpinnings of scientific expertise, ranging from botanists to psychologists to pediatricians to armchair "experts." In a 1908 piece entitled "A Few Words about the Hygiene of Young Girls," "Doktor Nikolia," a doctor who published a well-known article "3–4 years ago about the mechanisms of the body," explains that since the well-being of a child develops "little by little," the care for his or her body "must begin from the very start of childhood." He offers a lot of advice, based—the reader is constantly reminded—on scientific study. This includes the notion that children are not to be coddled. Parents should not carry their children too long "because they must learn to put one foot in front of the other."[134] The concept of the "emotional hygiene" of children was among common wisdom in these years. To some degree, the following of these ideas depended not only on individuals and their educational level, but also on their class and socio-economic circumstances more broadly defined. Nonetheless mothers would have been inundated with pamphlets and other materials that reflected the "cult of emotional hygiene" that dictated it is *not* advantageous to shower an infant with love but rather to teach them to be independent from an early age.[135] Perhaps this was the equivalent of today's ideas about "tough love."

Scientists of many varieties were tapped to guide parents and the reading public on matters of upbringing.[136] In the "Woman-Mother" section of *Zhenshchina* readers found an extensive article entitled "Questions about Children" that reflected a consciousness of the epochal changes afoot and the role that childrearing played in this.

> In the past time [or in recent times] there has appeared a new specialty among those advanced scientific types, which is bound to grow and form into a new scientific specialty. I am talking about the "pedagogy" of the science devoted to the study of children.[137]

This area is compared to zoology for the study of animals. Like animals, children must be understood through scientific methods, including those by the American doctor Oscar Krisman in this journal forum. "Botanists study their science; zoologists have their animals […] and so children must be studied with object criteria – called pedagogy." In other words, pedagogues must study children as "botanists study plants and mineralogists study minerals."[138]

Psychiatrists too naturally took up the question of childrearing. The Moscow Society for Neuropathology and Psychiatry sponsored a talk in 1908 by scientist A.N. Bershtein on the "Questions of the Sexual Life in the Course of Family and School life," in which Bershtein recommended not to conceal the truth from children, as children should learn about intimate sexual life and "about embryology." And by the sixth and seventh class in middle school, students, especially female ones, he contends, must learn also about sexual hygiene.[139] Scientists of many stripes took an interest in childhood and children as Russia was racing toward a modern future.

At the same time, experts were aware of the new dangers and challenges afoot inspired by the very modern environment that encouraged scientific inquiry. Modern conditions, thus, created new challenges and threatened to stop the march of progress. Although there were many signs of such concerns, perhaps it is most pronounced in stories about children. A story follows entitled "The Susceptibility of Children" about an incident in Ekaterinburg.[140] The story describes in detail the incident of students engaging in a very dangerous game. They were to dare one another to hang themselves and then, at the very last moment, beg to be cut down. The article that describes this incident emphasizes how such immoral and horrible acts could only occur *now*, today and in the modern era. In the past, such games among children would not have occurred: "In past times, children's games were innocent and useful for the participants themselves."[141]

This question of epoch, of modernity and of time reverberated throughout discussions of childhood and children. Children were, after all, imagined as a tabula rasa, not yet formed, vulnerable and in need of protection, while simultaneously embodying the promise of the future. The very same magazines and advertisements that taught women and sometimes men how to set up their domestic space and build current, modern interiors, instructed parents on how to bring their children from "darkness into light" through the creation of a present-day-oriented child's sphere within the home.[142] This connection between time and childhood extended to the entire nature of childhood itself. As elsewhere, there was a "central tension" between imagining childhood as innocent, a time of "wonder," which deserves to be "preserved intact for as long as possible," and children and childhood as the "material of future adulthood."[143] Put differently, and in temporal terms, children were imagined as of the past, in early biological time, not yet formed, nascent people, always in the "becoming" stages. At the same time, they had to be protected and nurtured in order to develop into autonomous creatures and thrive as the little adults that they were and who would be the key to the future. At the Russian fin de siècle, both of these ideas about children—past and future—existed in tension with one another. Modern science sought to protect and encourage the child stuck in the past as well as the child who represented tomorrow. One arena for this nurturing and instruction was the home.

A general consensus about the dangers of the present on the creation of a healthy home environment lurked everywhere, including in discussions about children's domestic space. Children were envisioned as possessing particular vulnerabilities. A piece entitled "General Hygiene of Dwellings," which appeared in 1908, stated that unhygienic domestic as well as public areas were especially bad for children in the midst of the filth associated with insufficient infrastructure, ubiquitous construction and factory life.[144] The article emphasized that in cities there were always unhygienic areas. Particular attention had to be paid to the construction of urban, residential dwellings. Russian cities had apartment buildings that were a danger to everyone, but especially to children, whether due to dryness, dampness or a general lack of light. "It is important especially when children are involved that sanitary concerns are met or else there will be infections about." Comparisons were made to mid-nineteenth-century England in places such as Liverpool or London, where there were hygiene committees that came to inspect apartments and as a consequence the government destroyed many buildings that were considered unsanitary. Other pernicious risks included apartment buildings where children lived in basements or lower, below-ground floors or in attics. There had been many deaths of children living in these situations. Childhood mortality was a serious concern in this and other articles. Among the preventions mentioned were the hygienic conditions of the child's room. Children, it was believed, should get the best room in the apartment, replete with sunshine and fresh air.[145]

The advice given on this proper set up and decoration of a child's domestic space emphasized the potential encroachment of the dark, unclean past on the present and future. If not properly set up, bad, unmodern habits could crush an innocent child. "So, let Russian parents give their children in the first years of life—bright, happy and healthy impressions all around them." These feelings will reverberate "for generations" yet to come.[146] The only way to look toward the future is to banish the "slovenliness of the past" that had the potential to "crush an innocent child" of today.

In an era when childhood was valued, defined and studied by professionals of all stripes, as the backbone of society and as representative of all of the ills and successes in contemporary life, children's domestic spaces proved to be of the utmost importance and a means through which to understand the values of the present moment.[147] Editors and writers in journals and magazines across the journalistic spectrum—highbrow through lowbrow publications—weighed in on how to set up, and maintain, a child's quarters. In 1916, amidst world war, readers and writers debated the decoration of a young person's room. The advice began with a discussion of how to set up a young child's first independent room, even before he or she is ready to occupy the space: "Save the best room for the future child [...]. Remember, there better be room in the apartment and prepare it early so that it is bright, and has windows that point to the south."[148] The set up and decoration of the room had to reflect the modern values of cleanliness and time saving. The use of materials that required some efficiency were suggested:

> If you are able, paint the room bright with oil paints and the floor with linoleum. It will allow you to achieve ideal cleanliness in your child's room [...]. Once a week wipe the walls with a wet cloth, and of course wash the floor each day.[149]

Each aspect of a child's physical domestic space was approached with the same great care. Part of this care involved simplicity and explicitly not the accumulation of unnecessary material objects and decorative items. A 1916 *Zhenshchina i khoziaka* article highlights the value placed on simplicity, cleanliness and comfort:

> Do not clutter the child's room with unnecessary furniture [...] nothing but the most necessary items should be placed in the room. Put in there a child's bed, a bed for the nanny not far away, but not too close so that the child can move around and get out of bed from all angles [...]. The best of all would be to have the child's bed in the middle of the room [...]. Choose all of that from the simplest woods and paint it yourself with white oil paint. That allows for frequent cleaning.[150]

Potential dangers of contamination always lurked just beyond the boundaries of the controlled environment. These included not only moral corruptions but also dust and grime. Each aspect of a child's domestic space was to be controlled by those in the adult world. Such advice regularly includes suggestions such as these:

Do not make the room totally dark when a child goes to sleep. It will bring capricious and demanding dreams; and in such conditions he [*sic*] will not be able to sleep [...] do not attempt to create absolute quiet in the apartment when the child is going to sleep [...] it is natural to demand that your body be accustomed to some noise when sleeping. He should get used to not paying attention to the noises around when going to sleep.[151]

In Figure 2, we see the ideal scenario for the creation of a child's domestic space within an urban apartment: a small sleeping quarters attached to the "child's room."[152] The furniture appears very simple, wooden and without cloth to either wash or dust. In the caption we learn that there is also "a lot of air and light" in the space, making it conducive to health and general well-being.

Journalists, backed up by doctors and other scientific experts, emphasized how the contemporary moment required cleanliness as a way to avoid a disastrous future and to distance one from an insufficiently hygienic past. In a 1913 *Damskii mir* article, the readers learned that

The ideal quarters for a child should consist of two rooms: a child's which consists of just a bed, a small table, and a cabinet where the child can put his things for washing, etc., and a corner where his nanny can feed him. There should be no baskets or chests for clothing [...] all of that is forbidden in the sleeping room.[153]

The actual acquiring of two rooms and their interior material objects reserved for children, as in Figure 2, even if all household children share the rooms, would have been beyond the reach of almost all urban dwellers. Yet, the idea of keeping children separate from the nanny—and the nanny's dirty clothing— does highlight the degree to which hygiene trumped all other concerns.

The reason for the simplicity also primarily revolved around a concern for dust and grime. Dust could collect where there was an abundance of furniture and other objects in the room, causing unsanitary conditions. "Ease of cleaning"—or efficiency—also played a role in deciding "which materials best suited today's needs." For example, we learn that: "in our contemporary times" furniture for children is done "in a simple style, with rounded corners on the table and chairs, painted with white oil paints, which is easy to restore to cleanliness, or if there is a small spot is simple to clean." Likewise, "the floor [of the sleeping room] is preferably carpeted on top of linoleum [...] because it is easier to clean and disinfect." These considerations of hygiene and efficiency reflect the same fears that existed in the adult world—the aggressiveness of the past and its potential encroachment on the transformation of children into modern, fully formed subjects.[154] The qualities that must be reflected within

Спальня, соединенная съ дѣтской. Мебель новаго стиля подъ дубъ. Много воздуха и свѣта. *(Рис. по фотографіи)*.

Figure 2 "Child's Sleeping Quarters," *Zhenshchina* 1 (1908): 5–6. Public domain.

the child's domestic space are: "simplicity/austerity; the absence of unnecessary luxury; comfort; and industriousness."[155]

Authors setting the limits for the set-up of children's domestic spaces, like those writing about the kitchen, turned to discourses of scientific expertise to undergird their advice. This scientific language of professionals made its way into almost every column written on children. In the very first issue of the practically minded publication *Home and Family* there appeared an article on "Laws for Heating Rooms" (January 1910), which essentially advised readers how to fight the dampness of city, apartment living in St. Petersburg. The editor offered particular advice in the case of a child's quarters. "In order to have healthy people, the temperature in a room should not exceed 20 degrees Celsius, but [...] in a child's room it should be a little bit less," according to present-day scientific knowledge.[156]

Other journals provided much more elaborate descriptions of how to decorate and set up a child's room. In a longer piece on "How to Decorate Your Apartment" the authors of *Damskii mir* emphasized efficiency and cleanliness, with particular attention to the temporal nature of the advice: it was being given now at this particular "modern" moment.[157] These days, the advice proceeds, children had to have a "cozy, and above all, a hygienic child's room: fresh air, light, a minimal amount of stuff, all of which should be useful."[158] The furnishings, too, were expected to reflect up-to-date, scientific research in the areas of hygiene and safety. "Modern medicine rejects former rocking beds, cradles, and thick canopies; most of all a simple English bed with a not so soft mattress; one where the side comes down so that it is very easy to lay down and pick up the child."[159] The author is clearly aware of the fact that there are new standards and ideas, based on modern science and safety. Children are meant to thrive at home and grow up to live healthy, hygienic lives.

Children were thought to be vulnerable to the exposure of unclean city living. They needed help. One of the homemaker's most crucial tasks was to set up the child's room. Scientists and other "experts" explained in an article entitled "Hygiene of a Child's Room" that "[a child's room] must be the sunniest in the house" for both psychological and physical reasons.[160] The exact reasoning went as follows: "A child must occupy the absolute best room in the house [...]. From a psychological perspective, sun in a child's room is even more important [...] a dark room would cause sadness in the heart of a child."[161] In 1913 *Zhurnal dlia khoziaek* featured a series of linked pieces on the relationship between a properly ordered domestic life and a child's emotional and psychological well-being. They consulted experts, parents and readers, who wrote in with their own experiences. All emphasized the close connection between "children's rooms and its impact on the well-being of children."[162] One author pointed out, in particular, the connection between the aesthetic charms and decoration of a child's room and the happiness of the child. He wrote:

> Simplicity, hygiene and the absence of superfluous things are essential for a child's room [...]. Everything in a child's room should be light and subtle [...]. All must understand that the child's room must be the sunniest and brightest room in the home. Where there is sun – there is no illness, say the Japanese.[163]

Parents are implicated in the failure to provide these conditions for their children. A "dirty" and "noisy" household and a "disorderly" room will breed discontent and "pessimism" among children.[164] Like the bedroom more generally, the children's room is the most important room in the house, experts advised. "Perhaps you thought the living room is more important, because it is where you entertain others. But the bedroom is where you spend the most time [...]. In the bedroom you spend half of your life! [...] and being clean is essential." And this was most true when children were involved.[165] There was a time consciousness on multiple levels in this small piece of advice: the awareness of "half of your life" spent in a single room, on the one hand, and the insistence on saving time in cleaning the bedroom, on the other.

It is worth noting that these discussions and presentations of the home in women's magazines did not end with the Bolshevik seizure of power. A discussion in an early revolutionary issue in 1918 of *Zhurnal dlia khoziaek* about how the work of psychiatrists proved that there was a connection between the emotional and the physical environment for children within the home. In particular the expert described how the make-up of a child's room was of paramount importance. The angles of sunlight and the placement of furniture would have a concrete impact on the child's mental health. The expert continued: "only in a sunny room with light, with colorful curtains and cheerfully colored pictures will [children]" be inspired to have pleasant life outlooks. In one particular textual representation, there appeared a spiritual dimension to home design. Experts expressed the belief that there is a significant emphasis on "the influence of the physical on the spiritual life" of the child. Children's space, experts explained, should be separate, if possible, from the world of adults: "a child's room must be quiet so that the child has the opportunity to rest at night. A child should not be exposed to adults' trivialities at night."[166]

Readers frequently wrote in to these publications and expressed their concerns about the relationship between the interiors of their homes and the health of their families. Indeed, readers' letters frequently occupied the final pages of women's magazines and journal issues. Readers asked questions about the minutia of everyday life, *byt'*, and often they were answered by so-called experts, whether the journal editor or an authority who might have signed "doctor." In one instance, the editors addressed a reader's concerns along these lines. This reader of *Zhurnal dlia khoziaek* asked: "How do you design your home so that you feel good and cozy in it, so that you establish a corner where you can hide and forget about anything unpleasant [...]?"[167] This exchange is fascinating because the reader poses the question of how to establish a home that is shielded from the outside world at the very moment that the mass marketplace intruded on the home. In other words, as homemakers tried to keep the past and the contemporary grime at bay, they also defined the present: it was not the dirty and unhealthy yesterday, but a clean and efficient today. The editor's answer to this query revolved around two characteristics: coziness and beauty. The goal was to achieve "a harmony in the room." It was therefore "very important to choose the tone and color of the room. The tone and the color are the two most important elements in setting the mood of the room." On the question of "tone" the editorial response included the following: "The general rule is that the bedrooms and the child's room must have a bright tone. The office and living room can be darker and the dining room should be nicely done in middle tones. But I myself personally prefer the dining room to be darker shades."[168] There also appeared a lot of advice on how to decorate the walls and with which colors. Readers were advised that the bedroom should be blue-gray, the child's room should be a soft pink/rose, the living room should be dark red, the office dark gray, and the dining room should be brown, the color of oak. Moreover, "the furniture must be the simplest you can find [...] and the curtains, the least likely to collect dust on them."[169] The curtains, like the rest of the interior, were required to be clean, hygienic and dust free.

In 1903, all of these values and modern demands of children's domestic spaces were put on formal display before a public audience. At this moment, when the International Exhibition of *"Detskii Mir"* was installed in St. Petersburg, the intimate domestic interior became a concrete part of the public discussion of modernity. There was a separate "department" devoted to children's hygiene, which focused primarily on domestic spaces and habits.[170] Reporting on this exhibition came in the form of a multi-issued "listok."[171] This exhibition "Detskii Mir" was meant to have an exclusively modern character (*sovremennyi*) and draw tremendous interest from all of society. "In our times, the majority of exhibitions show the modern conditions and successes." This particular exhibition, of course, emphasized "the practical results of raising children well."[172]

The exhibition, like the myriad publications described above, emphasized hygiene, highlighting practices in the home, and its impact on daily life in general and on rates of infant mortality in particular. The leaflet that reported on the exhibition contained many references to the "hygiene department of the exhibition" and made multiple references to the "contemporary" or "modern" [*sovremennyi*] condition of hygiene among children as far from ideal, so that engagement with hygienic issues in society, even among members of the intelligentsia, is "insufficient and not common enough."[173] The emphasis of the pavilion revolved around the practices of childrearing in the home, from birth until around age eight or ten. The piece on how to raise children echoed the sentiments in the journals and magazines aimed at decoration of the home: cleanliness, efficiency and taste were valued above all else. These were the qualities, wrote Professor N.P. Gundobin, which could decrease infant mortality. "The close relationship between maintaining hygiene and death [...] makes the purpose of the exhibit very clear."[174] Staving off the passage of time and the encroachment of past time clearly resided at home and within the realm of daily habits of eating, sleeping, dressing and tidying one's apartment and teaching one's children.

Some conclusions

The connections among interiors, aesthetics and time evident in the multiple examples explored above highlight fin de siècle Russians awareness of time, of the present moment and of the ever-proximate past. Embracing the present—its expectations, its habits and its material objects—offered an escape hatch from the drudgery of the past, even if in one's imagination alone. This was, though, no easy task. The past—embodied by its dust-collecting chairs, inefficient homemaking and rural landscape—lurked around each and every corner, making it very difficult for those in the present to completely disengage. Moreover, the past, in newly urban Russia, loomed especially large in comparison to other European capitals at the same time. Russia's transformation, albeit never all-encompassing (until the Stalinist era), happened at breakneck speed. In Moscow and St. Petersburg, where residents included recently arrived peasant-workers and members of the growing middling classes, in the modern imaginary, the cloak of the past continued to shroud the landscape, in the form of rural habits, such as uncleanliness, darkness and chaos, even as Russians moved to cities and aspired to create modern, urban lifestyles.

Present time at first glance appears natural, an immovable given, a fixed frame. Yet, the meanings of the present moment, and its relationship to the past as well as the future, modern philosophers and scientists contend, transform in each context and over time. The very recognition of temporal change and its contextualization itself marks modernity, as moderns were conscious of how temporal frames are "riddled with issues of power and hegemony."[175] Understanding the contingency of the present moment also meant a hyperawareness of the proximity of the past. Both markers of a modern moment in time.

The discourses embedded within advice literature on the domestic interior aimed at aspiring urban women reveal a consciousness of temporal change, transformations both large-scale (epochal time) and small-scale (everyday time). Urban Russians, as historian Mark Steinberg articulates in his study of fin de siècle St. Petersburg, were aware that they were experiencing epochal shifts characteristic of "modernity" that would transform their everyday lives. The precise nature of these changes, of course, was not always transparent. As Steinberg points out, for instance, there is no exact word for "modernity" in the Russian language.[176] Some artists and architects used the word from French, *moderne* in Latin letters, but that was rare and the meaning narrow. Rather, the commonly used Russian word was *sovremennost*, which properly translated means "of the present time." But, just as *moderne* began to mean "a particular epochal time" in the French context, the word *sovremennost* in Russia at the fin de siècle began to signify "the distinctive times" and was understood to mean "contemporary times" or "modernity." Ultimately, *sovremennost* indicated the particular conditions that were emerging in Russia's capital cities. The prescriptive tracts available to these urban dwellers— journals, magazines and advertisements—endlessly referenced "in our times" (*v nashem vremeni*) or "in our modern times" (*v nashem sovremennosti*), reflecting modern historical consciousness.[177] Russians encountered these prescriptive discourses as they absorbed the new expectations of urban life: norms shaped by modern, temporal concerns.

At the same moment, temporal shifts were felt in the daily and mundane activities of everyday life, whether through efficiency or cleanliness or the simple standardization and measuring of minutes in the hour and hours in the day. The particular way in which one was to live "in our times" was the subject of countless articles, images and editorials at the turn of the century. These texts were imbued with a modern time consciousness that reflected the anxieties of the age: not only that they lived at a time distinct from the past but also that they feared that the past was always in dangerously close proximity. The pages and pages of advice literature all pointed to this growing notion that in Russia, and especially for residents of the two capital cities, a new era was dawning. "Modernity" was ushering in a new day, a new now, "in our times," a time that belonged to "us," the urban Russian reader.[178] This "our" or "us" contains a "theirs" or "them," who were likely to be the rural peasants stuck in the old ways of the past. Discursively, thus, the past was imagined as dangerous, in part because of its association with Russian rural realities and embodied by the peasant, who threatened the creation of a modern, urban now. There was no place for the past—the peasant, the dirt, the chaos and the unpredictability—in the modern, domestic interior of "our times." Yet, a nostalgic sensibility seemed to lurk in the shadows, even as the dust of the past was being slowly swept away. The residue of dust remained. This residue was no small matter. Rather, as the next chapter will reveal, whether in the form of nostalgic portraits of estates in glossy magazines or memoirs of childhood steeped in filial landscapes or the preservation of ruins or the reinvention of peasant domestic crafts, images of yesterday and the decades before that, proliferated simultaneously with the embrace of the bourgeois-like hygienic and scientific interior.

3

The Past in the Present: Nostalgic Portraits
of the Russian Home

At the very same moment that newly urban families looked toward the future and embraced modern domestic expectations described in the previous chapter, from the cleaning of their bodies to the washing of their sheets, others in and near Russia's urban centers gazed longingly backwards. When the wealthy merchant Savva Mamontov and members of his artistic circle, for instance, walked into his recently purchased Aksakov family estate, Abramtsevo, in the waning decades of the nineteenth century, they immediately realized they were stepping into another era. Fin de siècle merchants and artists, such as Mamontov and his circle, understood that they "had to show profound respect for the previous owners". Although he expanded the footprint of the house and created "a new wing" to accommodate his family, Mamontov kept many objects—tables, dressers and chairs—where they were and did little to change the visual landscape. The past was, in this sense, everywhere: it was embedded in the domestic material objects, in the furniture or in the "Aksakov old things." And it resided in "a kind of spirit reflected in the Aksakov stories told by the servants," whom Mamontov retained.[1] And yet, even as elements of the former era continued to thrive, "a new, young, energetic life" simultaneously emerged.[2] Multiple epochs existed at once at Abramtsevo and were sensed in the walls, in the objects and in the memories of those who had lived there.[3] In this memoir we see how the spirits from the past were characters in the present, embedded in spaces and objects of domestic life as Abramtsevo and Russia as a whole entered into a new phase at the fin de siècle.

Philosophers, historians and scholars of many disciplines tell us that modernity brought with it the notion that the past, often preserved and repurposed in the present, itself is neither still nor unitary. The past, in its layers of meanings and material manifestations—a chair, a memory, a commemorative monument—is constitutive of the now. At Abramtsevo, as

Aksakov described it, the past became part of a contemporary moment where even as a new wing was created the old hallways were preserved. In this sense, as Henri Bergson, the French philosopher whose writings are about the meanings of temporality in the modern world, indicates, the past and the present in the modern era formed a coherent whole, one that was never linear, but always circular and selective. As Mamontov embraced parts of the Abramtsevo past, other aspects were partly discarded or simply ignored altogether. In this sense, the layering of past and present in Aksakov's descriptions of the estate, as he perceived it, echo what many philosophers have called "modern time," a notion of temporality when "people began to reflect on historical time itself."[4] The past played a central role in the formulations of the modern present. As one of the foremost scholars of temporality indicates: "The association of historical reflection with the consciousness of forward movement allowed one's own modernity to be marked out only by reference to a previous period."[5] The past was everywhere.

Russian nostalgia and modern time

This omnipresent past appeared in a multitude of objects and spaces, whether in the pages of childhood memoirs, the celebration of bygone estates or the embrace of craftsman-like wooden spoons with peasant designs, all part of the Retrospectivist impulse in art and design of the age.[6] While this "historicist" sensibility was not entirely new at the fin de siècle, it now appeared in full force.[7] The imagined eighteenth and early nineteenth centuries, divorced as they were from the sometimes brutal realities of daily life, began to inspire nostalgic longings for an invented past. This nostalgia included an imagined eighteenth century replete with a calm and peaceful aesthetic, which stood in stark contrast—and served as a welcome counterbalance—to the realities of the Russian early twentieth century with its massive population movement, crowded cities and impending war. In other words, regardless of the lived experiences of those eighteenth-century subjects, its fin de siècle representations imagined bygone decades as an era of beauty and relative calm. Writing on the meaning of the eighteenth century in later eras, Luba Golburt explains that often "presents are changed into pasts not in a linear way, but inconsistently and incrementally with parts being forgotten, remembered, and invented along the way."[8] In this sense, whether it was an embrace of the eighteenth-century estate or the early nineteenth-century burgeoning city, the later nineteenth century brought with it a paradigm shift in how the past was seen: "historical consciousness begins to frame and explain experience on all levels."[9]

Fin de siècle educated Russians were conscious of the meanings of time and some became enamored of Henri Bergson. Bergson's notions of duration echoed Russian Orthodox ideas about temporal flow. He argued that modernity brought a heightened epochal consciousness, and that with this heightened awareness came not simply a rejection of traditional understandings of time as quantifiable and progressive, but a simultaneous embrace of a second notion of time: "real time." "Real time," for Bergson, signified flow and flux. He believed that "past and present states [form] an organic whole," and that time cannot be completely scientifically calculated. This Bergsonian notion of time relied on intuition and unknowability, ideas that were very appealing to a Russian Orthodox audience.[10]

More contemporary cultural critics helped elucidate the various meanings of nostalgia at the dawn of the twentieth century. From Bergson and his ideas about temporal unknowability to cultural studies critic Svetlana Boym and her post-Soviet reading of nostalgic impulses, philosophers and scholars have long helped shed light on the fin de siècle nostalgic embrace of the past. For Russians living in the late nineteenth and early twentieth centuries, the nostalgic gaze existed, as Boym suggests, "somewhere in the twilight of the past or on the island of utopia where time has happily stopped, as on an antique clock."[11] Although Boym wrote amidst post-Soviet, early twenty-first-century anxieties, they mirror a phenomenon familiar precisely a century earlier: writers and readers found themselves within equally tumultuous transformations, including the Russian state's industrial drive and the subsequent migration to cities, the Revolution of 1905 and the entry into the First World War.[12] One hundred or so years prior to Boym's reflections, in the middle of countless political and social upheavals with the future uncertain, nostalgic writings and portraits surged.

The very idea of nostalgia itself reflects a modern temporal sensibility, which insists that echoes of the past are inherent in the present, whether through memory, material objects or commemorations. There is always, thus, both a sense of loss and of continuity with bygone eras. Peter Fritzsche, writing in the context of the European nineteenth century, explores how modern selfhood necessitated a sense of loss, and part of that loss included a nostalgic longing for a past that may or may not have ever been. In this sense, "nostalgia [...] [is a longing] to return to home, but it does so [...] with the knowledge that home is lost and loss is what remains."[13] Of course, the notion that Russians at the turn of the century had a fascination with the past is not new. Walter

Benjamin, upon visiting Moscow in 1926 to 1927 noted that "beggars" imagined as the embodiment of "the past in the present," roamed the streets of Moscow. These "beggars" "testified to the lingering presence of the past" and "all of the promises of modern life left unfulfilled." Artists, writers, commentators—all—embraced a sense of past in their art and writings, and beggars haunted their every thought.[14] Luba Golburt describes the involvement of early twentieth-century artists—such as painter Mstislav Dobuzhinsky, who created cityscapes that reflected a sense of urban decay—in reimagining "sets of the past," which hung in estates across Russia. Part of these depictions included renditions of the eighteenth century, which were insistent not only on its "pastness" but also on the strangeness and "incompleteness of the pastness" that was integral to reckoning with large-scale change in the present.[15] The eighteenth century, as seen through the eyes of later nineteenth- and twentieth-century admirers of art, became both "ancient" and "modern" simultaneously.[16] Dobuzhinsky was both an early member of *Mir iskusstvo*, an artistic group comprised of university students who embraced modern concepts of art at the fin de siècle, and also a contributor to *Apollon*, a St. Petersburg-based poetry journal founded in 1909. His participation and ideas were emblematic of the movement and of this era more broadly. There was an impulse to ward off the impending modern moment by embracing a sense of the past. This past became manifest everywhere, in artistic subjects, in aesthetics, even in the materials used. The use of mahogany in the re-creation of peasant crafts (*krasnoe derevo*) was implicitly a critique of the anxiousness of modern life. And yet, far from warding off the past, it was as if at the fin de siècle "gazing into the past has become part of modern life" itself, whether as a way to ward off the unknown future or avoid the violence of the present once the First World War began.[17]

Central to the time consciousness was the appearance of widespread "public nostalgia," which emerged as part of this embrace of modern intuitive notions of the flow of time and stasis of the past. This sensibility, as scholars have noted, was born in the cities, especially St. Petersburg and to some degree Moscow.[18] It manifested in a number of ways. A case in point are the displays and writings associated with the Jubilee of 1913/1613: the Romanov tercentenary. It was celebrated not just with pomp and circumstance, but also with tchotchkes and trinkets. The past was on display for various publics to enjoy, to see and to feel. They could gaze upon the re-creation of seventeenth-century churches and admire the sartorial choices of noblemen and noblewomen in the seventeenth century.[19] The past could be held, felt and, if desired, thrown away without much consequence. Indeed, the erecting of Stepan Krichinskii's Tercentenary Church in 1913 in order to mark a hundred years of Romanov rule serves as a very public and large-scale example of nostalgia on display: the church building was an exact replica of its seventeenth-century counterpart, a "Rostov" wall church.[20] The past haunted those who came to admire and to worship and celebrate what would soon become the last of the tsars.

Nostalgia had spatial and material dimensions. Nostalgia derives "from *nostos*—return home, and *algia*—longing" and denotes a desire for a place, a home, that no longer is around or in some instances has never been. The nostalgic impulse, thus, both indicated a sense of "loss and displacement" and simultaneously reimagines precisely what was lost and relocates it where it should have been. There is an inherent temporal simultaneity involved in nostalgic impulses. They require a kind of "double exposure," which becomes "stifled within the conventional confines of time and space."[21] Multiple time frames coexist in memory and consciousness. Representations of home, its architectural exteriors and domestic interiors, emerged as a central arena where nostalgia flourished in the early decades of the twentieth century, as Russians struggled to understand their place in the constantly changing environment.

Living in an environment of uncertainty and change, Russian fin de siècle writers situated their nostalgic portraits within the familiar domain of the domestic sphere in estate life or city mansions, replete with luxury and wealth. As modern nostalgia mourned that loss of the possibility of return, and the loss of a time more carefree, predictable and orderly, writers and readers (re-)created the past through textual and visual signs, where the domestic space signaled that mythical world. In this sense, the rapid pace of industrialization and urban transformation increased "the intensity of people's longing for the slower rhythms of the past, for social cohesion and tradition" in their daily lives.[22] This occurred, of course, through the use of modern technologies of display, both textual and visual. As historian Mark Steinberg has described, this was an era of melancholy, where longing seeped into the corners of apartments and frustrated desire walked the streets.[23] All this longing could be felt and viewed in newspapers, journals, self-writings and exhibitions across Russia's two capital cities.

Nostalgic narratives of time and space: The childhood home

In an age saturated with history, childhood, as Fritzsche describes for the broader European context, "acquired the same romantic status as the castle ruin, and both became containers to hold the 'good old days.'" And these "good old days" were integral to the creation of the everyday in the present. In this sense, the ruins of the past "extended into personal lives" and into the interiors of home and hearts.[24] If nostalgic narratives writ large reach for a past, albeit idealized in some form, retrospective narratives of childhood engage individual pasts as a way of reconciling with a present moment, whether with longing or desire. For some, the embrace of childhood and its resurrection in the present expressed the degree to which individuals "constructed their [contemporary] identities out of a sense of displacement" and loss.[25]

In the final decade or so of the nineteenth century, urbanization took hold of Russia and city life began to hit its stride. Individuals, families and groups were uprooted. Their sense of home changed. These signs of modern transformation were everywhere: the increasingly mass-scale politics and the mass circulation of newspapers as well as the dirt and overcrowding of urban life, to name a few. Peasants, many of whom had continued after the emancipation of the 1860s to live in rural regions and towns beholden to collectivities and landlords, made their way to the cities. While many of these newcomers to Moscow or St. Petersburg continued to have strong ties to their villages, they still found themselves in a drastically new environment where they refashioned themselves into workers (or peasant-workers). They lived in squalid quarters or served as house servants for the wealthier residents of the cities. Many from modest gentry backgrounds also found themselves uprooted from a familiar domestic world as they sold their estates and moved to newly constructed apartments in the capital cities. These decades, before and after 1905, thus, brought drastic transformations in the daily, and domestic, lives of Russians across the socio-economic spectrum.

These large-scale transformations, impacting much of the population in and around cities, served as the backdrop for the strong nostalgic impulse of the age. The reification of the home as a repository of nostalgic sentiments of long past days reflected the changing domestic landscape for many newly urbanized Russian citizens at the fin de siècle. In particular, the transforming domestic circumstances, the move to apartments and the massive scale change manifested in political upheaval, urbanization and industrial growth, not to mention full-scale war. Estate life was waning as gentry homes fell into disrepair or were divided up—as Anton Chekov masterfully described in *The Cherry Orchard*. Peasants were becoming workers in the cities and the emergent middling classes occupied city residences. As writers looked toward an uncertain future, they reached into the past to create a story that helped them come to terms with their present. This story involved conjuring a mythical time when the social order was intact. Authors dreamt of their own childhoods and of domestic life, with its hierarchical relationships and its relative predictability. This distinctly modern embrace of historical time—and nostalgia—included a sense of their place within the forward-looking narrative of Russian tradition, present and future.

Many of the facets of modern life—alienation, corruption and cynicism, overcrowding, filth and mindless routine—saw their counterpoints highlighted in the nostalgic writings about childhood and the home. The images of childhood explored in these self-writings emphasized the emotional intimacy of home and childhood, the cozy spaces of domestic interiors, the beauty and calming of the natural world, and the innocence and orderliness of daily life. Taken together, nostalgic portraits of childhood centered on the intimate and ordered spaces of the domestic realm, places free of the ever-encroaching and ever-transforming, corrupt and alienating modern world.

The impulse to narrate one's history and the lives of family members took hold in Russia in the years after the Emancipation of the Serfs (1861) and the other Great Reforms. Scores of writers filled pages upon pages of their diaries, autobiographies and memoirs written from the mid-nineteenth century through the first decades of the twentieth. They revealed, among other things, that the trope of happy childhood so celebrated in the Stalinist 1930s had much earlier roots. Lev Tolstoy's *Childhood*, the first of three parts in a cycle of autobiographical texts, written in 1852, was perhaps the first such text. In this novelized autobiography, Tolstoy participated in—and some argue created—this resilient "sociocultural myth" of "a happy childhood." It would resurface in Russian literature throughout the next one hundred years.[26]

By the turn of the twentieth century, the attention paid to the subject of childhood only intensified. With the increasing sense of societal change after 1905, recently minted professionals turned to the subject of childhood in their discussions of law, medicine and education.[27] They created a series of debates within the emergent civil sphere regarding children's bodies, education and proper rearing techniques. This emphasis on childhood within professional circles, though important, was not the only reason why self-writings about childhood years proliferated. The early twentieth century saw an upsurge of attention to real children and narratives of childhood during an era of modern rupture, where individuals felt dislocated from the past. And perhaps the most important expression of the dislocation among individuals was "the evocation of lost childhood."[28] This is precisely what the dozens of diaries and autobiographies express: the attempt to create what has been lost. For many Russians at the fin de siècle childhood occupied a place in time, at once gone forever and resurrected through nostalgic portraits.

The subject of childhood as a defined life stage occupied a very particular place within nostalgia's time/space narrative. Childhood, in fact and in memory, is a finite stage (albeit with historically contingent boundaries and borders) that exists in time and for a time. It is almost instantly a place of memory, a place of recollection and, in the modern context when childhood itself took on more defined meanings, a recurrent frame of reference in adult life. Depictions of childhood years became for many Russian writers around the fin de siècle a repository for their desires and an opportunity to recreate what had been lost or wished for, but never realized. In its individual depictions, childhood served as a treasure trove of long-past moments, which were recovered through memory and retrieved by words on paper. These pages reflected the romantic desire to return to an imagined past, cozy and intimate and innocent, in the face of the alienation of industrial and urban present-day life. Yet, these childhood spaces and memories irretrievably resided in the past.

Written from exile and after the revolutionary upheaval, first published in 1951, Vladimir Nabokov's *Speak, Memory*, a narrative about his life from 1903 until he left for America in 1940, celebrated the early years of his boyhood while living in a prerevolutionary St. Petersburg and at their country estate Vyra. Nabokov, a celebrated émigré author, recollects the domestic spaces that marked his youth. From his descriptions of being a child on the Batovo estate—where Pushkin dueled to the death and where the Nabokov clan took up residence decades later—to Vyra, their St. Petersburg estate, Nabokov injects his stories with the nostalgic impulse so characteristic of his era. He highlights how as a child he trotted "from sun fleck to sun fleck" in the environs of his family home.[29] Moreover he describes "the kind of Russian family to which I belonged – a kind now extinct."[30] Nabokov's emphasis might be more poetic and severe than others—as from the vantage point of postrevolutionary exile he not only mourns his childhood but also his loss of an entire prerevolutionary world[31]—but he is not alone. Early twentieth-century portraits of childhood homes, such as Nabokov's, reflected larger ongoing discussions of the emergence of the meaning of childhood and the role of the domestic. Authors re-created imaginary homes, replete with childhood joys, orderly routines and memories long past in order to make sense of the world shifting around them. Nostalgic portraits of domestic space—cherry orchards, bridges through gardens, grand parlors and cozy nurseries—thus proliferated as cityscapes were born and smokestacks erected.

Like Vladimir Nabokov, many of the most successful artists, writers and members of the Russian fin de siècle intelligentsia more generally wrote retrospective narratives of their lives as children; some wrote from political exile after the Bolsheviks rose to power, others in the last years of Tsarist rule from within Russia itself. In these pre- and postrevolutionary fin de siècle musings, the childhood home occupied center stage, often located outside of the filth and overcrowding of the urban streets and factories. Whether modest in size or elegant with sprawling corridors, country estates, city houses and apartments often appeared among the main characters in the narratives that memoirists created in the first two decades of the twentieth century. From an emphasis on nature to filial intimacy to self-consciousness about the passage of time, writers attempted to create a world of childhood remote from the realities of their daily experiences and their contemporary surroundings. Childhood, in the nostalgic time/space complex, was both then and there. Themes in the childhood reminiscences of educated Russians at the dawn of the twentieth century—ones that reflect an attempt to grapple with the modern present through depictions of an imaginary past—include an emphasis on nature, order and intimacy.

Like Nabokov's family estate, the spaces of childhood were housed in the past. Memories resided in the garden, the parlor or the child's room. This domestic landscape conjured a nostalgic, sweet and irrecoverable past. Childhood was recalled not only as a time in one's life but also as a place in one's personal history. The memories in autobiographical writings reflect this intersection of time and space. P.P. Semenov Tian-Shansky, a well-known geographer who managed the Russian Geographical Society, explained in his autobiographical musings from 1906 that the memory of his "old [one-story] house [...] built out of wood" was the "first visual memory of my childhood."[32] His childhood sat at the intersection of time and space.

The themes of modern life—alienation, loneliness, industry—all found their opposites in the depictions of home and childhood. In this sense, the invocation of childhood reflected the simultaneous embrace of past and present and the impulse to stop the hands of time and embrace the imagined calm of bygone days. The childhood home, for example, appeared amidst nature rather than in the hustle and bustle of town or city life. The peaceful tenor of natural places served as the backdrop for many childhood memoirs. These natural surroundings near the home no doubt contrasted to the industrial projects of the day and, thus, played a central role in childhood descriptions. Tian-Shansky commented on how as a boy in his family home "from the terrace you could see pretty flowers in the summer."[33] In his memories of childhood, P.N. Miliukov, historian and prominent member of the Constitutional Democratic Party, used images of his mother in the gardens and "picking apples in the fall."[34] He recalled walking around the trees as a child with his mother near him.

The natural environment, seen from within the vantage point of a domestic interior (through the window) or experienced outside, served as a calming backdrop to the orderly life inside hallways and rooms. Konstantin Stanislavskii, actor and theatre director, emphasized in his autobiography—written in postrevolutionary 1925—the perfection and sheer happiness of his early days, surrounded by family and by nature. His authorial voice, in his present moment, highlighted how his childhood years could never be retrieved. These irretrievable memories, as sweet as they are, haunted him in the present. "I stand here now resurrecting a moment from memory, a moment in my former child's life and I am again exactly young and I feel a familiar feeling." In these feelings he recalled the "morning of a holiday: a free day ahead, we could wake late in the morning – a day full of joy [...] nature demanded happiness on such a day, and we believed that anything to interfere with that was evil."[35] Such interruptions would have meant a challenge to the idyllic version of childhood: unfettered pleasure, freedom and joy.

Memoirists depicted how the cozy and comfortable physical spaces of the domestic interior, along with the natural world, served as central stages upon which childhood was enacted. Alexandra Shchepkina recalled in her memoir the closeness of physical domestic space during her own childhood years. "We, the two girls, slept in one cozy room with two beds, each close to the other."[36] Despite the obvious smallness and likely cramped quarters, Shchepkina, and others, used words such as "cozy," "comfort" and "coziness" to describe the feeling of being in their childhood homes. The closeness multiplied at Christmas time "when all of the siblings were at home."[37] "Coziness" appears here too, even when all ten children were in the house. She paused on the shared childhood between herself and the rest of the Stankevich family and provided a description of early childhood in the domestic realm: she and her siblings congregated in "our small room at the end of the corridor of the magnificent house. I remember, too, that we were permitted to run in the big hall with the clock, as long as it did not disturb the older siblings or our mother." Time was marked by the "big hall with the clock," indicating the ubiquitous nature of the temporal frame in her memoir writings. Modern time—marked by the mechanized and large-scale clock—contrasted with the cozy, close quarters of childhood at home. Time, in this example, reverberates through both object (clock) and space ("small room at the end of the corridor").[38] Shchepkina, too, emphasized the layered temporal nature of the home itself. She recalled how her father had a new wing built in the house, in part due to a fire that occurred, and how looking out on the balcony she recalled how she was "born in the new wing." This temporal layering of the home itself emerged as part of her memory itself.[39]

The portraits of intimacy among family members mirrored the descriptions of the coziness of the material realities of the domestic interiors. Writers included passages describing the parental and sibling closeness of their childhood years. Childhood, at least the early years spent at home before formal institutional schooling, was introduced through a series of loving sketches, each centered on scenes of intimacy among family and friends. These intimate moments served as counterpoints, sometimes seemingly self-conscious ones, to the alienation of contemporary modern life. Alexandre Benois, who was both the founder of *Mir iskusstva*, the magazine and the artistic circle, and the director of the Ballets Russes, reflected on time passages in his autobiography. He made his reader aware of the time/space lag between the events he remembered and the process of writing them down: "As I sit here by an open window, looking out on the practically native to me Seine [in Paris], in today's heat on a bright, June evening in 1934, I imagine myself being transported back as in a time machine to a time long ago, when I lived in my native city [St. Petersburg]."[40] His imagination moved back to St. Petersburg and his idyllic childhood years.

Like Benois, P. Florinsky, an historian, recalled in his memoirs—written in diary form throughout 1916 and entitled *To My Children: Memoirs of Days Gone Past*—how childhood filial intimacy served as a refuge from the world outside. It was a place of escape from the troubles outside. "I use the word heaven [*rai*] [...] I had the purest form of family life, I was raised in heaven, where there was never fear and never internal turmoil, or cold, or the taint of outside, external social relationships. There was no space for, no, it seemed, even death."[41] Florinsky dwelt on his childhood relationship with his father, the time they spent together at home and in its environs, and the intimacy between them. "My father often took me with him on strolls through the city [...] I remember when we were out together and he bought me my first doll (*kuklia*). I passionately loved that doll." His father brought him all comforts: "With papa I always had that unfettered feeling of intimacy."[42] On one occasion in particular, Florinsky recalled a family outing to the sea: "That sea, that blissful sea, blissful childhood [...] I already cannot see it now [...] it is gone, it left, truly where does time go? [...] I remember now my childhood memories."[43] They were distant, yet present in the current moment.

The spatial closeness—often within a domestic interior space—and emotional intimacy, such as highlighted by Florinsky's narrative, overwhelm depictions of childhood years in intelligentsia narratives. Konstantin Stanislavsky also described his early years as filled with love and intimacy among family members. He highlights too the affections between his parents: "My parents were in love with one another from youth until old age; they were so in love with each other and with their children, that they always kept them so close at home."⁴⁴ Memoirs of parental nearness also characterized many of the memoirs written at the fin de siècle and later. In the pages of Miliukov's *Vospominaniia*, he writes about his early childhood. There is an extended description of how his parents met. His mother was only fifteen, "in the innocence of her youth." When he was a young boy, he remembers a very "happy family life," with his parents' love shaping the family. That is, until his father died of cholera.⁴⁵ Finally, Florinsky too provided details of the daily life of his younger self within his "exclusive little world" of childhood. He wrote with affection: "my parents were home bodies" and my mother spent her life "tending to her children, of which there were ten."⁴⁶ These memoirs, only the very tip of the iceberg of recollections, highlight the degree to which childhood, and domestic childhood, emerged as a trope among nostalgic writers and their audiences. The imagery of closeness, both spatial and emotional, woven into these memoirs and autobiographical writings all reveal how modern time, and its nostalgic manifestations, were refracted through the spaces of domesticity and its familial intimacy. These themes, far from unique to the handful of memoirs presented here, were magnified in the particularly rich and detailed memoir of the daughter of a prominent merchant, Vera Nikolaevna Kharuzina (1867–1931), who was born and died in Moscow.

Kharuzina's autobiographical writings are at once exemplary in her subject choice (childhood and home) and exceptional in their detail and self-conscious authorial voice. Hers is, thus, a particularly lively example of nostalgic memoir literature on childhood and domestic life. Kharuzina was born the daughter of a successful Moscow merchant and Russia's first female professor of ethnography. Kharuzina grew up in an educated environment—her three brothers also became ethnographers—and taught ethnography in the Higher Women's Courses and at the Archeological Institute in Moscow from 1907 until 1923, including the years she was composing her autobiography. Entitled simply *The Past: Reminiscences of the Years of Childhood and Youth*, her memoir does not represent the high literary prose of Lev Tolstoy's fictionalized account of his own childhood but, rather, relies on detailed stories about daily life among her family and its close circles, perhaps with an ethnographer's eye. Kharuzina's autobiographical narrative has its own clear purpose: to pass on her memories of the habits and customs and the daily lives of members of the educated, privileged merchant class. In this way, her narrative, so self-conscious in its purpose, highlights the degree to which professionals in the 1910s, when she was writing, concerned themselves with questions of childhood and domesticity. Given Kharuzina's scholarly, scientific lens, her firsthand account of growing up in a successful and well-educated merchant home in the later part of the nineteenth century, surrounded by all of her siblings and tutors and nannies, throws into stark relief the experience of childhood, through memory's prism, at the start of the twentieth century.

There is something strikingly self-conscious about Kharuzina's own awareness of the temporal/spatial dimensions in her narratives of her childhood. She asserted in the introduction that: "If someone uses this memoir to understand childhood in my era that would be my greatest joy."[47] The entire project was written in the form of a diary. She pieced together her past in a series of diary entries spread over years. Her memoir began in 1910 and ended in about 1926; she stated herself that it was written "intermittently" and did not always follow a linear temporal sequence. Throughout, Kharuzina paused to remind the reader of her desire to preserve the past, a particular series of moments in her own life story, through these pages. "Here is a depiction of life at home – children's and 'bigger ones' [...] I want to say so much about my sweet past, about the sweet, warm and good people, who shaped our childhood – a happy childhood."[48] Her primary purpose is clear: she hoped her autobiographical reflections would survive and elucidate future understandings of childhoods long past.

Her narrative exposed the anxieties of the present from the vantage point of a postrevolutionary moment: the alienation, the corruption, the numbing routine and the chaotic sensations of dislocation. It invoked none of these markers of modern life; rather, her stories created an opposite feeling. She writes a nostalgic portrait of her sweet younger years amidst her family. This childhood at home includes the orderliness of daily life, the intimacy and closeness of human relations, and of physical space in her childhood years. With each evocation of innocence, of order, of intimacy, Kharuzina's words are reflective of modern sentiments and temporal understandings, whether intentionally or not. Not only does she gaze into the future and plainly state her desire to be remembered after she is gone, but she also presents the past through a multitude of presents, which collectively create an opportunity to reflect upon modern life. She is not insolating herself from her 1910s world but, rather, participating in creating a modern aesthetic that relies on nostalgic impulses evoked through time and space. It is the very absence of the outward markers of modern change that points to an awareness, conscious or not, of the profound changes afoot.

The mood of the overall writing vacillates between a feeling of deep longing (*toska*) and a much lighter celebration of her early years. Ultimately, her ambivalent, and sometimes vacillating, depictions of childhood reflect the multifaceted, dialectic nature of modern life. In one particularly melancholy moment, Kharuzina describes her memories of the loss of her favorite tutor. She was eight years old. This brought her "first woe." She recalls how:

> Out of the window of our small child's room with the rising moon just coming up in the early spring morning, we sat at our students' desks – itself an open card table: Kolya (her brother) sat in front of me with an open book in his hands and between us there she was, with her lovely, dear, pale face [...] she had to go and she would not remain with us for long.[49]

The feeling she remembers upon learning this news was a deep sense of *toska*. Once the tutor went, Kharuzina's girlhood melancholy only intensified. "Life went on as always, and we had to go on too, regardless of the woe; we learned this life lesson so early [...] the heart is broken by *toska*."[50] Her memoir is filled with lessons, whether sad or joyful, and she created a sense of nostalgic sentiment, with both a desire to return and the knowledge that it was not possible. In a sense, this example encapsulates many of the themes emergent in Kharuzina's narrative: the cozy, small spaces of memory; the safe, predictable routines; and the heightened emotional, nostalgic mood of daily life. The stories that Kharuzina narrated, like the one above, were centered on the home.

The physical space of the home itself emerged as a main character in her story, even if the actual location shifted over the course of her narrative, as her family moved among the Moscow apartment, the dacha outside of the city and later Arkhangelsk. Each time the family relocated, Kharuzina paused in her writing in order to provide minute detail about the physical landscape of the domestic spaces. Throughout her text, her memories included the mundane, physical realities of home life and its associated objects and routines of daily life, including the furniture, the wallpaper, the garden and the food. Her words were heightened with emotion in the passages where she concentrated on the experience of her parents purchasing for the first time a family house in the city (previously they had been renters of apartments). Kharuzina provided her readers with the children's reactions to their new urban house. They asked its color, shape and size. They wondered whether it had a garden or space to roam around. The house, through the children's enthusiasm (in her telling) became its own character in the story. "Sweet, sweet home, we did not yet know you, but we loved you." They called it "our yellow one" and declared, Kharuzina wrote, "that there is no one better than you." Kharuzina also provided a "life history," of sorts, its birth, life and death.[51] The personification of the home as a comfort reverberated in her depictions of the natural world in the environs of her home.

The domestic interior, in the vignettes that Kharuzina provided, were accompanied by her celebration of the domestic exterior, whether natural vistas seen peering out of windows or scenes of walking in the gardens. Kharuzina elevated her natural surroundings, especially those that were in close proximity to her home. Whether a self-conscious effort to hold back the tide of industrial growth in the Moscow of her present (the 1910s) or an attempt to associate her early years with the natural world, nature played an important role in the childhood memories she provided. Nature, often seen through interior windows, served as a counterpoint to the industrial landscape of Moscow: the cozy interior on the one hand was juxtaposed with the alienating transformations of urbanization, and the natural beauty was presented in contrast to the mechanical industrial change. This imagery, nostalgic in its tenor, is constitutive of modernity with its contradictory dialectical impulses: the past and its imagined peacefulness is embodied within modern transformations. Nature was everywhere in Kharuzina's storyline. She repeatedly emphasized both the education that she and her brother Kolya received on and in the natural world, and their subsequent love of nature, as they experienced it as young children. In an entry on June 13, 1912, Kharuzina paused over how much she and her siblings were taught to love nature. "Love of nature was established in us early. We loved nature in all of its aspects." Their time at the dacha, their home on the outskirts of Moscow, especially allowed the children to spend days feeling "harmonious with nature." Kharuzina writes: "When papa arrived at the dacha we would sit under our beloved bird cherry tree (*cheremukha*) in the garden, and we knew, without a word from him that the peacefulness of his silence meant that he was well among the green, the flowers and amongst us."[52] They were together and also comfortable with their natural surroundings. This image served as a counterweight to the alienation and aloneness so characteristic of modernity. Their mother too appreciated the "quiet evenings" out in nature "when nothing could bother us."[53] Nature, in her memories, surrounded her childhood with peace and quiet, and written from the vantage point of the 1910s, stands in stark contrast to the urban environment of the day, even as it is constitutive of modernity itself.

The invocation of nature was intertwined with her girlhood memories and created a juxtaposition between the industrial reality of the present and the natural environment of her childhood. The natural world enchanted her when she was young. Whether near Moscow or elsewhere, Kharuzina presented the intersection of time and space as she connected her girlhood with the forest that surrounded her home. Her time outside of Moscow, in the city of Archangelsk and its surroundings, was one such place. In the later part of her memoir, written in the mid-1920s, Kharuzina provides stories from her summers in Archangelsk with her aunt. "Our summer life left me with a sunny memory of the pure happiness of my childhood."[54] They lived on the grounds of the Yusupovs' palace, a well-known and long-standing aristocratic family. Kharuzina's family stayed in one of the many dachas on the grounds: "Our garden was the biggest [...] at least it seemed that way with my child's eyes." She provides long descriptions of the gardens and forests where they played.[55] "One beautiful summer morning, we walked through the park [...] noticing the high nature of the grasses and the trees."[56] Her descriptions of childhood, then—whether within the confines of the domestic interior peering outside or within natural surroundings themselves—created a nostalgic picture of daily life as calm and intimate, a counterpoint to the modern world of industry and alienation in which she presently lived as she wrote.

Modernity, with its many contradictions—the desire to create and to undo—touched Kharuzina's narrative in many ways. Nostalgia, of course, sits at the nexus of these two contradictory impulses. Modernity's creative impulses caused change and distance from the past; once in place, modern subjects longed for what was now gone for good. One such modern impulse in Kharuzina's writings is that she simultaneously reflected the transformative aspects of modern life and the desire to recover what had been lost: the familiar and predictable order of daily life. Order was invoked as a response, conscious or otherwise, to the alienating and chaotic changing surroundings. One reprise in the memoir was the ordered nature of relationships and spaces within the household: both between parents and children, and also between the parents themselves. There were clearly defined age and gender hierarchies at play in the assigning of domestic spaces. In a March 20, 1912, entry, Kharuzina explicitly suggested these hierarchical patterns: "Everything in the children's area [of the home] was clean and neat; everything was in its place." The parents too occupied separate spaces, each of which was marked by their own tastes and interests. The orderliness of the mundane was reflected both in the actual division of spaces and in the neatness of the objects inside each room. In fact, as Kharuzina told it, children and their needs were compartmentalized, including how the household was ordered: "Children were subordinated to the structure of the home. [...] Mama always worried about us children disrupting the order of the household and also telling me that things were 'forbidden for girls.'"[57] The age and gender hierarchy appeared intractable. The rooms assigned to her mother and father were also marked by gender. Kharuzina introduces her mother's quarters, "mama's special parlor [*gostinaia*]," as "the most intimate parlor in the home." It was described as a room that her mother spent a lot of time in and actually reflected her personal "likes and habits."[58] There appears a "*maminaia komnata* [mama's room]" and "*papina komnata* [papa's room]," each of which is distinct from the parlor (*gostinaia*) that was especially assigned to her mother. "So much is connected in my memory to that [mama's] room. It was, in those years, if you please, ours, mine and Kolya's, favorite."[59] The rooms, orderly and predictable, inspired their happiness.

Just as spaces existed in an orderly hierarchy, so did relationships. In a long entry from August 1919, Kharuzina presented the exact pecking order among the children. "We children were raised very differently from one another. Me and Kolya [Kharuzina's young brother who was close in age] were more progressive, and we had more interests than they did, and our mental horizons were wider."[60] Birth order was everything in determining one's spot in the sibling hierarchy. Kharuzina explained rather matter-of-factly that although she enjoyed time with her older sisters, her "playmate" was Kolya. In fact, Kharuzina refers to her sisters only as a pair, just as she almost exclusively included her brother in her autobiographical descriptions. "It was fun to be with them because at an early age Nastia and Nadia were being taught to be homemakers."[61] Kharuzina emphasized the sibling order in her descriptions about the ways in which other siblings reacted to their sister's death. Because of the nature of sibling relationships, this death was particularly hard on Alyesha, the closest to Olechka in age. "We were born in 'pairs' [...] Misha and Lena, Kolya and I, and Alyesha was paired with his small sister [Olechka]." Because of this pairing, Alyesha found himself alone and without a mate after Olechka died. Kharuzina presented it precisely this way: "And given the intimate friendship, which was felt among the pairs of brothers and sisters, to lose one's paired sister was in our eyes a huge unhappiness."[62] The descriptions of the death of Olga indicate not only the intimacy among siblings but also the degree to which their lives were ordered, as they lived in sets of two.

The orderliness and routine of daily life included the predictable and mundane rituals of the everyday (*byt'*). Kharuzina provided numerous details about daily routines and rituals, from breakfast foods to evening prayers. She wrote how "we wake early – Anna Martynovna woke even earlier than us. We would lie there and not get up until she told us to." Every morning they shared the same routine:

> We got out of bed, washed ourselves, got dressed, proud and without help. Anna
> Martynovna taught us all of this. Every step ahead we made was a huge happiness
> for us. Kolya tied his shoes all by himself! Vera learned to tie her bodice all by
> herself. None of this happened, of course, without hardship, without tears – but
> the joy at being independent soon meant that we forgot the struggles. The art of
> getting dressed [...] we all soon learned.[63]

The detailed stories about daily schedule, ritual and routine all throw into stark
relief the theme of time and the passage and structure of time. On numerous
occasions, Kharuzina highlighted the timing of various activities that she recalled
filling moments of her childhood day, whether morning, noon or night. Daily
routines created predictability each day: "That was how each day passed, day
after day more or less." Rather than monotony, that sameness inspired comfort.
At one point in her story, she paused on the calm, close and joyful memory of
the evenings:

> I cannot end my descriptions of our day without mentioning the evenings – those
> sweet evenings, when the grown-ups did not go out to friends, to the theatre, but
> stayed together with us at home. In the evenings, papa was home – that is most
> important of all. When papa arrived, he brought happiness to all of us. When he
> arrived, we flew to him [...] in happiness and excitement [...]. Papa loved his
> family, and returning home to it each day gave him a great deal of happiness.[64]

The routine of evening created a sense of calm and "happiness and excitement"
in Kharuzina, as she recalled. Midday, was another matter. Her least favorite part
of the day was lunch because it was a much more formal meal, where children
had to "sit properly" at the table, and when guests would often be present.

Childhood, in Kharuzina's story, was framed by daily routines and also
marked by closeness, both physical and emotional, within the domestic realm.
Kharuzina provides details of her connectedness to the physical spaces of
childhood. She identified with the space and the physical memory of her home,
whether in Moscow or otherwise. Her description of her "bright, very good and
cozy room" emphasized its smallness and warm, cozy memories. There were "two
small wooden beds, placed parallel – and close – to one another with only room
for a stool in the middle."[65] This childhood room "was like a place of refuge," she
wrote.[66] Throughout Kharuzina's stories about her childhood, which included
extended periods at the family dacha, she focused on the material reality, physical
space and often smallness—or coziness—of the domestic interior.

Images of corners, cozy, small, protected by the two walls framing them, recur
in her depictions. Recalling days spent at the dacha, Kharuzina depicted the

space that her family shared: "I loved that corner [of the room] [...]. The room was small, but warm and cozy." And there she always found a "soft, cozy bed with a pillow."[67] Although corners might be lonely, isolated places, in Kharuzina's narrative they were, on the contrary, places of comfort and warmth. Here she was not alone and sad, but in the company of her beloved Kolya. The bedroom was not the only close, comfortable quarters with corners. "We would go across the house to the living room, where there were no adults and it was immediately comfortable and cozy, we looked around and saw the malachite candlesticks and saucer with bright woolen flowers." Even when in a small space, she and Kolya found a corner. In the living room, Kharuzina remembers, "we went into the corner of the room. I loved that corner." Her parents' bedroom, too, was small, "but warm and cozy."[68] The emphasis on physical proximity and the celebration of corners reflects, in part, a nostalgic impulse to recall a past, now gone forever, that was safe and warm with its smallness and closeness, so very different from the increasingly alienating urban environment in the 1910s and afterward.

The celebration of physical closeness was accompanied by depictions of emotional intimacy, so central to her childhood reminiscences. There were endless passages about the carefree days and innocent early years, full of love. Her primary object of affection was her brother Kolya, with whom she shared cozy interior space as well as emotional intimacy, both in and out of corners. Their lives were so intertwined that Kharuzina perceives herself and Kolya as a single being:

> I write in these memoirs, the trivialities of my childhood and consistently repeat the word "I", I speak of my feelings, of my sufferings – and yet, at that time, I lived precisely NOT alone, but together with Kolya [...]. We lived, me and Kolya, one life, we were, in the full meaning of the word, inseparable, in our daily routines, our happiness, or woes.[69]

Vera and Kolya shared a past, they shared a childhood, a closeness and intimacy. "Everything I write about from this era was with my dear Kolya."[70] Elsewhere she writes that: "To say that Kolya and I were friends was not quite enough. We simply lived one life."[71] When Kharuzina describes her experiences, they were often shared. In a diary entry written from Dobavl(eno) on June 30, 1926, she wrote, "We loved [she and Kolya] to look out the window and see how papa and mama exited the house. I recall papa wearing a smart coat. He went to a very good tailor – in a black silk hat."[72]

There was affection among family members in general and among the parents and each other and their children. These feelings of affection, closeness and connectedness were heightened in a time of mourning. Kharuzina painted a dramatic portrait of the death of her little sister. She described the death of her "beloved, angelic" sister Olechka in 1915, many, many years after her death. "She was our small, dead, sister." Olechka died when she was only four years old and Kharuzina noted how their mother was never to get over this tragedy (even upon her own death bed). Her mother would often go and visit the grave of her young daughter, where she was buried next to her grandmother, Elena Afenas'evna Kharuzina. Olechka, Kharuzina emphasizes, was "a wonderful child, with dark hair, beautiful dark eyes and long lashes." She was "like poetry in our children's word." She described in heart-wrenching detail the long illness of her sister, how she sat by her side and how Olechka knew that she was dying. She would look up from her bed and, as Kharuzina recalled, "look at me with her beautiful eyes, and with the long lashes and smile at me – and that was Olechka."[73] Kharuzina also explains how Olechka was her angel and they would "talk quietly to one another" after she died. Olechka was her "light-curled Angel" and Kharuzina would say to her: "Are you here for me? Do you want to be my guardian-angel?" And Olechka answered in the affirmative. The happiness that Olechka brought to her sister Vera "lasted a very long time," including past Olechka's own time on earth.[74]

Childhood in Kharuzina's—and others'—memoirs existed in both spatial and temporal dimensions. Textual depictions of childhood years were enacted and remembered at home, amidst siblings and tutors and domestic interiors and gardens. Childhood, too, was a time in the life cycle, a finite series of moments (even if the particulars shift across time), which on these pages emerged as a nostalgic counterpoint to the fraught present.

The resurgence of estates

From the vantage point of the early twentieth century, the noble country estate, whether in a depiction of childhood or in a celebration of lost beauty, was becoming obsolete. Landlords sold their estates, which in some cases had been in the family for generations, peasants moved to cities and there emerged the desire to recover what had been lost, at least through memory and representations of an imagined past. From this point of view, as the country estate waned, just like childhood, it became increasingly visible by the early twentieth century. Writers and readers rehabilitated their modern sense of estate life centered on the eighteenth and early nineteenth centuries. This longing for an imagined past that may never have been was integral to the creation of a modern aesthetic, which merged disparate pieces into a single story about a place, encompassing past, present and future. In the early twentieth century we find an updated, modern version of an earlier dream, one familiar to those who study the eighteenth century: the pastoral idyll. By the early twentieth century, though, there was a shift from idyll, still and timeless, to a modern pastiche, built upon disparate, historically overlapping expressions and aesthetics. This modern pastiche, reminiscent of modernist ideas, reflected a sense of modern historical time, layering eras, striving for what had past and yet conscious of it being beyond return. In the early twentieth century, against the backdrop of war and revolution, the estate, like childhood itself, symbolized what had been lost and yet simultaneously began to embody the present: a modern understanding of temporal layering and rupture.

Over the past decades or so, there has been significant scholarship on the estate in the eighteenth and nineteenth centuries, the "Golden Age" of the nobility from Tsar Peter III's emancipation of the Nobility (1762), when noblemen were released from mandatory service and many returned to their family homes to toil and work the land, through the Serf Emancipation (1861), when the obligations between peasants and landlords changed.[75] In this sense, scholarly and contemporary reflections upon the pre-emancipation's "Golden Age" endorse an image of the estate as a place of symbolic meaning that looked quite different from the modern rendition of estate life found in early twentieth-century publications. Scholars, including Priscilla Roosevelt, John Randolph, Mary Wells Cavender, Stephen Lovell and Thomas Newlin, help us understand not only the realities of serfdom for landlords and serfs alike, which have been known for some time, but also the cultural and social meanings of the estate in its domestic dimensions. Writing on the eighteenth- and early nineteenth-century pastoral tradition within the Russian literary imagination, Thomas Newlin depicts a group of eighteenth-century noblemen who considered themselves part of an elite and enlightened gentry. These men attempted to "withdraw inward and homeward, into the self, into the family, into the benign, quiet, familiar landscape of the estate."[76] They were escaping the increasing presence of the growing spaces of public life in the eighteenth century. They just wanted peace. This impulse of retreat into the self—in literary terms—can be called "a pastoral impulse."[77] For eighteenth-century noblemen, the imagined estate represented a simplicity, marked by a certain timelessness and stasis. It was a world of no conflict. In the Russian literary tradition, as scholars have pointed out, the pastoral was often born out of a clash between the dream of the simple, calm, peaceful estate idyll and the mundane, daily drudgeries (*byt'*) of

Russian provincial life. This juxtaposition, or tension, was at the center of literary writings and autobiographical musings on estate life during the "Golden Age." Yet, despite the wide gap between the perception and its daily reality, the ideal of "the pastoral idyll remained strong within the Russian literary imaginary."[78] The pastoral, in its literary guise, encompassed depictions of fences, gates and other structures marking boundaries, whose transgression created anxiety. Time and movement were thought bounded in the pastoral imagination.

One important aspect of the pastoral, in this temporal sense, was its embrace of "old time": a kind of eighteenth-century idyll as a one-dimensional version of the past. Here, in the pastoral idyll, we see a consistent desire for stillness, even as movement flows in a circular rhythm. The pastoral ideal incorporated a dual sense of flattened time, mixing both stillness and stasis of movement in the peaceful country with an emphasis on the circular rhythms of daily routine, which although moving do not march forward in time. In this dual sense, the pre-emancipation estate perfectly conforms to the Bakhtinian "idyll chronotype." According to literary theorist Mikhail Bakhtin, such an eighteenth-century idyll included the binding together of:

> The unity of the life of generations (in general, the life of men) in an idyll in most instances primarily defined by the unity of place, by the age-old rooting of the life of generations to a single place, from which this life, in all its events, is inseparable. The unity of place in the life of generations weakens and renders less distinct all the temporal boundaries between individual lives and between various phases of one and the same life. The unity of place brings together and even fuses the cradle and the grave (the same little corner, the same earth), and brings together as well childhood and old age (the same grove, stream, the same lime tress, the same house), the life of the various generations who had also lived in that same place, under the same conditions and who had seen the same things.[79]

Bakhtin highlights how the blurring of all the "temporal boundaries made possible by a unity of place also contributes in an essential way to the cyclical rhythmicalness of time so characteristic of the idyll."[80] This rhythmic sense of time marks the "old time" understanding that Russians would transform at century's end.

At the center of this dream, this desire, this invented tradition stood both the manor house with its vast lands and the city mansion with its Grecian columns and French furnishings. Writers and readers in the early twentieth century crafted a modern domestic ideal that reflected not the lives lived by earlier generations but the desires and dreams of the writers and readers themselves in the years amidst significant change, including urbanization, industrial growth and mass-scale political dissatisfaction. Put differently, the phenomenon of modern nostalgia found in the pages of fin de siècle journals and magazines— even among current political and military conflict—was not so much a longing for a real past as it was a function of the centrality of loss of an imagined past to the modern condition. Notions of nostalgia, with their embracing of movement, change and rupture, all reflected the modern circumstances of urbanization, mass production, political upheaval and industrial change. This historical consciousness transitioned from an earlier, pre-emancipation emphasis on the pastoral timelessness of life on the estate to an emphasis on the permanence of the past, along with open, endless vistas in the future.

Gentry homes, in particular, so often sprawling estates embedded within acres of natural surroundings with Italian designs, fill the pages of late nineteenth- and early twentieth-century Russian writings about the passage of time: novels, poems, memoirs and, at the turn of the century, specialized journals and magazines. Anton Chekhov's *The Cherry Orchard*, perhaps the most famous, if farcical, portrait of waning estate life during the rising tide of new economic and social power at the twilight of the old regime, written in 1903, is one such example. It was at once a tragic and comic example of how gentry homes occupied a central symbolic role in longings about the past, desires in the present and desire in the future. As the aging Madame Ranevsky returned to her beloved childhood estate after a long hiatus of miserable indulgence in Paris, she ran right to the nursery of her childhood exclaiming: "The nursery! My lovely heavenly room! I slept here when I was a little girl! [weeping]."[81] We soon learn that she had squandered her fortune through sexual impropriety, whimsical travel and romantic tragedy, she had failed to pay her debts and she frequently indulged in self-pity. Yet, we do have sympathy for the fact that her beloved cherry orchard will be bought up by the peasant-cum-entrepreneur Lopakhin. In Chekhov's play, it is the former peasant, morphing into the landowner, who buys the old dying gentry lands. Madame Ranevsky, indeed, has no home, as the spaces of her childhood have disappeared, and she is left only with her memories and desires: a tranquil life on a sprawling estate with happy peasants serving their masters. Yet, such a nostalgic, and perhaps comic for readers of the time, vision of loss marked the culture of the age. The past slipped out of view even as it was retrieved in the world of desire.

Chekhov's tale was but one instance of the fin de siècle emphasis on the changing of the tides and modern awareness of time. Fin de siècle portraits of childhood gentry homes, such as Chekhov's most famous one, were part of a larger desire for the imaginary estate, as educated Russians strove to make sense of the world shifting around them. On the one hand, the world of brutal estate life was receding as peasants moved to cities and landlords lost their properties to debt. On the other hand, nostalgic portraits of domestic space—cherry orchards, bridges through gardens, grand parlors and cozy nurseries—proliferated as Russians found themselves in new, often disorienting urban environments. At this moment of great displacement and change, writers and readers embraced an image of the estate that—given the brutal realities of estate life—existed in memory alone. As with depictions of childhood, the estates themselves provided plenty of fodder for nostalgic musings in autobiographical texts. Descriptions of the very Abramtsevo of this chapter's opening was longingly described in several memoirs, including one by N.V. Polenova, an artist and participant in later workshops there. In her 1922 historical overview of the intellectual circles that thrived within Abramtsevo, Polenova provides a portrait of the gentry lost landscape "The Ambramtsevo-type home, assembled with old furniture [...] provides a picture of a life of old gentryfolk with their coziness and patriarchal character [...] there it lies, over the artistic small river the estate Abramtsevo [...] in the midst of steep mountains [...] an old gray manor house with a mezzanine, the type evocative of the 1840s [...] near a shady park."[82]

This portrait, as with many written before the revolution, reflects the fact that as peasant-workers packed their bags and moved to cities and former landlords sold their fields to move to smaller quarters, there was a renewed interest in estate life. This resurgence, unlike its eighteenth-century counterpart, involved the creation of an ideal that was both at odds with the reality of a waning gentry life and the result of a growing modern aesthetic, one that launched Russians solidly into the new century. By the late nineteenth century, the word *usadba*, or country home, was used as a signifier of Russian national culture. The picture that emerged (and reemerged in the post-Soviet years) bears little resemblance to the realities of serfs and the majority of serf owners in the pre-emancipation era. Yet, memoirs and journals brim with depictions of and desire for a life that never was. It is in this era that the Russian estate "began to acquire a history."[83]

Town and country

Elite Russians, aware as they were of their waning centrality to the increasingly modernizing Russian landscape, turned to the past as a legitimizing mechanism for their place in the present and significance in years to come. One way in which the past—as well as the present and future—echoed in the homes of this elite was through their reading of a multitude of journals and magazines.

This recapturing of the past included the documenting of the collecting of antiques or the propensity to walk through ruins, which were considered "central to modern life."[84] Moreover, the literary landscape increasingly included many nostalgic publications that celebrated the past and the estate—*Mir iskusstvo, Starye gody, Stolitsa i usadba*—and preservationist and collection-oriented organizations, each of which celebrated the desire for a particular past. These nostalgic images, and their textual manifestations, flourished among turn of the century educated Russians in their journals, magazines and individual personal writings.[85] The embrace of nostalgia too could be found in the growth of preservationist and architectural organizations, chartered to preserve the past landscape in the present, modern city. Some embraced existing ruins and others invented what was required. As Andres Schonle puts it: "modernity fabricates ruins in order to dramatize the difference from the past."[86] Ruins, fabricated or otherwise, were thought to be a reminder of "the endurance of the past" in the present moment.[87]

This moment was also defined by the creation and embrace of a variety of publications that celebrated Russian art, both past and present. One important venue for these preservationist impulses of the day was the magazine *Starye gody*, which was published from 1907 until 1916 in St. Petersburg, in tandem with the emergent architectural and preservationist societies. In a January 1910 issue of *Starye gody*, there was a significant spread celebrating the gentry estate. And it was often the estate and its domestic interior, as Peter Fritzsche highlights in the French example, where fragments of the past take up residence.[88] In particular, several articles appeared on the estates of the Golitsyn family, which are located on the outskirts of Moscow. The author bemoaned the passing of "our old estate." He writes that "this is an estate about which little is known. And, by the way, with each passing year, all that is, is in the past [...]. This beautiful life of the Russian gentry is becoming less and less accessible to the historian of art and of life."[89] There was a certain tone of inevitability about the passage of time: "The question becomes not whether daily life (*byt'*) of our old gentry life is dying; that is the order of things. Certain cultures outlive others, they make room for the new demands of life."[90] The author, with some resignation, explained how proud he is of being involved in this project to preserve the estate. One article in particular meandered through the rooms, halls, grounds and church of the Golitsyn estate—Dubrovitsy—and paused on the eighteenth-century pictures on the walls, the furniture on display and the luxurious vases and ceramics lining the windows.[91] This early twentieth-century readership was inundated with faraway aesthetics, ones that included objects and mementos from a multitude of eras, together constituting the contemporary moment in time.

The nostalgic observer, whose writings flourished in magazines and memoirs, painted a picture of a time and place long gone, replete with its objects and spaces of memory—whether a vase, a garden or a childhood room. Safely at a distance, these spaces and objects reminded the reader both of their own time as separate and of the past that was irretrievably gone. The descriptions of domestic space, one can imagine, brought the reader beyond the present moment and provided some comfort in an era of dramatic transition. The domestic arena was at the center of many reminiscences and portraits. These interior spaces, with their many domestic objects, served as an imagined repository for nostalgic sentiment amidst present-day anxieties. Time was thus refracted through space and embedded in material objects.

One such magazine, which celebrated the domestic interior of the past, was the beautiful, if anomalous, glossy lifestyle magazine, *Stolitsa i usadba*. It was aimed at an exclusive and elite audience of luxury and leisure seekers. It embraced the past, reified a present and sought to remain relevant in an ever-changing world. Published from 1913 to 1918, it was one of a kind in the Russian context, although there were other magazines that specialized in architecture and advised about the home. This publication chronicled the period with its layouts of elite domestic spaces, social commentary, its celebration of luxury and leisure, and its sleek advertisements. Published twice monthly, it had articles on individual estates, portraits of weddings, layouts of horse riding and photos of balls, as well as the occasional gussied-up dog.[92] During the war years, a regular column "Petersburg at the Time of War" emerged alongside articles on gastronomy, horseback riding and estate life. Throughout its run, the audience numbered about 1,500 at any given moment and included the waning aristocracy and the emergent, ambitious middle classes. V.P. Krymov, its editor and publisher (out of the publishing house: *Biblioteka Mezhdunarodn'i Institut Antikvariata* [ASG]), believed that the magazine's mission was to report on the beau-monde life of St. Petersburg and Moscow.

This trade-based magazine promised its readers on the very first page that it would bring them "the good life." Part of this good life among the Russian elite in the waning days of empire involved the very aestheticized form of the magazine itself, with its eclectic and Art Nouveau or Style Moderne. This aestheticizing was evident even in the building in which the offices were housed: the House of Singer on 28 Nevsky, a modern, Art Nouveau-style building. Replete with elaborate covers and photographs to spare, *Stolitsa i usadba* modeled itself on publications found in capital cities across parts of Europe, including London, Berlin and Paris. In addition to the famous "photographs of society ladies," the writers and editors feature pictures and descriptions of "ancient estates" as well as contemporary ones in every issue.[93] Depictions of countless pre-and post-emancipation estates, detailed in the pages, include winding garden passageways, tall ceilings and elaborate chandeliers. Flipping through the magazine, readers encountered interiors of parlors, views of rolling hills and lush gardens, as well as close-up images of family portraits and ancient vases. Even as they packed up their bags and moved to tiny apartments, the past haunted the imaginations of newly urban Russians. By simply picking up a magazine in the city, Russians could imagine a past, live in the present and project a future in which they played a central role. One of the magazine's explicit mission statements included the charge to always "preserve the past," whether that past was real or imagined or resided somewhere in between.

This magazine's aesthetic was itself a product of innovative strategies of visual and textual display. The present, both in its daily realities and in its technological manifestations, was found on each page alongside images of the past and the future. Flipping through pages of beautiful images of estate life, readers found photographs of nurses returned from the front or advertisements for vacations on luxury ocean liners. The audience of this journal, thus, was simultaneously staking a claim on the past, the present and the future. It was precisely this layering that made the magazine a reflection of modern aesthetics and temporal narratives. The magazine grounded these temporal narratives in the space of the elite home.

Stolitsa i usadba evoked a nostalgic sensibility on almost every page. Articles and pictures of upper-crust Russian life and leisure peppered each page. The estate stood at the center of these narratives, including columns devoted exclusively to the familial and architectural histories of the estates themselves. These columns included "Estates: Then and Now," "Old Petersburg" and the lengthy portrait of a single estate that appeared on the first page in almost every issue. Readers encountered, on page after page:

> Cozy estates with old, legendary dark alleyways, with surrounding fields [...] Old spacious rooms, in which coziness and comfort reigned through the generations [...] and many old things which reflect accumulated wisdom; old help, old members of the family, old family portraits, are all interlaced with new life, strongly sewn together with an old, former life.[94]

There is a self-consciousness about the temporal flow that marked the tenor of the magazine as a whole. In the inaugural issue in 1913, the editor begins with the following portrait of fluid, epochal time and its movements.

> Not long ago, the Russian countryside, with its way of life, exited into the past. The life of the city changes very quickly, much gets better and some things get worse [...]. We've buried already many types of art, philosophy, social thought, honorable traditions, beautiful artifacts like old country estates [...] which have been destroyed either by time or by people themselves.[95]

This editor's lamentation continued as he commented on the overlapping tendencies of past and present. As the beautiful life had not completely disappeared from view, the magazine aimed to paint a picture of the past "over time" and "to underline the beauty as it exists today."[96]

Most issues of *Stolitsa* began with a multipage spread on an individual estate. Many of these portraits were written by individuals who presented themselves as self-conscious seekers of the past. They positioned themselves as detectives and historians piecing together many layered bits of a story. As amateur historians, these columnists wove together stories about particular buildings, gardens and objects scattered around estates in the Russian countryside and in closer proximity to the city. Their stories, like the buildings and the objects they described, were pieced together, ultimately resulting in a present that encompassed a many-layered past. In one such 1916 example, a columnist peeled back layer upon layer of the textual and material remains of a Muscovite home, the Riumini mansion, on the verge of decay: "Many secrets are buried in an old home. Many strong feelings are aroused in one's soul when we see the rooms, where a wealthy aristocrat grew up over time."[97] The early twentieth-century reader, amidst massive urban flux and war, could pick up this magazine and be transported to the mansion where the old aristocrat collected his vases, adorned the walls with family portraits and admired the natural surroundings of his home. These references to home, to the past, to the emotions stirred by viewing the halls of former grandeur or pictures of the natural surrounding beauty, all emerged amidst the challenges of transition from a world in which the elites in their estates were at the center of national narratives and economic power, to one where new social realities were emerging throughout the early twentieth century.[98] This writer—and many more like him—was searching for stability in an ever-changing world. Describing his archival-like activities, he wanted his readers to know that he put the past together bit by bit. Similarly, in the inaugural issue, movement that marked the passage of time was everywhere: from the "exit" into the past to the "passage of time." The past haunted—and defined—the present. At Gomel'skaia, "the soul of the landowner's whole past daily life" resided still at the estate, even long after it was sold, some objects discarded, others remaining. Even after the estate was sold and transformed, many wonderful and mysterious secrets were "archived in the palace."[99] Here, then, the author declared that the estate itself was a space containing the past, while simultaneously carrying on in the present, as new individuals and families took up residency.

In another 1916 article, the author became the protagonist of his own historical narrative. Rather than reporting on the state of affairs associated with former noble life near Moscow or even in his own day, he took his reader through the process of how he had discovered and uncovered "former Moscow comforts." He moved into the past and narrated how he walked the blocks of central Moscow to catalog and consider the history of the mansions he encountered. He described, in particular, how properties changed hands, and how, in his times, many family homes were being sold off to the highest bidder.[100] He took a trip backwards in time, through his own personal history as he described himself as a child and then a youth. As a boy he strolled down the Moscow streets and wondered about this city mansion that he was writing about now. He reminisced about his childlike perception of how the building stretched down Nikitinskii Boulevard, in the center of Moscow, and how he wondered what its history might be. He asked himself: "when and which family bought it after 1812 [and the fires]?"[101] Revealing a consciousness of history and of the passage of time, not only vis-à-vis the buildings but also in terms of the author's personal time and individual life narrative, the author wrote: "Inside the home, amidst the potted plants, the stunning chimes, and the canneries, all seemed as if from another era […] and before us would be a man in stockings."[102] The author highlighted one final temporal twist: he explained how on his journey, he studied the old images of the rooms and the exterior that he encountered, he found that the photos were not old but relatively recent. The pictures were taken a little over twenty years ago in 1874: an illusion of time long past.[103]

Another trope in the multipage explorations of estates and their histories included expeditions into the past through archival discoveries. Similar to the wanderings around Moscow, the author who described Pokrovskoe became an archivist-historian, as he traveled to archives and libraries in an attempt to fill in the pieces of the historical puzzle.[104] He started with a series of questions.[105] When (was it built)? In which year was it built? Which architect? According to what plans? Who were the brave and original artists, who created on the wall of the hall and living rooms such incredible beauty and even more fantastical, the frescoes? Who lived here? Who in the 1830s came and occupied these halls? "It's the usual story. One finds in Russia such a picture: the sad fate of many palaces of well-recognized architects who produce first-class architecture. But sadder still is the history of similar estates that gradually go into oblivion."[106] This was one such estate, one built by a well-known architect that survived the decay of time. To answer some of these questions about the details, the author turns to a family history: a history of the Engelgardts. Engelgardt wrote a lot about this estate, which belonged to his family from the eighteenth century. The images on the multipage spread were obtained from an historical museum in Smolensk, and the information in the text was gathered by the author based on memoirs and diaries and family archives. Our resident historian and archivist paused on the domestic interior, and on the temporal pastiche found within. It is not clear when the estate was built. It may have been "15 or 20 years after the death of V.A. Engelgardt," but seems clear that we may never find out, as "there may be alternative versions of this story."[107] The ambiguity about precision combined with the insistence on the layering reflects how modern time functions. Part of the answer to this question of precise timing resided within the interior, in the furniture itself. The living room furniture, for instance, was "from a later time."[108] The objects within can teach readers about the past; at one point, the author wondered: "what does the fireplace teach us?" about the history of the place and the inhabitants inside. The very narrative of the time and place was unfixed and required the crossing of a "stone bridge" or the climbing of a staircase to a faraway land.

Another common theme revolving around the past in the present was the persistent narrative of occupancy and renovation or renewal of the built environment, of the estate buildings themselves. On page one of the very first issue in 1913 appeared a piece that highlighted the manor house that belonged to early nineteenth-century poet Mikhail Lermontov's grandmother and subsequently to a cousin of the Lermontovs: A. Stolyina. This magazine piece included one of Lermontov's poetic stanzas from approximately a century earlier. His words, in a sense, set the mood for the magazine as a whole. He recalled his childhood journeys to Srednikovo, the home of his grandfather. His stanza described how it was an "ancient manor house with a partly destroyed greenhouse and a garden just beyond a drowsy pond." He paused on its garden: "The garden beyond the drowsy pond, the ancient manor house [...] is strong and simple in its classical beauty."[109] After opening with the poetic words of Lermontov, which connected this piece to Russian literary tradition, the author of the column emphasized the changing ownership of the estate, as it was passed down from generation to generation. Lermontov's own memories were augmented by a more contemporary commentary by A. Stolypina, who grew up, at least in part, amidst the beauty of Srednikovo. For Stolypina—and also her readers—the interior and exterior spaces of home invoke the desire for an imagined past: "For me personally Srednikovo is on the road of memories about my early childhood."[110] Within the space of a brief article, the reader encountered at least three generations of occupants, as each moved through the space of the manor house and recalled time spent there. The passage of time and flow of generations were highlighted by the changing ownership itself. The past, irrecoverable, resided within the domestic interior, within its objects and its very structures.

Some of the estates appeared to include buildings that were built at disparate times, sometimes decades and other times centuries apart. Eras were literally layered on top of each other. This was the case with the estate Selyeznevka in Ekaterinoslav.[111] The authors described how in the eighteenth century, during the time of Catherine the Great, Russians had no interest in this southern region of the country where Selyeznevka was found, and only foreigners expressed a desire to explore these areas of the country. Russian families shied away because they insisted "the region was uncultured and demanded a tremendous amount of work." But in the second half of the nineteenth century foreigners again appeared to cultivate the land and build homes. Even if the best Russian families owned the land, they did not live on it. But, in the last few years, there has finally been local (read legitimate) interest. This is how the article described the land and estate today (in 1916), now that Russians have shown interest: "In a cozy and artistic hollow, where a fresh breeze passes by in the summer months, there emerges a small river and a vast shadowy park."[112] There were two estate homes on the very same land. One was built "15 years ago" and provided little interest, and the second was old and rebuilt not long ago by a European architect. Eras are layered on top of one another in a kind of pastiche of style. [113] This mixing of times remained a theme throughout. Reading about the Mikhailovka estate, one learns that "on the lands of Mikhailovka, there were two mansions, large and small. The large one has two stories [...] and has been preserved until this day." The other smaller part was falling apart. "And so, the modern [*sovremennyi*] large building [*dom*] in 'Mikhailovka' is pasted together from many parts." A discussion about the piecing together of the larger structure over time followed. The author wondered whether or not the windows all match up given the varying times at which they were installed. "From the side of garden – to the portico there is built a vast terrace and a staircase, which is obviously from a later time."[114] The reader encountered the multiple manifestations of differing temporal moments in the very structure of the estate. The author of the articles on Mikhailovka appeared cognizant of the temporal pastiche. "Combining excellent, first class antiquities with modern comforts – that is the motto of Mikhailovka."[115] The nostalgic layering of past and present—"first class antiquities with modern comforts"—is constitutive of modernity. Homes, at least those longed for and missed, were imagined as museum-like templates for the layering of multiple temporalities.

Descriptions of estate interiors and their objects as museums highlight the multitude of styles and eras. A bedroom, for instance, might resemble "a museum," with its multiple objects and decorations within.[116] In explorations of contemporary, early twentieth-century homes, one author remarked that "if they were built by people with taste" then the owners aspire to combine "into one whole or another" a variety of tastes, places and styles. There are, the author tells us, in great contrast to the peaceful image first evoked, homes with many different styles, which include "a love of smashing" or breaking with the past in one moment, and an embracing of its aesthetics in the next.[117] The following lengthy article described Muranovo and its environs. It began with a nostalgic mood and offered the reader image after image of the interior and its objects within, and in some cases, its portraits on the walls and shelves.

> The old spacious rooms are where comfort and coziness were housed for generations: [these include] the old stuff, which have their own lives and physiognomy, the voluminous library shelves with accumulated wisdom of the generations; the old servants, the older members of the family, the old family portraits, mixed together with the new life, strongly woven together with the old life.[118]

Reflecting the joining of styles and the emphasis on the flow of time and history, parts of the home were in the style of "the eighteenth-century genre" and included "Austrian luster" and "subtle French moldings," which contributes to the feeling that permeates the whole house: "a subtle smartness character."[119] There was a self-consciousness to the embrace of temporal layering in *Stolitsa*.

Mikhailovka evokes the same sense of multiplicity of eras and also the degree to which estates do function as temporal museums of history. Appearing amidst the war, the reader encountered Mikhailovka, an estate that "came into being during the Petrine times."[120] The historical roots of the estate and its importance were declared: "At Mikhailovka, until our day, there stands an oak tree that was planted in the days of Peter the Great. That oak is now the tallest of all trees."[121] Like the estate as a whole, the objects within it heap era upon era. There was a "gallery of portraits" of many hetman and also those who have lived in the estate over the centuries. There too were art and domestic objects, which betrayed the multiple temporalities represented. "A candelabra from Nicholaevan times" sat near the stone-tiled oven in the style of Louis XVI. Down the hall, "in the dining room [...] [there was] a wonderful chandelier from Petrine times." And, finally, in the living room one could find a "remarkably comfortable big and somewhat unusual form of a chair [...] from a Nicholaevan factory, marking it as likely nineteenth century."[122] And also "in the other living area (the portrait one), in the library, the office next to it, there are many wonderful and even rare pieces of furniture from the very beginning of the nineteenth century." The article ended by emphasizing the eclectic nature of objects within the estate. The author wrote: "Combining excellent, first class antiquities with modern comforts – that is the motto of Mikhailovka."[123] In a certain sense, the estate was like a museum, except for the fact that many rooms were occupied. Writers and readers of this publication, thus, contributed to the flourishing of a modern aesthetic that reified not just the lives lived by earlier generations but also the desires dreamt by the writers and readers themselves in the years amidst significant change, including urbanization, industrial growth and mass-scale political dissatisfaction. This resurrection of an imagined past was integral to the creation of this modern aesthetic, which merged disparate pieces into a single story about a place, encompassing past, present and future. This pastiche, reminiscent of modernist ideas, reflected a sense of historical time, with its many eras represented, striving for what has past and yet conscious of it being beyond return.

While the longest estate portraits came in the form of self-conscious journeys into the past, in almost every issue there appeared a section entitled "Usadba v proshlom i nastoiashchie" (Estates: In the Past and the Present), which had the singular purpose of narrating, through words and images, the story of an individual estate and its transformations over time, often resulting in a pastiche aesthetic. These brief articles, more visual than textual, highlighted both the tenuous nature of estate ownership and the physical transformation of the landscape and buildings over time. Readers learned about the interior and exterior design of a particular historical estate and the inhabitants within: then and now. In some instances, temporal flow appeared as a central theme. The column on the Seleznevka estate began with a discussion of its historical origins, its birth under Peter the Great, and moved through a discussion of how the estate transformed from generation to generation, ending in the contemporary early twentieth century. The most recently built bits of the estate, the author warns, are "not very interesting."[124] Yet, the furniture and objects within the walls of the estate came from a variety of eras and cultures. "In the living room [*gostinaia*], for instance, which is cluttered with objects from a multitude of eras [...] includes the tea cups and tea pot made from 'old Dresden/Saxon china'."[125] In a similar column from January 1914 there appeared a discussion of estates that had weathered the passage of time, including whole buildings and, in some instances at least, walls from the 1760s.[126] These columns marked the passage of time in concrete ways, whether through descriptors such as "all of the rooms have old furniture, pictures, and portraits" or by mentioning events indicating a particular temporal frame, such as the Russo-Japanese War.[127] The emphasis on the multiple temporal narratives resident in domestic interiors and their material objects, from the archivist-like author to the portraits of estates "then and now," reflects the modern aesthetic and its impulse to look backwards with longing in order to reckon with the rupture of the present moment.[128]

From noble quarters to peasant huts: The past, the present and the portending of future

As part of this backwards-gazing impulse, there was a sense among educated, and especially artistic, elites that peasant traditions in particular were fading before their very eyes. They feared the loss of aspects of peasant life that had long been part of the elite imaginary: peasant domestic arts and crafts, the backbone of Russian national consciousness and definitions of self. Writers, artists, merchants and other urban elites worried about tradition fading away, even as many peasants themselves embraced the industrial and urban changes going on around them. In other words, it was not necessarily the peasants who yearned for the fading past, but rather the artists and other elites who feared the consequences of dramatic loss. The past, with its rural aesthetic, should be preserved and integrated into contemporary life. One means of slowing the movement of time as the past and future collapsed into the present, spearheaded by merchants and artists of various kinds, was to ensure the continuation of peasant domestic handicrafts by offering peasants employment in a traditional craft context and overseeing their work. Peasants were selected based on their perceived honesty and integrity and skills to make traditional designs and objects under the guidance and direction of elites. The designs and aesthetics, thus, were determined by the artists' own taste and sense of authenticity, not to mention their desire to meet modern consumer demands. Ultimately, the peasant handicrafts would fetch high prices in the open market.[129]

The market impulse to turn toward the past, to save it from fading away, was captured by new aesthetic impulses. Artists and their patrons found themselves very involved in the broader artistic movement that resembled the Art Nouveau in France and elsewhere in Europe: the Russian Style Moderne and the artistic circle and its journal the *Mir iskusstva* (World of Art) best represented this Russian style, with its European echoes.[130] The beautiful art journal *Mir iskusstva*—which ran from 1898 to 1904—was eclectic, featuring Russian and European Arts and Crafts, reviews of exhibitions, furniture, domestic interiors, architecture, pottery, design, jewelry and articles and letters by artists and their associates. The embrace of traditional peasant objects and crafts, many domestic ones, was part and parcel of the broader nostalgic impulse of the fin de siècle. By sketching out a peasant hut for the *Mir iskusstva* readership or employing peasants to make a baby's crib in a traditional style, these artists and journalists struggled with the changes around them. These changes manifested in other realms as well. If peasant crafts were assumed to be fading from view, commentators imagined that the gentry estate and noble living had practically disappeared. While engaged in a variety of styles and projects, including "organic motifs, botanical flourishes, and graphic references to animal and vegetable world," practitioners of the Style Moderne in some instances emphasized "simplicity and efficiency" in the design of domestic interiors and objects within.[131] They too embraced the peasant naturalist aesthetics in much of their work. The past proved integral to the modernist aesthetic found in Style Moderne. Its proponents believed, in particular, that the nineteenth century had essentially undone many of the accomplishments of the eighteenth, with special attention paid to the era of Catherine the Great. Some, including those in the World of Art movement, professed the urgent need to "recapture the mastery and artisanship of the Russian eighteenth century," which flourished under Catherine's patronage.[132] The World of Art also accused nineteenth-century artists of essentially neglecting their own ancestors and allowing older artifacts and treasures to fall into disrepair. Members of this modernist artistic circle launched a campaign "to promote and save Russia's eighteenth-century heritage." One way in which they did this was to support new journals that celebrated the ruins of the past, including *Starye gody*, the art historical/architectural preservationist journal tied to the Retrospectivist movement.[133]

Retrospectivism and the World of Art group embraced a romantic understanding of the peasantry and its craftsmanship by elevating especially domestic objects and their written manifestations, in the form of magazines and other materials. Nostalgic impulses—and no doubt, in some cases, economic considerations—of the age inspired some among Russia's elite artists and merchants to embrace this impulse and to halt the fading of peasant domestic crafts from the aesthetic landscape. Artists, thus, recast peasant domestic designs and styles in hopes of curtailing the future by reaching into an imagined past. As peasants became landlords and landlords sold off their estates, and the ideal of rural life transformed, many educated Russians not only longed for the luxurious estates of their imaginations but also became nervous and mourned for what was not yet past. They looked to the peasantry to quell their fears. They feared the loss in particular of aspects of peasant life that had long been part of the elite imaginary in Russia: peasant domestic arts and crafts, from slippers to spoons and other domestic objects, symbolic of Russian national culture. Writers, artists, merchants and other urban elites worried about these traditions fading away, even as many peasants themselves embraced the industrial and urban changes going on around them. Scholars agree that it was less the peasants themselves who grasped for the fading past as the ground shifted beneath them, and more the artists who worked to elevate peasant aesthetics. These elites predicted that the focus on peasant styles would not only placate their anxieties but also prove appealing to a wider audience and provide financial gain.

Historians have commented on the fact that peasants welcomed changes that were part and parcel of modernization and urbanization, from mechanization and the new job opportunities it created in cities to the possibility to travel and leave the village.[134] On the one hand, there was the emergent discourse about "elevating the cultural level of the masses" among professionals who would have encouraged the changes. On the other hand, there was also discussion of "deep concern about the loss of folk traditions and communalist habits."[135] Other ideas, too, circulated around and contributed to a sense of loss, anxiety and possible opportunity for the peasantry in the newly emerging environments. One theme, though, that runs through discussions about peasants coping with the changes is that educated, urban members of the middle classes tended to romanticize the peasantry and imagined a peasant past that was "less complicated, more clearly defined, and less threatening" than the circumstances at the fin de siècle. Among the elite, even as peasants were in open rebellion in and after 1905, there emerged distinctive nostalgia for an imagined simple, rural past. The present, which felt unstable, anxious and unknown, created a deep desire for stability, certainty and the familiar. This inspired a "deep longing accompanied by a sense of melancholy" for the past now gone.[136] Inherent in this nostalgia was a desire for proximity, closeness with the peasantry reminiscent of another age. It was artist colonies and crafts' workshops that elites imagined would solve their existential desire to hold the past in place.

The impulse to employ peasants in the traditional domestic crafts, woodworking and embroidery, in places such as the Abramtsevo workshops, mentioned in the opening section of this chapter, thus, came from members of merchant and artistic circles who had a "commitment to folk traditions and communalism."[137] The goal, as artist Elena Polenova elegantly wrote, was "to capture the still-living art of the people, and give it the opportunity to develop." This sense of urgency of loss, too, is captured in Ivan Bilibin's 1904 words, highlighted by scholar Alison Hilton: "There is no doubt, Russian folk art is dying, it has nearly died. The currents of modern life sweep it away, and only in a few places deep in the most remote areas, do its last feeble sparks still smolder."[138] A sense of loss for an era that was feared receding and without a future, and a craft that was feared doomed to extinction, thus, inspired those in these artistic and merchant circles to invigorate peasant craft production. The past had to be preserved and reinvented, market-ready, in the present moment.

Abramtsevo became the summer home of the railway magnet Savva Mamontov and his wife Elizaveta. The married pair enticed the artist Elena Polenova to direct the carpentry workshop at Abramtsevo, which she did from 1885 until 1893, only years before she died. Abramtsevo, a modest estate, stood about forty miles northeast of Moscow. Starting in the 1870s, Mamontovs began to invite artists to come to their estate in the summertime. They had guests ranging from Vasilii Polenov, Viktor Vasnetsov, Il'ia Repin and decades later Elena Polenova, Valentin Serov, Mikhail Nesterov and Mikhail Vrubel. Elena Polenova, along with Mamontova and Mariia Iakunchikova, as well as the male artists, began to research folk arts and contributed to their revival in a variety of forms. At Abramstevo, one of the main workshops devoted to the revival of artisan peasant domestic crafts, Elena Polenova and Elizeveta Mamontov, among others, created and oversaw the making of objects, whether practical material and/or artistic in nature, which reflected peasant aesthetics and harkened back to some imaginary past. In this sense Abramtsevo, which housed a multitude of already known artists who as part of their repetiore made a study of local folk art, "distinguished Abramtstevo's group's interests from the more common pattern of mingled historicism and nostalgia." Folk art forms were incorporated into their work, and beginning in 1881 at Abramtsevo, these objects included carved wood ornaments, textiles and utensils.[139] These aesthetics existed in numerous time frames simultaneously: the era of traditional craftsmanship itself and the fin de siècle desire to preserve at least an imagined version of tradition in the contemporary marketplace.

This was one means of creating proximity: slowing the movement of time by investing in the continued production of peasant domestic handicrafts that Polenova and the Mamontovs had begun. The most celebrated venue for this impulse was of course the Abramtsevo workshops. When, in the late nineteenth century, peasants were ready to cease their crafts and arts, women from prominent merchant families, such as Mamontova and members of her circle, began to engage peasant craftsman in projects of preservation; they asked the peasant craftspeople to remain in the countryside (or nearby towns) and to continue their traditional crafts under new, artistic direction (weaving, lace making, furniture) rather than to participate in the increasingly industrialized society. In particular, artists drew sketches of peasant *izbas* and peasant craftspeople built chairs and desks in "traditional styles" under instructions of artists and merchants and others. There was nothing covert about this co-optation. And it was not surprising that it was women artists who took the lead in recreating peasant handicrafts and artistic aesthetics, especially with their emphasis on domestic crafts. Writing to a friend about her goals for the employment of peasants in traditional crafts, Elena Polenova—the artist most responsible for the Abramtsevo furniture-making workshop—remarked: "Our goal is to capture the still-living art of the people [peasantry/*narod*] and to give it the opportunity to develop." Polenova and her fellow travelers looked for, as she put it herself, "inspiration models mainly by going around the *izbas* and examining things that are part of the environment."[140] And this is precisely what Polenova, Mamontova and others did at Abramtsevo in the years surrounding the turn of the twentieth century. They found capable peasants—some craftsmen by trade and others inexperienced—paid them, educated them and instructed them on how to create "authentic" peasant crafts, including household furniture, tablecloths, toys and in some cases full-blown peasant huts.

Peasants were selected based on their perceived honesty and integrity and skill to make "traditional" designs and objects under the direction of elites. The designs and aesthetics, thus, were determined by the artists' own taste and sense of authenticity, not to mention their desire to meet modern consumer demands, as ultimately the peasant handicrafts would fetch high prices in the open market.[141] The impulse to employ peasants in the traditional domestic crafts, woodworking and embroidery, in places such as Abramtsevo, thus, came from members of merchant and artistic circles who had "deep concern about the loss of folk traditions and communalist habits."[142] Nostalgia for an era that was feared receding and a craft that was feared doomed to extinction, thus, inspired those in Mamontov's circle and others to invigorate peasant craft production. They attempted to recapture aesthetics in the workshops of Abramtsevo and elsewhere, as the past collapsed into the present.

Artists and architects searched out traces of rural, peasant life as sources of inspiration, whether the *izba* where peasants lived or the cloth that they stitched and wore. Polenova and others would travel the countryside and live among the peasants in search of artistic inspiration. In a letter recounting her days among the people, Polenova writes: "Today I went to the countryside, where Semen worked. I was so happily surprised at our encounter [...] so real [...] that *izba* where [...] the two peasant boys sat at the table, being instructed by Semen, who passed on what he learned from his grandfather and aunt."[143] Despite this touching passage, in the end, practicality won the day, and since "Semen had no real talent" he was fired and the artists began finding their own designs and orchestrating production themselves.

This Russian folk revival is well known and has very interesting parallels in the British Arts and Crafts movement and the French Art Nouveau.[144] Its connection to the birth of modern temporalities is less often remarked upon. The insistence on peasant (and peasant-like) aesthetics was, at least in part, imbued with a fear of loss, a search for authenticity and for some a return to childhood fantasies of innocence when serfs and then peasants roamed estates. The so-called "simplicity" and "honesty" of peasants' nature emerges as a theme in the letters of Polenova and others who described their daily lives together with the peasants. In a letter about these days, Polenova explains how she felt herself "close to the peasants [*narod*], to their worldview." This led to the strong desire to keep alive their artistic processes through the opening up of workshops such as Abramtsevo. The artists themselves commented on how intimately they related to the peasants: "they felt like family relations' and we were very connected together."[145] Polenova's Abramtsevo existed in numerous time frames simultaneously: the era of traditional craftsmanship itself and the fin de siècle nostalgia for tradition, while stemming the tide of change.

Temporal discourses surfaced in discussions about the peasant arts and crafts at Abramtsevo and elsewhere through the infantilizing—at least in words and images—of the peasantry. Peasants were imagined frozen in time, both in their embodiment of the "tradition" and in the course of the life cycle itself: they were often infantilized and imagined as childlike. Polenova described her involvement with the peasant-craftsmen/craftswomen as a kind of "retreat into a child's imaginary world." One avenue of interest for both Polenova and Mamontova was educating children. They each wished to pass along their knowledge of peasant crafts to the children in the Abramtsevo school, "joinery for boys and needlework for girls." They taught children the skills of craftsmanship and ultimately set up means by which their pupils would sell their wares at local markets or at first at the Moscow Zemstvo Kustar' Museum in 1885, and later in a store devoted to the work of the carpentry studio at Abramtsevo, established in 1890. Polenova herself wrote that the furniture and domestic wares and crafts made at Abramtsevo and sold had "novelty, originality and style," although some did question the authenticity of the styles and designs.[146] When working with the peasantry, Polenova became inspired to write a book of fairy tales that recalled her own childhood experiences. She entitled the piece her "Abramtsevo Cycle" and published it in 1889 as "The War of the Mushrooms." The stories themselves, children's fairy tales, were collected from among the peasantry. Childhood, too, was invoked in the increasing emphasis on children's toys at the various craft workshops in place by the early years of the twentieth century. Due to the growing interests in the "cult of the child" around the fin de siècle, toys served as a connection to the past and the fading folk tradition, and to the future and the education of future generations. Moreover, Russian crafts had a domestic bent. Polenova was commissioned to design a "Russian dining room" for Maria F. Iakunchikova's country house in Nara outside of Moscow. It was the first fully created interior in a definitive "neo-Russian style" intended for actual living rather than display.[147]

The emphasis on peasant artisan domestic handiwork did not emerge in a vacuum. Small-scale peasant production, or the *kustar* industries, including some items of decorative value (spoons, cloth, etc), thrived in the Russian countryside both before and after emancipation, although with more autonomy after the serfs were emancipated. As late as on the eve of the First World War, a peasant producer was "as likely to work in a peasant home or small village workshop as in a large factory."[148] Although cottage industries made up a significant portion of the overall industrial production throughout the fin de siècle decades, it was not until the 1890s that the kustar industry took on new, aesthetic meanings among Russia's elite circles. The opening of the Moscow Kustar Art Store and the Kustar Museum are reflections of this later trend. Many elites, beginning in the 1890s, began to embrace the notion that the decorative arts brought "direct access to the spiritual and imaginative world of 'the people,'" which ultimately inspired them to fully embrace peasant crafts.[149] In the Russian imaginary, the kustar industries became part of a national cultural narrative that insisted on generating a material culture that would "give authentic and unmediated expression to both individual imagination and collective national culture."[150] It is therefore worth noting the prevalence of kustar industries, in a variety of guises, throughout this period. On the one hand, there was a longer standing tradition of kustar production, including the making of domestic items, which made up a significant portion of the Russian economy in the post-emancipation era. By the 1890s, though, there emerged a more artistically oriented effort to preserve or, more accurately, create aestheticized versions of some of the kustar arts and crafts as a way of counteracting the forward movement of time, on the other. Despite fears of the loss of peasant skill, labor and designs, kustar workshops continued to exist and thrive throughout this period. Rather than imagining the preservation of "tradition" in the face of modern change, though, the lens of time allows for an exploration of the contingent nature of concepts such as tradition and modernity as the elevating of the kustar aesthetic reflected an acknowledgment of the past in the present.

Practical considerations were central to the artistic movement celebrating peasant domestic arts. Money was certainly on the minds of those involved in peasant craft production. The Moscow Kustar Museum, for example, engaged in an intensive marketing effort to interest the public in handcrafted objects, including very prominently children's toys. In order to maximize the authenticity quotient in toy production at Bogrodskoe workshop, its director, Batram, instructed the peasant artisans to model the styles on the old *lubki* and icons.[151] There was also an exporting business, which made sure there was a profitable overseas market for Russian toys. The Moscow Kustar Museum sold many of the items made at various workshops, prominent of which were those at Sergei Pasad. Many exhibitions meant to showcase the work done at Sergei Pasad and elsewhere: in 1902 the First All Russian Congress in the Kustar Industries in St. Petersburg and the Exhibition of Architecture and Industrial Art in the New Style in Moscow.[152] Yet, these commercial concerns only demonstrate the widespread reach of nostalgic sentiment. Artists, merchants and managers alike understood the allure of the domestic craft object imbued with the promise of authenticity and able to hold back the passage of time.[153] Some of the common features included organic forms, which were partly a reaction to industrial change. In both the artistic group and the magazine, artists took nature as a source of inspiration, a way to distance themselves from the mechanized world; they combined this with some elements of traditional decorative arts/design/peasant aesthetics, etc. The aesthetic impulse within this artistic group, much like the larger movement of peasant crafts, was a rejection of linear temporality. The embrace of the lubok and the "new primitivism," for instance, was both inherent in Style Moderne and "inevitable within the framework of modernism."[154] At the time, in 1898, both the Solemenko and the Abramtsevo workshops were considered Russian responses to the European-wide Art Nouveau movements. There was a sense among the artists and merchants (who would make a profit from these projects) that they/artists were trying to somehow fabricate the creative and emotional world of the traditional peasant.

Proponents of Russia's Style Moderne wrote critically of their own era and believed that the nineteenth century had essentially undone many of the accomplishments of the eighteenth, with particular attention paid to the era of Catherine the Great. Some, including those in the World of Art movement, professed the urgent need to "recapture the mastery and artisanship of the Russian eighteenth century."[155] The World of Art also accused artists of the nineteenth century of essentially neglecting and allowing to fall into disrepair all of the many artistic and architectural treasures of the eighteenth century. They launched a kind of campaign "to promote and save Russia's eighteenth-century heritage." One way in which they did this was to support new journals, including *Starye gody* and *Mir iskusstva*, the first of which was an art historical/architectural preservationist journal and the second reflected the impulse to bring the peasant almost-past into the modern present.[156]

The broader context for the impact of *Mir iskusstva* is worth rehearsing here. The impulse to stop the forward passage of time and celebrate peasant domestic arts was not unique to Russia, although it had its own national variations (the *matrushka* doll was invented at this time). Russian Style Moderne was part of a pan-European and transatlantic phenomenon. Like the French Art Nouveau, for example, the Russian movement embraced eighteenth-century aesthetics and celebrated nature, while it attempted to "reunite the artist with the artisan" and to emphasize the domestic interior as a canvas for artistic expression.[157] "By 1900 in France, the new Style Moderne was a means of celebrating not technological innovation but ornamentalism, nature and the home. The French, like the Russians, wanted to bring together art and craft to create a modern aesthetic. Yet, in the pan-European context, each nation had its own emphasis, even as some basic aesthetics were shared across borders. In the French case Art Nouveau included the "search for lost golden age" when French craftsmen were in charge of good taste. In the German context, by contrast, the decorative arts movement emphasized applied arts and celebrated "new machine culture."[158] Finally, in the in case of Polish and Irish contexts, these simultaneous movements of the revival of peasant crafts was politicized and part of struggle for "home rule." Russia, too, had its own set of political and social circumstances at play. By contrast, in Russia, the kustar crafts movement harkened back to the eighteenth century before Peter the Great and his successors had fully buried the true "Russian" culture. In Russia, these artistic forms found their most faithful expression in the beautifully designed art journal *Mir iskusstva*.

In 1904 an article appeared in *Mir iskusstva* that overtly meditated on the meaning of the loss of peasant domestic arts. Ivan Bilibin, an artist and illustrator and frequent contributor to *Mir iskusstva*, wrote about the fading of "folk art."[159] He begins by declaring that: "peasant art is dead." Yet he continues to explain that although there can be "no doubt that peasant art is dying or is already dead," that is "as it should be."[160] Why, though, would Bilibin, a proponent of the decorative arts movement, approve of the death of folk art? Perhaps because artists wished to reimagine the rural aesthetic themselves and embrace this new version of peasant crafts at the very moment when an interest in craft production was waning among the peasantry itself. As Bibilin pondered: "The current of a new life is sweeping away the old" and so as the old "folk art decay and its final sparks are put out" a new spark is born. Bilibin, in his article, equates the old art with "a former childhood" that must grow into "young adulthood," thus transforming and maturing rather than dying completely. This perception of changing and temporal movement with occasional ruptures is not unique to the present day, according to Bilibin. "Just 40 years ago, Russia was full of echoes of the seventeenth century, a time wonderful for the folk art if nightmarish politically."[161] "Folk art, just like life, never stays in the same place; it always appears in new guises, which sometimes harkens back to the old [...] or at others look toward the future." Bilibin then ends after a lengthy discussion of church architecture and folk dress: "I am ending my essay, but I want one more time to say that it would be a crime against the future, if we lost one grain in the fields of Russian folk art in the next centuries." He explains how one "must give sprouts, and not grow mold in provincial magazines. And that grain should search for some kind of path forward with all of the other grains." We must, Bilibin insists, "wait and not waste time."[162] The future was upon Bibilin and his colleagues; the past could not be allowed to escape from view.

One particular article in *Mir iskusstva* featured long passages from a correspondence between Elena Polenova and, the much younger artist, Maria Vasilevna Iakunchikova. Their writings reveal the intense nostalgia contained within their aesthetic sensibilities—at Abramtsevo and throughout their lives. Polenova taught Iakunchikova when was she was a child; and the young pupil would come to her mentor's home in the country in the 1880s and 1890s. Iakunchikova recalls in her letters, published in *Mir iskusstva*, how when she met her mentor in her home she felt as though she were stepping into the past. "You live in the past [...] where it is [...] to wake early and pick mushrooms."[163] Abramtsevo and Polenova, as its chief artistic representative in these years, embodied a desire for the past, a past that was—in part—celebrated through depictions of the home and its interior.

The domestic interior, as many of the above examples illustrate, occupied a particular place in the time-space narrative. The inside of homes, whether the layout or the objects within, were featured—in textual or visual form—in *Mir iskusstva* and other publications of the time. The themes so central to the peasant arts and crafts workshops were ubiquitous in this art journal throughout its run. One 1904 issue of *Mir iskusstva*, for instance, featured a picture of a "child's crib" with panels of paintings of rural, peasant scenes. It combines the woodworking and simplicity of 1904 with the echo of a traditional peasant past.[164] With a similar impulse for bringing the past into the present, another 1904 volume featured an image of the *terem*, or old Muscovite boyar women's domestic quarters, painted by a Russian artist.[165] These images combined scenes from different eras and, thus, defined modern time. In a 1900 issue, in another instance, there appeared an extensive spread of the domestic interior scenes from the Russian Pavilion at the 1900 Paris Exhibition, featuring precisely the kind of traditional peasant aesthetic style so characteristic of Polenova and her circle, at the time: Style Moderne.[166] The emphasis of domestic arts and interiors from other places around the world also became very common in the magazine. In a 1902 volume, *Mir iskusstva* had a multipage spread of reprinted images from the German decorative arts journal *Die Kunst*. It included a picture of a "bedroom." Other household furniture, dishes, embroidery/cloth patterns were all taken from the Turino Exhibition of Decorative Arts that took place in 1902, the first large exhibition of decorative and applied arts.[167] Some issues include picture after picture of simple colorful embroidery designs, whether for napkins or table clothes or other items.[168] Pictures of churches too were common, including wooden ones from the era of Catherine the Great.[169] Finally, there were pictures of peasant huts or *izbas*, appearing under the rubric of "typical village."[170]

The embracing of traditional peasant objects and crafts, such as domestic woodwork furniture, was part and parcel of the broader nostalgic impulse of the fin de siècle. By sketching out a peasant hut for the *Mir iskusstva* readership or employing peasants to make a baby's crib in a traditional style, Russian artists, such as Polenova, and merchants, such as Mamontov, were coming to terms with the changes around them. These changes manifested in other realms as well. If peasant crafts were assumed to be fading from view, commentators imagined that the gentry estate and noble living had all but disappeared. At the very moment that Polenova and her close collaborators were repurposing the old Aksakov estate, many members of the fading gentry elite were selling their homes and making their way into the city to find new homes and new lives.

Closing thoughts

In 1992, on the seventieth anniversary of the founding of the Society for the Study of the Russian Estate (founded in 1922), a group of scholars gathered in Moscow to share their research on, and ideas about, the Russian estate. One outgrowth of this ongoing project is a catalog, produced by the Russian Academy of Sciences in 1994, listing all of the estates featured in early twentieth-century publications on estate life. Inside the front cover of this thin catalog is a poem, taken from an early issue of the glossy lifestyle magazine *Stolitsa i usadba*, which highlights the centrality of ideas about the estate to the educated, and likely elite, public of the time: "As if a legend I recall, how I love that sweet and ancient, white estate home."[171] This poem, with its place in late imperial and post-Soviet imaginings, reflects something of the role that estates and nostalgia played within the creation of a modern Russian historical consciousness at the fin de siècle. As peasants were picking up and searching for work in factories and the gentry elite were receding, a segment of the urban population embraced an image of the pre-emancipation estate and of peasant aesthetics that seemed to reflect neither the harsh realities of serfdom nor the fact of peasants' own desires to move to cities and seek their fortunes. Instead, many educated elites hung on to versions of the past that reflected a deep nostalgia for the way things were or might have been. And the domestic—whether in scenes from childhood, in the spaces of the manor house and its surrounding grounds, or in peasant crafts—was the site for nostalgia's fullest potent articulation.

And yet, just at the moment when narratives of the past integrated into narratives of the present, the future appeared ready to make demands. As Koselleck writes in his *Futures Past*: "the more a particular time is experienced as a new temporality, as 'modernity', the more that demands made of the future increase."[172] Over the course of the nineteenth century, family parlors became "memory places" that embraced a past in hopes of defining the present, and in this sense "the past was endowed retrospectively with the formal contingencies of the future."[173] And after 1917, once the Bolsheviks found themselves at the helm, it was the future they sought. Yet, early Soviet proponents of a Soviet new everyday found themselves knee-deep in the dust of the past, and it proved impossible to sweep away.

Revolutionary Time

In the beginning: Mythical time

Time narratives crafted by the Bolsheviks, like those in the magazines and memoirs of late imperial actors, could not shake the past. Yet, the emergence of narratives of everyday Soviet life also included an emphasis on not just yesterday and today, but also tomorrow. In the famous dystopian novel *1984*, George Orwell's character Winston Smith thought to himself:

> And if all others accepted the lie which the Party imposed—if all records told the same tale—then the lie passed into history and became truth. "Who controls the past," ran the Party slogan, "controls the future: who controls the present controls the past." And yet the past, though of its nature alterable, never had been altered. Whatever was true now was true from everlasting to everlasting. It was quite simple. All that was needed was an unending series of victories over your own memory.[1]

Vladimir Mayakovsky, one of the most prolific and well-known Soviet bards, upon the death of Vladimir Lenin, wrote of revolutionary time; he wrote the following lines that echoed throughout the streets, kitchens and halls in the early revolutionary days:

> Lenin—lived.
> Lenin—lives.
> Lenin—will live.[2]

These lines reflected the revolutionary moment: erratic, dramatic and fundamentally shifting temporal and spatial perceptions. These early years brought with them a kind of mythological, revolutionary temporal flow, at once utopian and grounded in the present moment and embracing the past. In their project to create a mass utopian society, members of the Bolshevik propaganda team attempted to control time, revolutionary time, and as bogged down as it was by the past, it also had to be quick on its feet, speedy and efficient. And, most of all, in control. As Susan Buck-Morris suggests, in *Dreamworlds and Catastrophe*, of revolutionary, modern time regimes, the central "collective dream," the "dreamworlds"—a notion she borrows from Walter Benjamin— included an emphasis on the transience of modern time, the constant fluctuation of our temporal field of view with the unwavering belief that "the future will be better."[3] Therein lies the dream.

Lenin's notion of time, similarly, included the idea that Soviet society would be ahead and advanced of all others. It was the job of his new regime to finally overcome the lag in development so characteristic of the tsarist regime. His was a relatively linear notion that included progress and triumph above all else. Lenin's idea of progress included an emphasis on Russian and then Soviet backwardness and the need for rapid fire catch up, the origins of which go back to at least the era of Peter the Great. This historical dynamic, where Russians were always playing catch up, or put in temporal terms, "behind the west," was shared by Alexander Herzen in the nineteenth century and then Leon Trotsky in the twentieth century. Trotsky, in contrast to Lenin, was famous for his commitment less to linear progress than to "perpetual revolution" and a dynamic understanding of history, where "the future would not be monotonous" and would always be in movement. Trotsky also wrote about combined development "to describe how 'backward' countries might skip over stages traversed by advanced nations in order to arrive at the socialist goal without enduring the requisite intervening development. These ideas implied the coexistence of elements associated with separate time periods in the Western sequence."[4] Russia was to experience several phases, temporal in nature, at the same moment. Part of the quick-paced movement, thus, involved sacrifices in the present. One common revolutionary impulse, amidst the chaos of restructuring and creating a new state and society, was, unsurprisingly, a reset of the temporal narrative. From the French Revolution, with its temporal reset, to the Russian, with its changed dates on the calendar, one way in which revolutionary regimes create meaning and assert control is through the mastery of the temporal narrative. Like the changing calendar in France after 1789 (where from 1793 to 1805 and also during the 1871 Paris Commune, the French government changed the calendar to reflect revolutionary values), the calendar in the Soviet Union changed. The Bolsheviks, in 1918, dropped thirteen days: February 1, 1918, became February 14, 1918, which meant the Soviet Union did away with the Julian calendar and became aligned with the Gregorian one. In this sense, the Bolsheviks controlled the very passage of time. But this was not the only way.

When Vladimir Lenin had his final and fatal stroke in 1924, all movement and history stopped. For a moment, time stood still. All daily noise and activities were ordered ceased. At 4:00 p.m. on the day of his death, January 25, 1924, the radio announcer declared that time stopped. All were instructed to stand still for five minutes; the trains stopped; telegraph lines went silent, all of Russia was at a standstill: "Stand up comrades, Illich is being lowered into his grave." And, of course, in a further attempt to stop time, to control time, his body was embalmed as he was never to fully die: "Lenin's Body Should Last Forever."[5] These early days of revolution, thus, rather than solidifying a uniform march toward the utopian future of communist dreams, unhinged temporal understanding from concrete linear patterns and instead played with the idea of reversal, standstill and pastiche, from Sergei Eisenstein's *October* in 1927 when film sequences ran backwards to express the desires of political reactionaries to the embalming of Lenin himself, halting time and banking on a better tomorrow, temporal flow ran both backwards and forwards simultaneously.

Soviet state builders' impulse to create new temporal and everyday narratives, and centrally domestic ones, in the early days was part and parcel of a conscious attempt to make Russia and then the Soviet Union modern. Becoming—or being—modern has a multitude of dimensions, including the creation of a new relationship to temporal flow and spatial layout. The birth of modernity across Europe and the United States was always tied to particular notions of the movements of time across space. The layering of time in general and in domestic discourse in particular is nowhere starker than in the early revolutionary Soviet Union, when the refashioning of the everyday and living space was on the minds of individual citizens, state propagandists, artists, architects and others. This adolescent state, with its growing propaganda machine, aspired to foster the birth of new Soviet men, women and children, who would occupy the communal domestic spaces of the present as they built a communist future, imbued with the spirit of a new era, with its technological efficiency and utopian-like communalism.

The dream to create a revolutionary society, one whose private and public spaces, intimate and civic, reflect revolutionary—even utopian—values, where "the utopian desire for social arrangements that transcend existing forms" won the day. In this sense, the revolution itself, with these goals for a better tomorrow, reflect modernity's impulse toward "dreamworlds where time is transient and constantly in flux and where the future will be better" as social arrangements will be created within the utopian space that "transcend existing forces."[6] With its utopian visions, "the revolution entered the phenomenal world of the everyday."[7]

The revolutionary ideologues and activists crafted ideas and programs meant to transform individual daily life at its very core, from how one loved to how one furnished one's apartment.

Utopian discourses were not entirely new with the Revolution. A heyday of science fiction and dystopian (and utopian) visions abound in the early years of the twentieth century, including well-known tales by Alexander Bogdanov, from *Red Star* to *Engineer Meni* as well as the continued power of the prerevolutionary avant-garde who played with the idea of time and tomorrow. Most famously, of course, were the Russian futurists, modeled on the Italians, who wrote one of their seminal Manifestos in 1913.[8] Their emphasis was on movement and time, circular but always forward and fast. Filippo Tommaso Marianetti glorified speed and technology and, of course, youth. "We stand on the last promontory of the centuries! [...] Why should we look back, when what we want is to break down the mysterious doors of the Impossible? Time and Space died yesterday. We already live in the absolute, because we have created eternal, omnipresent speed."[9] Speed defied conventional understandings of time and space. These modern ideals of time and the utopian impulses to gaze toward tomorrow reverberated in early Soviet prescriptions of daily life. In this sense, central to the Soviet project was the ambition to create new narratives of time and space.

There is rich scholarship on the revolutionary everyday, including histories on the lives of women and gendered performance and sexuality in the early Soviet era.[10] The work on women and gender is decades old and includes Elizabeth Wood's study of Bolshevik gendered ideals to Wendy Goldman's discussions of the transition from Leninism to Stalinism and Amy Randall's exploration of consumerist impulses in the 1930s, as well as edited volumes on everyday life and masculinity and also work on sexuality and sexual ideology in the first decade or so of Soviet power. Monographs on space and place, especially the building of new communal spaces and creating of a new Soviet domestic ideology, have also informed understandings of everyday life.[11] Fewer works have examined time and new Soviet temporal visons, but there is a nascent scholarship on the meaning of speed and the avant-garde in the early revolutionary days. This book, attempts to build on these long and deep scholarly traditions and bring together questions of how time and temporal narratives were refracted through its spatial dimensions, with particular attention to the home. Just at the moment when proponents of revolution were attempting to create new habits and ideals of everyday life, and traditional gender ideals and familial arrangements were challenged, revolutionary temporality emerged, with its focus on speed, efficiency and its gaze toward a utopian tomorrow. The home, and its interior landscape, became one of the stages upon which new ideas of time was performed.

New understandings of time, and the economy of time, sat center stage, whether the Fordist-inspired insistence on efficiency in daily life or the compression of time and space as a result of industrialization and trains and the like. The Soviet Union, especially in its early years, embodied the revolutionary desire to transform time and space, and to create, albeit with far too few resources, interior spaces that reflected the spirit of a "new life." Part of the crafting of this new life involved building revolutionary—and utopian—domestic spaces: communal, efficient, clean and modern. Celebrated in magazines, newspapers, memoirs, prescriptive texts and literature, this new life, manifested in the home, included the creating of significant distance from nineteenth-century conceptions of gentry sloth. The new Soviet person, with eyes intent on the future, had to be the antithesis of Ivan Goncharov's infamous Oblomov. Unlike the domestic scene with this title character Oblomov lying on the couch, indulging lazily in his bodily desires, the ideal Soviet home might be peopled with new Soviet citizens, who like the radical nineteenth-century characters from Nikolai Chernyshevsky's *What Is to Be Done?*, would be busily and efficiently creating socialist habits and building communal homes that were crafted with clean lines, efficient, collective and ultimately serving the larger ideological purposes of the building of socialism to achieve revolutionary transformation; minutes, hours, days and so on were respected and not "wasted" lounging on the divan.

Authors of Soviet domestic discourses, in their writings and production of images, expressed anxieties about the present and its relationship to the past. These apprehensions took the form of backward, filthy peasants living disorderly lives. Tracy McDonald begins her prize-winning study of the Riazan countryside in the first years of revolution, *Face to the Village*, with this sense of disquietude among revolutionaries vis-à-vis the peasantry. Her introduction quotes A.M. Bol'shakov: "The most difficult is before us / The countryside is the most important and the most difficult [...] [it is peopled by] the ignorant mass [and with] backward agricultural technology."[12] The past, in this case in the form of the peasantry, was always felt to be proximate; lurking in the shadows; around the corner; within sight. The urge toward uniformity—the syncretizing of time—presented a solution to combat the past and its peasants and its seeping into the present.

The path to the future, though, was far from straightforward. The urban apartment, a quintessentially modern space, embodied the anxieties and dreams of this present moment with its emergent temporal narratives. Spatially, apartment living inevitably demanded making one's home in close quarters with one's neighbors, as it did in preceding decades, and often not of the same life circumstances. It created a proximity in daily life, although separate and compartmentalized. Moreover, the dangers of the past—the dirt, the old habits of food and living, the inefficiencies—were just next door in the apartment buildings. Anyone could be living next door; the potential for overcrowding, dirt and general "backwardness" were omnipresent. And as the postrevolutionary years proceeded apace, and the number of communal apartments expanded, these dangers were closer still. The phenomenon of the migration of the peasants from the countryside into the cities and into apartments was, in effect, bringing the past into the present. Whether or not most peasants actually stayed in the cities or lived in apartments is another matter; peasants' presence in the urban imaginary impacted the narratives of modernity. They had to be transformed to conform to modern expectations. The past, in other words, was partly embodied by the countryside, its peasantry and the Russian particularism of those arrangements. By contrast, the present was the city, which should be routinized and syncretized, and finally made efficient.[13]

New modern scientific approaches to domestic dilemmas could be found in the prescriptive literature of the day, including editorial columns in women's magazines. Readers were inundated with advice about how to combat the past and build environments that conformed to present ideas of efficiency and uniformity, much like in the prerevolutionary years but with a new urgency and insistence on the part of the state apparatus. Readers were advised that as peasants left the countryside and members of fading gentry families migrated to Moscow and St. Petersburg to find work and new residences, newcomers should adopt daily domestic practices that reflected modern definitions of time, of the present and of proper, modern home life. The domestic became one central repository for ideas about the now, both its large-scale seismic shifts and its everyday mundane manifestations. In Russia, perhaps even more so than in other parts of Europe, the past did not recede so delicately, as the countryside continued to dominate the landscape and recent migrants from peasant villages populated the city. The urban infrastructure could not keep up and modern standards were hard to implement in any widespread way. Yet, that did not stop those who worked for the aspirational press from publishing issue after issue and writing column after column instructing Russians on how to live in the modern, present day.

Gender works

None of these ideas about the New Soviet Woman or revolutionary gendered ideology is new to scholars. We know an awful lot about women, gender and femininity in the early Soviet days. There is no need to rehearse the dreams of Alexandra Kollontai or Nadezhda Krupskaya, with their plans for communal kitchens and collective day care. The home was to be transformed entirely, freeing up time for Soviet people, and especially women, to concentrate their labor in ways that were productive for the state, whether directly to move into new labor forces or in order to free up time to study Marxism-Leninism or be active in the Zhenotdel, the women's arm of the Bolshevik Party. Although despite these ideologies and attempts, tastemakers themselves in the 1920s acknowledged both these goals of efficient and collective housekeeping, and emphasized its incompleteness. In a 1927 issue of *Dom i khoziastvo*, an author explains that even though "we are ten years from the revolution, there is still much work to be done."[14] Women's domestic burdens are far from alleviated. On the contrary, she writes that often women who are employed have to use so-called "free time" to do housework, that is, "hours that are uncountable as working hours." Thus, the author suggests, it was key for those hours "by rights and rational principles" to be "normalized/rationalized/made efficient." And since it is "unacceptable to be late to a meeting" or to "burn the soup," in order to expect so much of women, and "to do this properly, technology must be known and used," and efficient movements mastered. There is a kind of plea for readers to write in and to share their own experiences and offer advice on how best to master this time efficiency. The object of all of these prescriptions were women. It was women who were reading and writing, for the most part, these prescriptive texts.[15]

Gender was always central to these revolutionary narratives of daily life and the mastery of time. One key element in the reconfiguring of daily life and domestic life and its temporal narratives was the reframing of gender norms. Despite the fact that the women of the collective were the ones meant to ensure the economy of time in the everyday, one prominent trope of gender performance was the notion that early Soviet society was one of *Men Without Women*.[16] This argument is contingent on the idea that all signs of femininity were to be erased and the quintessential Homo Sovieticus was a masculine, perhaps androgynous (in the Zamyatin *We*-like variety) laborer who devoted himself to building the Soviet state. The quintessential Soviet person was masculine; the state had taken over (in theory) the duties of traditional womanhood and so only men were required to build the glorious Soviet state. Who, though, would tend to the home, in this singularly masculine universe? Women, of course. Soviet notions of gender performance included temporal elements, where the economy of time and space emerged triumphant so that women-homemakers had sufficient time to learn to be better members of the collective.

And yet, even the ideologues themselves could not quite envision such an androgynous, gender-free or feminine-free tomorrow. The now, the moment of Soviet becoming, could not shed the traditional gendered past. Lenin is quoted as having said: "there are very few men, even proletarian men, who think about how best to ease the pain and care for your wives or even totally ease their burden by helping out around the house."[17] In this same prescriptive tract, A. Radchenko quotes Anatoly Lunacharsky, the Minister of Enlightenment, in a similar vein: "If I entered the apartment of a comrade and saw a man with a beard rocking a baby in the cradle, because his wife was out studying or at a meeting, what would I say? I would simply give him my hand, like a proper Leninite." Even the most strident of prescriptive texts that emphasize gender equality imagine the domestic realm as one where domestic labor is ultimately or first of all, naturally, feminine, if momentarily masculine, to help the larger cause. This prescriptive piece, in particular, compares the Soviet attitude toward domestic duties with that of foreigners. The author emphasizes how in foreign lands (America and Germany) men only do housework for their bosses if they are somehow "others," whether (as the tract lists) "negroes, Indians, Chinese, etc etc." This is juxtaposed to the Soviet case where the roles assigned to Soviet men were primarily non-domestic and at best what essentially equates to being helpmates for women and to "care for their housewives."[18]

Women, in the end, remained the authority and performed the bulk of the labor in the home in the early Soviet present and thus women had to be attentive to the efficient use of time and domestic space. Tricia Starks, in her monograph on hygiene practices and ideologies, explains that "in plays, posters and even in weeklong propaganda campaigns, reformers considered women the authorities within the home and the ones capable of substantial change."[19] Writers indicated that the women were responsible for the home and for organizing "the collective laundries, kitchens, and nurseries to free them from domestic slavery." In this sense, Stark turns to prescriptive texts on proper hygiene to highlight how, across various prescriptive genres, the so-called traditional concerns of "women, hearth, and home were consequently more deeply entrenched." In the end, prescriptive writers deemed men incapable of "changing the home themselves."[20] Moreover, in addition to tending to their homes, women were assigned the community tasks of inspecting domestic spaces. In the most extreme cases, men not only resisted the domestic sphere but also were portrayed as drunken and beating their wives.

The Soviet home, thus, despite its radical gender ambitions of equality and the unburdening of women performing domestic tasks—in part as a way to ward off the past backwardness and its gender oppression—remained in a present moment that held tightly to older notions of masculinity and gender hierarchy.

The reified gendered hierarchy reared its ugly head in women's and home magazines with regularity, both those that continued their runs from prerevolutionary days and newly created Soviet ones. If home-oriented magazines, including health advice for the communal domestic realm, featured whole sections of magazines and pamphlets entitled "woman mother; woman housewife, woman worker" and so-called experts on home life explain that men are there to help their wives and mothers, then norms of masculinity remained mired in the past. Thus, even though Marx declared that the main source of women's backwardness was their place in the home and domestic labor, and Lenin wrote that woman would "remain a *domestic slave* in spite of all liberating laws as long as housework remained isolated labor conducted in the home," gender itself remained tied to the past with a communist twist, where all citizens were to work and contribute to the building of the new society. This did not equate to liberation from housework or childrearing for Soviet women. Likewise, new notions of manhood, defined by a technologically more advanced, communally oriented future, never emerged within the domestic imagination. Although women and the home were important tools of propaganda in the 1920s and the home itself took on increased public meaning, its gendered ideologies did not significantly transform, and thus when the 1930s rolled around it was not far to "return" to past gendered hierarchies based on traditional notions. The question of "return" itself is fraught. Many scholars have argued that there was a significant transition from the New Economic Policy (NEP) era ideal to the Stalinist one. Others, more recently, have disagreed and contended that since the revolutionary moment itself was not very transformative, the traditionalism/conservativism of the 1930s was not a dramatic change. In either case, the past loomed large. However, not only the past but the future too, in this utopian-oriented Soviet society, had its role to play.

Bringing utopia home/Concrete utopia and the everyday

In the well-known 1929 play "The Bed Bug," Vladimir Mayakovsky provides his readers with a portrait of life fifty years hence, in a sort of dystopian future after the fervor of revolution has subsided. Ivan Prisypin, the protagonist of Mayakovsky's drama, finds himself in a frozen state, having survived a fire at the time of the revolution. Once unfrozen, he becomes reacquainted with his former lover and the new regime captures them both and puts them on display in a zoo for all to admire, two creatures from the past. People are frightened of them. The director of the zoo (a scientist) is discussing these two "beasts" and says: they are different in size, but identical in essence. Both of them have their "habitats in the musty mattress of time." They are both "parasites" who "made their homes in the dirt."[21] The dirt of the past.

This portrait, like so many to come out of the early years of revolution, reflects the Soviet socialist impulse to gaze toward the future, whether bleak or bright, even as the past tugged on the present moment. The future, often utopian in nature, included fantasies of efficiency, speed and technology. Yet, at the same moment, the utopian future had a complicated relationship to the past, one that included Mayakovsky's bedbugs, who themselves reappeared as vestiges of the past, freaks to be caged and gazed upon by a society already building a revolutionary dreamworld.

In this sense, and others, early Soviet temporal narratives were replete with contradictions. On the one hand, many theorists and philosophers, including Karl Marx himself, both before and after the revolution, conceive of utopia as "a promise by the state that can never be fulfilled."[22] Yet, despite the illusive quality of utopia itself, as design scholar Tom Cubbins, in his work on Soviet design aesthetics and collectives posits, utopias in the early revolutionary context were not "escapist nonsense" but rather "a fundamental part of human culture" that ultimately shaped the ways in which ordinary, revolutionary citizens crafted their daily lives. Cubbins,[23] in his work on the Senezh Studio, an experimental design studio of the 1960s, turns to Ernst Bloch in order to understand the ways in which utopian discourses manifest in the everyday. He distinguishes between "abstract" and "concrete" utopias as a frame for making sense of the disjuncture between abstract ideologies and concrete everyday prescriptions and practices. His emphasis is on small actions, what he calls "concrete utopia" as juxtaposed to overarching abstractions and ideologies enacted by individuals or collectives. In his understanding, concrete utopias are part of a process of the continual production of the future in everyday life whereby "the unfinished nature of reality locates the possible within the real."[24] Cubbins also points to Paul Ricoeur's notion of "constitutive utopia," which has similarities to Bloch's "concrete utopia," but places particular emphasis on culture that directly or indirectly imagines forms of social existence and presents alternatives to the status quo. A constitutive utopia is an important part of the cultural or social imagination. In this thinking, the social imagination is *constitutive* of social reality. The presumption here is precisely that of a social imaginary, of a cultural imagination, operating in both constructive and destructive ways, as both confirmation and contestation of the present situation. It is precisely this set of constitutive utopian ideas that, in the early Soviet context, is a part of the "continual production of the future in everyday life."[25] The early Soviet social imagination included an embrace of the future—as well as the past—as a means of confirming the distance between the past and the promise of the future.[26] It was through everyday actions and behaviors and ideologies where utopian ideas held sway. Utopias "seek out what is deficient in the present and produce alternatives."[27] Life, in this revolutionary era, was always becoming, always in process and made up of the everyday manifestations of new ideologies. This becoming, however, never meant a rejection of the past, rather the past was harnessed to give meaning to the present and its striving toward tomorrow. The answer resides in a number of cultural and social arenas of everyday life.[28]

In her comparative book on fashion in communist Europe, Djurdja Bartlett confronts the question of the Soviet tastemakers' relationship to the past. She begins her discussion on dress and utopianism and writes: "no other revolution rejected tradition more strongly or attempted so vigorously to provoke an absolute break in continuity between past and present."[29] The past is imagined as unrecognizable to the early Soviet ideologues and culture producers.[30] The past, whether manifest in aesthetics, norms of everyday life or political ideology, is imagined as remote from the present. Yet, the early Bolshevik period was not without its contradictions. The years of the NEP brought the emergence of avant-garde artistic trends, the celebration of—and reemergence of—materialism and consumer desire alongside the creation of a socialist, ascetic, communalist aesthetic, each of which resonated with aspects of the past. The past itself became woven into the utopian dreams, whether in the form of avant-garde artistic trends or the celebration of the nineteenth-century estate. In this sense, the past, with its multitude of material and ideological manifestations, haunted the Soviet era, even as it was being forced aside by new aesthetics and everyday morals. The centrality of the past in Soviet presentations of domestic and filial spaces might at first glance appear unexpected. Yet, this celebration of nineteenth-century practices appeared as a way to embrace the past, a particular national past, to move toward the future; early Soviet tastemakers turned their gaze backwards as they defined what might come next. These seeming contradictions reflected the larger dynamics of NEP-era aesthetics and daily life.

The years of the New Economic Policy overflowed with all types of aesthetic and ideological contractions, including the relationship to the past, the meaning of the present and aspirations for the future. Throughout the 1920s, individuals were "surrounded by cubism, futurism, Bauhaus, jazz, commerce, films and advertising." The embrace of all of the modern movements took place "against the backdrop of sweeping change brought about by the Bolshevik revolution."[31] In one sense, the past was vilified, it was to be discarded and daily life redone. The focus rather was on the creation of a particular, communist, future. "The Bolsheviks' condemnation of the past presupposed that the present reality would soon be replaced by a new world, inhabited by New Men and New Women modeled on the Nietzschean superman."[32] This relationship to the past and future was indeed relevant in all aspects of everyday life, whether a reconfiguration of family life or the design of furniture.

Domestic interiors were no different. Journals of interior design and architecture in the 1920s emphasized the creation of a New Domestic World Order including efficient construction and spatial layout. In an article—whose title makes this point quite boldly—entitled "New World" and "Neue Welt" as well as "Novyi Mir," the author emphasizes how it is technology that will bring Soviet society into the future, whether in the form of the flight of Lindberg as in America or the ship rotation of Fletner or other such examples across the globe. Regardless of the stage, "a diagram of modernity [*sovremennost*] gives us a complicated picture of the social and economic arena [...] both straight and crooked [...] that characterizes the movements of science and technology."[33] This New World Order shows "the clear and earnest VICTORY OF A CONSCIOUS PERSON OVER AMORPHOUS NATURE."[34] And, the reader is instructed, "such an outcome reflects all inherited value and converts all earlier created forms; it gives a clear formulation of our new world. This new world order included roads and automobiles," and as the declaration in the magazine insisted: "At the same time [...] all of this abidingly unceasingly expands the impression of "time" and the impression of "space." Life is faster: "We live faster; consequently, we live longer."[35] Speed, too, is a value in this new domestic future: "The feeling of speed is more acute" at certain moments of the day. Moreover, speed on the roads itself is not enough, hygiene and efficiency were key uses of Soviet technology as "hygiene permeates these domestic dwellings: porcelain bathtubs, bidets, WCs [water closets]—it is a new genius of sanitary ceramics." New interiors live, "Life and death by the laws of hygiene!"[36]

Architects, tastemakers and, of course, political ideologues had particular ideas about how to construct this utopian inside, within domestic interiors. In a 1929 issue of *Sovremennaia arkhitektura* there appeared "A statement: Thesis on Housing" that contrasted prerevolutionary housing with housing of contemporary times. Prerevolutionary housing meant "a means of maximizing the exploitation of workers" and "class warfare between the bourgeoisie and the proletariat." During the early phase of revolution, the proletariat lived in barracks or in dormitories, in general. The individual apartment was always under suspicion. It was imagined, in particular, that the apartment "is a material form of petit-bourgeois ideology" and served as the "basis of the structure of the capitalist economy." Although economically it may be profitable with a "high coefficient of living areas," ideologically it has no "social meaning." The purpose of collective housing, on the other hand, was to satisfy the mass of workers and to connect them to one another and, also, to create temporal and material efficiencies.[37]

In the Soviet homescape, utopia became a matter of *practice*, constitutive of the everyday.[38] Since utopias seek both to define that which is deficient in the present moment and to imagine alternatives to those deficiencies in the future, the temporal landscape of Soviet daily life included notions of past, present and future all wrapped into one.[39] The Soviet project to create new housing structures and norms, which was premised upon an ideology of communalism, reflects the building of a concrete utopia in the everyday. And also Soviet socialist utopias had a particular temporal quality in that the future—with all of its promises of progress and modernity—was always embedded in present narratives. The present was the cauldron of the future; each action, mundane or otherwise, embodied the dreams of what would come.

The present moment: Efficiency, cleanliness and the dawn of a new day?

Utopian notions, both in ideology and in their concrete forms in practice, manifested in the particular prescriptions for the domestic interiors in new Soviet living spaces. Efficiency and cleanliness were the requirements for the creation of a modern household, along with a sweeping away of the dust of the past, no matter how persistent it may have been. The efficient use of time, of days, of hours, minutes and seconds, played a very important role in Soviet early prescriptions of domestic life. Stephen Hanson in his monograph *Time and Revolution* argues that in the Soviet context the goal revolved around the transcending of modern time discipline in order to avoid becoming beholden to the clock (as in the capitalist West), and ultimately dispensing with the clock altogether, in order to conquer time, in all of its manifestations. Hanson begins his discussion with a quote from Valentin Kataev in *Time Forward* (1932):

> The clock was accurate but [engineer] Margulies did not depend on it. He was not asleep. He always rose at six and was always ahead of time. There had never yet been an occasion when the alarm clock had actually awakened him. Margulies could not really have faith in so simple a mechanism as a timepiece; could not entrust it to so precious a thing as time.[40]

Hanson highlights how this hero, an "archetypal Bolshevik engineer," is "unimaginable in the western context," since the idea that time is "too precious" to entrust to a watch would be unthinkable within the Fordest culture of modern Europe. Here, our Soviet hero has a highly developed *internal* sense of temporal flow and ticks on a clock. He has, in a sense, mastered time in the present, in all of its modern machinations, and in doing so, left the past behind.

Yet, even as Soviet ideology demanded a mastering of time through the internalizing of temporal rhythms and the efficient layout of homes and furniture design, Aleksei Gastev, the quintessential Soviet Taylorist, emerged as the father of Soviet Time.[41] Gastev was the founder and inaugural director of TsIT (Central Institute of Labor), which was "dedicated to the improvement of industrial efficiency."[42] With this embrace of a Taylorist sensibility, Gastev and his comrades emphasized a totalizing efficiency that led to a simple aesthetic style for quick paths to cleanliness and labor, whether in the factory or at home. Gastev wrote ditties about how the body must be cared for like a working machine and had to be carefully monitored like a clock. The clock, for Gastev and his followers, ruled daily life.[43] Gastev was widely known as the Prophet of Time in Russia, as his followers created charts of how to spend daily time, including doing housework according to a deliberate time regime.

Regardless of whether the ultimate goal of early Soviet ideology involved the precision of Gastev's clock or the internalizing of time discipline, which Gastev also advocated for, Soviet citizens had constant reminders at their fingertips of how to make their lives more time efficient, at least partly in order to find more time free from domestic labor to devote to the building of the Soviet collective. If postwar 1950s Soviet domestic culture, as Susan Reid suggests,[44] demanded the assertion of individual filial time regimes, early revolutionary ideology relied on a modern, collective temporal sensibility. Women's magazines and behavioral booklets demanded—in form and in substance—collective, embodied and efficient time regimes. The notion that "we must defeat the old everyday" echoed in the hallways of Soviet apartments across towns and across the capitals, and included calls for collective efforts to ensure that the new Soviet era would be efficient, scientific and communal.

This impulse toward efficiency and control moreover meant a reliance on technology and science as key mechanisms for setting up new domestic interiors. As one magazine editor wrote: "the meaning of technology for housekeeping is in its ability to allow for time efficiency."[45] And this "economy of time use," a constant refrain in the prescriptive and instructive literatures, whether referring to the kitchen, the dining room or the collective *dvor*, appeared as a frequent principle in prescriptive domestic tracts. It was meant to be observed in all areas of housework, whether the placement of shelves in kitchens or the type of paint on the wall that was easily and quickly cleanable. In one article on housekeeping entitled "Conversations About Housekeeping," for example, the author reminds her readers that the "Regime of Economy—is the law/rule of our day." Using economy (of time) "marks novyi byt" as does "reasonable economy" in housekeeping.[46] And, too, one of the main principles of contemporary housekeeping includes the expectation that the "knowledge of technology of housekeeping allows for the economy of time, which is essential for modern women, who must carry in new skills to refine the labor that is called 'housekeeping' or 'housekeepers' and replace what was there before."[47]

The careful parsing of daily time not only indicated a modern sensibility in general terms, on par with nations to the West, with its emphasis on technology and cleanliness, but also meant more time to invest in the Soviet collective project each day. The Soviet prescriptions for efficiency at home, moreover, often emphasized that individuals were meant to internalize time regimes and even adjust their movements to accommodate the most efficient way of dealing with domestic tasks; they were advised to collectively embody the Soviet time ideal. An article on food preparation in the kitchen, entitled "The Economy of Time," for example, emphasizes the importance of individuals adjusting to how they move within the domestic sphere to minimize extraneous movement: "Particularly, it is very easy to spend a large amount of time on food preparation" and so you must adjust your time expectations and your movements within the kitchen.[48] Similarly, articles in prescriptive texts emphasize the need to efficiently clean rooms within the home. "In these cases, there is often a large amount of movement required," but women are advised not to "make a fuss." This is because "often what needs to be done is the cleaning of a single room: to wash the floor, the windows, to create clean pathways; to wipe away the dust; and only then go to another room and begin cleaning all over again. – the corridor, the kitchen, etc." The advice that follows is to clean entirely differently and with much more efficiency. This older way is "a lot of extra work." Under the heading of "the plan of work," the editor explains that it is necessary to establish "the following order for cleaning your home"; this order included the advice that window washing not be part of the morning routine. This article quotes a *Practical Guide to Housekeeping* by Frederik, a popular guide at the time among Russian educated urbanites, and emphasizes how a housekeeper must plan to use time efficiently and wisely: she must "prepare everything necessary for her work and her dishes ahead of time," so that she can minimize movements around the apartment. To create an efficient space, she needs "enough kitchen shelves for dishes and food" that are conveniently located to allow for minimal bodily movements and she also should prepare meals in bulk, "as it is simply inefficient and ineffectual to do them day by day and one by one." The author advises that she never purchases each item separately, as that would "take too much time." Rather, she should "spare time and money" by buying one's groceries in bulk or in "large quantities."[49]

The overall Soviet project of electrification, and its penetration into the domestic interior, contributed to the success of time-efficiency practices at home. Women, who are often the ones to take care of the home, benefited from mechanization and electrification as it ensured that it would take "about five times less time" for housework, and most especially if the tasks "were performed collectively." These statute-inspired efficiency schemes were all meant to ensure that Soviet citizens learned how to "distribute [their] time properly."[50] In an article from 1927 in *Dom i khoziastvo* on "The Electrification of Housekeeping," the readers learnt that the factory Electricity engaged in the "Electrification of All Things," including housekeeping. One example is the electrification of the tea pot, which was touted as a big improvement, because among other reasons, it "guarantees cleanliness, hygiene, not dangerous vis a vis fire problem, and it allows for the saving of time and labor."[51]

The efficiency and technological change benefited the home in general, and women in particular. Article after article in domestic-oriented magazines emphasized how women had to change their habits in order to inspire the "reduced consumption of time" in their daily lives. This impulse to "economize with time" and the sense of efficiency, too, extends to advocacy for the collective.[52] In the article entitled "How to Ease the Work of the Khoziaka?," the author traces the history of the practice of having communal kitchens and cafeterias. She argues that these communal spaces lessen the burden on women and are more economical of time. A single woman, who is devoted to the collective, might perform tasks that were performed by multiple women in their individual households in the past. The author quotes from a manual on how to set this up.

It is also money saving and time saving. "In this time, every apartment has a kitchen from the old times, but which may not fit the new living needs of communal kitchens" to create efficiency of housekeeping.

Science and technology marked a new era and facilitated the implementation of this modern commitment to time efficiency, which brought a doubly modern aesthetic: at once technologically innovative and time efficient. Soviet-era writers of prescriptive texts detail how technology both confirms Russia's modern status and inspires the efficient use of time. In 1925, *Dom i khoziastvo* put out a series of articles on technological advances within the domestic interior. This series provides vignettes on various innovations for the domestic interior: "simplified machine for washing clothing"; "door with an ironing board"; "new electric stove."[53]

The small article on the washing machine states that "household work for the housekeeper is laborious and tedious. These days one can often facilitate these efforts by using various electric appliances—tea kettles; hot water heaters, etc., which are made in our soviet factories." There is also a picture and description of a door with an ironing board built in; the magazine emphasizes the efficient use of space. The small article explains that this is what you find inside of American homes: the "rational use of space."[54] Soviet apartments too were to be economical and rational in their design and in their use in order to maximize space use and to minimize movement to preserve energy and save time.[55] In the recurring column "Help for the Khoziaka," the author writes all about technology, from a "machine for potatoes" in order to guarantee "quick cleaning," to a "machine to prepare noodles" quickly and without much mess. "This machine helps to quickly prepare noodles [...] with one hand you hold the machine, with the other you crank the dough/noodles through the machine."[56]

Furniture was also at the forefront of the battle to combat the waste of time. Furnishing throughout the apartment, like the kitchen, was meant to be economical and rational. A 1928 article in *Dom i khoziastvo* highlights how to properly furnish the apartment as a whole, including stating that Soviet apartments must "update" and "rationalize" furnishings, but that the current available furniture might not be sufficient.[57] The design itself emphasized having space. Many were encouraged to make what was called "Double furniture," which takes up little space and is efficient; "they fit together and have modern parts [...] like stacking chairs." The concept was simple: one object would do the job of two creating spatial and temporal efficiencies.[58] Soviet furniture design was profoundly transforming to meet these current values of efficiency and economy:

The current furnishings, most of all, are cumbersome and non-economical in the use of space, and in current, cozy domiciles play a large role. And, in my own internal opinion, it remains true that this contemporary furniture is like the "traditional" furnishings in that commodes and shelves are made in legitimized frozen forms, the style is – not comfortable and not simple.[59]

If the furniture was not simple, it also could mean a lack of easy cleaning and ultimately at the sacrifice of hygienic practices.

In some instances, practices in nations to the West are invoked in order to provide inspiration for Soviet audiences. In a 1928 issue of *Dom i khoziastvo*, there is a picture with the caption: "Kitchen in the Room" (see Figure 3), which describes how Germans have worked toward solving the domestic space crisis.[60] The picture and article emphasize how Germans are able to efficiently use domestic space, and especially the space in the kitchen. "What kind of a kitchen should we [Soviets] have?" in order to "simplify and facilitate" the efficient use of space," asks the author of the article on German kitchens. The answer includes a plea to internalize time discipline. Since it is the place where the

Figure 3 "Kitchen in the Room," *Dom i khoziastvo* 11, no. 45 (1928): 2. Public domain.

housekeeper spends most of her time, everyone should attempt to "maximize time and be as conscious of using each moment and movement as carefully as possible." In other words, "the kitchen should be "both small and spacious," with its interior organized to minimize bodily movement.[61] French households are also invoked to emphasize efficiency of time and space. In two small articles in *Dom i khoziastvo*, the Russian audience learned about the "rationalization" of housework in France.[62] One in particular mentions an exhibition in France that focused on the efficient use of space within the household. The article gives four specific examples: "1. The buffet-kravat [...] the bed comes out of the buffet, saving space. 2. Using very deep cabinets/cupboard for food; 3. Have not very deep doors so that they do not take up much space. 4. A room/kitchen table/shelf again combining to save space and economize."

The use of modern furniture in the home, practical and enabling an efficiency in daily movements and easy to clean was a central aspect of state policy on building the new *byt*. L. V-ii, the author of an article simply entitled "On Furnishing Apartments," suggests that the proper furnishing of apartments is comparable to a military offensive. Furnishing apartments, it articulates, is "one of the remaining tasks on our 'apartment front' [kvartarnogo fronta]." Not enough has occurred "on this front up until this time." Rather, soft, old furniture was allowed to remain and even flourish in apartments. This article insists that modern, Soviet "hygienic practices go against soft furniture."[63] In an article entitled "Finishing and Decorating Rooms," the author emphasizes how configuring a room efficiently and then living in it each day should only "take a very short period of time," because it must be efficient and fairly uniform.[64]

Furniture and their aesthetics, thus, became central aspects in the Soviet story. In the article "Furniture Care" chairs and couches are not only personified but also grow old with time: "Old, cranky furniture, with cracked paint, with an unattractive appearance, and refusing to listen, very often it is possible to update/refresh one's home oneself."[65] Time is always of the essence. In a similar piece, "On Furnishing Apartments," the author explains ways of fixing furniture oneself as well as the efficient use of time. "From time to time [...] wood furniture must be updated," since newer woods "take less time to clean." It is a matter of efficiency.[66] Revolutionary efficient ways are compared with old-fashioned North American ones: "There was a time not too long ago that what counted was that everyone relied on their own physical strength (before mechanization) within the household." In this sense, this celebrates the mechanization of equipment for everyday domestic life. "Mechanization and technology should be used."[67] Part of the explicit goal was to leave the past behind. There is a "real thrust" toward transforming "primitive technologies in today's world," which would inspire a successful and utopian tomorrow.[68] This emphasis on efficiency and modernity is also highlighted in descriptions of children's furniture. In one piece from *Home and Housekeeping*, the author explains how a mixing of past and present styles in the crafting of children's furniture may yield the best results. The author explains how there is a carpenters' workshop at Abramstevo, which makes the best kind of kids' furniture. This furniture is "a new type of furniture that mixes the contemporary with the former pre-revolutionary aesthetic." This is the same peasant-inspired aesthetic that was discussed in Chapter 3 in this book. There is a duality to the furniture style, in both its prerevolutionary and Soviet renditions: one that mixes past and present.[69]

The layering of temporal frames, thus, was everywhere, in both the material and the behavioral. There appeared an article entitled "Living Life on the Clock, as a Basis for the Correct Way to Live," which outlines in no uncertain terms the proper ways in which time operates in the context of the upbringing of children and the timing of an orderly Soviet household.[70] The author concentrates on how mothers, in their daily routines with their children, must perform according to the clock; time must be used efficiently and wisely. "If you do not eat in time then you will suffer severe and frequent bouts of gastrointestinal pain," for example. There is a certain urgency to the claims of using time correctly and with intention. "Time is running out and taking our lives, and therefore time – provides the ability to live, without time there is no life! We must teach our children to have the correct approach to time! We must give them the correct approach to time!" This occurs from the moment of birth: "When a baby eats correctly, calmly and deeply sleeps, the mother is able to have time for work, and time for rest. Isn't that important?" Paying close attention to time and how to live by time allows for better living: "If we don't learn to live with those close to us: with our children, with our wives, and then perhaps we will be better citizens? Never! We must live together [...] we must teach our children how to best approach time, having taught them the order of time from birth."[71]

And yet, the past persisted. It was nearly impossible to sweep away. Soviet tastemakers, like the Russian ones, emphasized the degree to which a new day was dawning in the early days of Bolshevik rule, a new era emerging and the past receding. In the case of the fin de siècle, modernity—with its industrial spirit—itself demanded an emphasis on newness and progress as the past was left in the dust by speeding trains and new domestic technologies. The past had to be swept away. The same was true when the Bolsheviks came to power. The past had to go. And yet, its echoes were around every corner.

When Walter Benjamin traveled to Moscow in 1926 to 1927, he observed these tensions in the state's project of building a new society—whether one steeped in communal utopian ideas or one focused on strengthening a strong middle class in the era of the NEP. There was—and yet never is—in a sense, an escape. Like "a Bauldelairian flaneur, simultaneously very close to and very distant from what he hears and sees."[72] Benjamin describes how Moscow's streets and shops and apartments are replete with the contradictions between "modern technology and old-fashioned ways."[73] The physical layout of the city reflects this layering:

> In the streets of Moscow there is a curious state of affairs: the Russian village is playing hide and seek in them. If you step through one of the high gateways-they often have wrought-iron gates, but I never find them closed, you stand on the threshold of a spacious settlement. Opening before you is a farmhouse or a village, [...] wooden staircases go to the backs of homes, which look like city buildings from the front.[74]

He finds that Moscow is layered with modernity and "tradition," with urban and rural, and with present and past.

Benjamin also articulates these contrasts and contradictions within the domestic sphere. Benjamin comments on the Bolshevik abolition of "private life" and the lack of availability of space in the now. Whereas in the past "apartments that earlier accommodated single families in their five to eight rooms now often lodge eight [families]."[75] The aesthetics of the domestic interior had also shifted, from the petit bourgeois "completeness" with pictures crowding walls and puffy cushions on sofas that collect dust versus the now. Today there are "bare rooms" and a "radical means of expelling 'coziness' along with melancholy." Lenin's activities, Benjamin highlights, "accelerated the course of events" in that much recedes swiftly into the past, albeit the dust can never be completely swept away.[76]

Yet, despite the hidden courtyards of the past with staircases that led to bare and crowded quarters, much of the Soviet rhetoric revolved around leaving the past behind. The rhetoric surrounding International Women's Day, for instance, reflected this. March 8th was always an occasion to mark the ways in which women, and therefore families and the domestic culture, had made great strides forward, and especially in the home. One 1926 article entitled "Attack on the Everyday" in *Hygiene and Health in Workers' and Peasants' Family Life* [*Gigena i zdorov'e rabochie i krest'ianskoi sem'i*], a journal geared toward both workers and peasants, celebrated International Women's Day by attacking the "Old Life": "The Old Life still had chains that fettered women," which included individual families—women being in charge of children and kitchens, their washing, cleaning and raising children. All of this work and expectations obscured from view, this author tells us, "like a wall, the majority of women from actively participating in the societal life and the building of socialism." This, however, has begun to change, but takes time and effort. Women now, though, "look toward the "future": "Our *byt* is still extremely inert, not healthy, full of prejudice, dark, full of ignorance: we must improve, we must change things. We can see that there is a huge amount of work going on everywhere to build "*novyi byt.*" Women are urged to continue their great work on the front of change and especially as it relates to domestic tasks becoming collectivized.[77] The past must be confronted and swept away.

As Lenin himself suggested, the past must be swept into the dustbin of history. The image of the Soviet state sweeping away the past in order to welcome the present and strive toward the future is familiar to most who have studied the creation of a Soviet Revolutionary Culture. The oversized broom rids society of the everyday grit and grime so associated with bygone years. The broom sweeps away bad old habits of yesterday, whether religious beliefs, bourgeois tastes or domestic trash, as in Figure 4, a poster that appeared in *Bezgodnik*.[78]

Interior spaces, including domestic spaces, were far from immune to this cleansing. Even while the domestic spaces of Soviet life, as some have argued, served as an unofficial refuge from the storm, a place where private thoughts

Figure 4 "Sweeping," *Bezgodnik i stanka* (1926). Public domain.

and feelings could flourish and whispers could be cautiously uttered, Soviet tastemakers wrote endlessly of how to set up modern and efficient kitchens. Apartment interiors were always the subject of heightened official (and unofficial) prescriptive discourses and desires.[79] The Soviet home, far from being in a private realm outside of politics, always was central to an imagined Soviet present and future.[80] Within Soviet discourses, the ridding of the past, including the old domestic order, would make way for a communal Soviet future, out in public and at home. One of the early Soviet tastemakers who authored the book *For a Healthy Everyday* wrote that: "You must always remember the words of [Vladimir] Ilich [Lenin] that in order to crossover into socialism, we must make a complete about face. We need whole transformation of cultural practices for all of the masses of people. This about face included sweeping away the past in our own homes, with its dusty reminders of bourgeois life and backwards fields."[81] The new Soviet life, modern life, was manifest in everyday domestic objects and behaviors, whether the type of furniture one had or the methods one used to clean out the kitchen sink. A soft, comfortable couch, for instance, had the potential to carry with it the dust and the aesthetic of the old society, and to interrupt the planting of the seeds of the new society in the preset moment. Discussion about the problems with old-fashioned "soft furniture," such as Benjamin pointed out in his Moscow strolls or articles on inefficient layout of kitchens, abound in the prescriptive texts of the early Soviet era.

In an attempt to reimagine the Soviet domestic interior absent of the bourgeois penchant for "cozy for cozy sake," writers insisted that readers rejected all of the "old prejudices!" that governed domestic life, most prominently including tastes of the "old domestic interior of an apartment."[82] In several instances, the domestic interior of the past is pictured as cluttered, curtain-filled, messy with soft and overly cozy furniture.[83] All Soviet citizens, women most of all, were instructed to rid themselves of old habits and acquire furniture that conforms with modern hygienic design.

Part of creating domestic spaces and respecting the power of the now included a direct attack on the past, even as it refused to recede entirely. Many articles begin with the battle against junk in order to create "authentic living spaces and culture." They point to how architecture/layout weighs on the question of cleanliness, etc. and how there are "new demands" for the "new architecture and furniture." There is a discussion of the difference between "traditional spaces" versus "modern apartments."[84] As was discussed above, there was inevitably a gendered dimension to understandings of domestic interior aesthetics. It was understood that this process first of all involved women and was gendered in its division of labor and aspirations despite discourse about equality. "The improvement of domestic life demands upon the improvement and ease of women's lives."[85] Women are imagined "ignorant of their own situation." They do not realize how enslaved they are in their contemporary apartments. "They give away their lives everyday and every hour, they never stop working: they cook, they wash, they clean, they sew, etc etc." Women, too, are asked to perform emotional labor: "The largest role is played by feelings." Women wish to establish "comfort [...] for themselves and their families."[86] The old "comfort" of traditional spaces is no longer acceptable, as now there is a new Soviet understanding of "comfort." A "modern comfy exists." The modern, new ideas of living comfort and beauty emerge in place of old "pretentiousness." Now, the Soviet magazine insists, there will be "simplicity, outspoken and clear corresponding form of living quarters and its inventory of purpose."[87]

From Soviet tastemakers' bidding farewell to the past and embracing of domestic aesthetics and technology in the present to prepare for the future, older bourgeois ideas of coziness and comfort, ideas which were already challenged at the end of the old regime, no longer held sway in Russia's capital cities. This Soviet deliberate construction of new domestic interiors and new ideas about time were reflected in the impulse to sweep away the past, put its faith in progress, technology and efficiency.

Dust

One of the main enemies of the efficient Soviet apartment was dust, perhaps dust in a particularly Soviet form. It was Soviet dust per se, a dust that was associated with the ordinary dirt and grime in the urban—ever-industrializing, modern—present, on the one hand, and contained residue of the past, on the other. Thus, the war against dust, which we saw in the earlier era, resurfaced time and again in the prescriptive tracts of the 1920s and early 1930s. As Carolyn Steedman writes in her masterful account of dust in the archives, twentieth- or twenty-first-century dust embodied "the immutable, obdurate set of beliefs about the material world, past and present, inherited from the nineteenth century." [88] While Steedman's story is one about the archives, and the residue left for us to discover and make sense of in the present, her insistence on dust's simultaneous embodiment of the irreducible traces of the past and reflection of an industrial present resonates with the understanding of home as an interstitial space—neither past nor present—meant alternatively as a refuge from present chaos and as a beacon of ideological hope for the Soviet present. Dust, like the home itself, takes on these dual, often contradictory meanings. This paradoxical relationship of dust to temporal narratives is echoed by Mark Steinberg in his monograph on fin de siècle St. Petersburg. Steinberg states that dust is both "a paradoxical product of both St. Petersburg's development and its backwardness."[89] This paradox emerges too in dust's relationship not only to narratives of progress but also to understandings of time more generally. Dust, as Steedman reminds us, contains tiny, small specks, residue of the past, a past that has no place in the modern present. Yet, dust also embodies the progress, industrial and otherwise, of the present day. Meanwhile, the Soviet home itself emerges as, on the one hand, the quintessential manifestation of Soviet ideological priorities: communal, efficient and clean. On the other hand, the home, the space of familial intimacy, served as a reminder of the old world, stuck in a state betwixt and between and a place where no matter how much technology was used, how many hours spent, the past floated in through the window or entered on the bottom of a shoe.

The rapid pace of industrial change, too, not only produced endless seas of dust but also destroyed natural environments, leaving children to grow up in cities. One author bemoans this new reality: "It is true there are parks, boulevards, squares, where you can spend time with your children, near your homes; your cooperatives. However, increasingly, in our own times now, they are few and far between [...] Children from a young age are on streets and experience the dirt and dust of the city." This author points to the impact of industry on the health and welfare of the youngest of the Soviet citizens.[90] Of course, the author reminds the reader, nature too can be dangerous, if left unchecked.[91]

The goal of creating a dust-free, efficient and clean domestic environment was implicated in many of the prescriptive texts, which themselves imagined that the achievement of good and cultured health included the refashioning of domestic interior décor, from the layout of spaces to the design of furniture. "In order not to obscure the light and to stir the dust, it is better not to hang any kind of curtains."[92] Fluffy and soft décor not only aesthetically reflected cozy indulgences but also invited dust into windows, onto floors from the bottom of shoes and within the nooks and crannies of curtains, chairs and lampshades; dust, with its traces not only of the past but also of the industrial present, was an unwanted visitor in Soviet apartments. The very act of "stirring the dust" invited the residue of the past into the home of the present, a home that struggled to embrace the technological and hygienic communist modern moment but could not quite help but serve as comfort and a refuge from the rapid change outside.

Domestic interiors were obvious sites of dust's presence. The soft and velvety arm chairs of old had to be sacrificed for the modern clean design. Readers of prescriptive texts learn that "on the furniture, you can never allow dust to remain."[93] A Soviet citizen must always "avoid dark, cluttered furniture that creates a dusty home."[94] Furniture must be appropriately placed and made from proper materials. The urge to create cozy spaces, which evoked the past, caused the most consternation for Soviet tastemakers:

> Usually, people are in the old habit of creating spaces that are cozy, in other words, they consist of the softest furniture, they hang curtains, lay down carpets, which take the sun and light from the room (prevent it from coming in). Additionally, carpets, are difficult to clean, always stuffed with dust inside. It is especially bad to turn a sofa (divan) into a bed at night, and in the day, and hide all of the dust inside during the day; it is gathering dust, and not getting ventilated.[95]

An article on "Housing Care" begins by laying out the challenges of apartment living, with particular attention to the interior of homes. Inside today's apartments, there are too many people and there is "not enough attention to clearing the dust [!]." The author asks "what are the hygienic considerations" for communal and individual spaces. The answer is threefold:[96]

1. "Clean air" is number one: "dust and dirt are brought in the room along with the firewood logs." There must always be fresh air in the room. In the daytime one can have the windows open 24 hours; in the winter the fortochka can be opened three times a day, in the morning, for *obed* and night. And each time not for less than a half hour.
2. The second battle in one's domicile is "the battle against dust." All about the dangers of dust and how one is too easily subjugated to those dangers— the cause of illness—and how they are hard to avoid. "Dust on the floor is impossible to rectify."
3. The third is dampness.

"We must fight all three of these to avoid illness and have a healthy apartment."[97]

The past, embodied by soft, comfy and cozy domestic material objects, had to be swept away to make room for a revolutionary today and Soviet tomorrow. Once the dust-prone past receded, a space opened up for the dawning of a modern day. The epochal moments that ushered in the modern day in the first days of the Soviet times, however, had strong reverberations in the earlier days of the fin de siècle.

Magazine editors and columnists recognized the fact that even new Soviet construction brought the possibility of dirt, grime and indeed dust entering into apartments. Inspectors of Soviet apartments found "places with a tight/confined/narrow (tesnyi), dark and moist character" and declared that "there must be new residencies made, ones that have a breeze, sun and light, surrounded by green, deprived of tiresome noise, dust and smoke, dirt and grime." Inspectors were concerned with developing and establishing "hygienic norms of construction [and] new normative construction rules." The state also insisted upon "regular and thorough inspections of domiciles, which will give advice and ensure the health of all members of the laboring classes." And with well-known military language state inspector reports suggested that there "must be a standing army in defense of all evils associated with bad living places."[98] Dust was the enemy and had to be defeated.

For some writers and readers, the biggest danger associated with dust was disease and sickness. In the 1929 journal *Hygiene and Health in the Workers' and Peasants' Family Life*, Dr. M. Dubianskaia elaborates upon her thoughts about "Dust and Home": dust is "a small physical structure with all kinds of different chemical composition substance; dust comes from dead and living nature. In dust you encounter microorganisms, their buds, their seeds."[99] In another article addressing how best to defend yourself and your family against the onset of tuberculosis, the author points to the essential need for clean and healthy habits.[100] A caption to a picture of a family in disarray: "Never spit on the floor; sweep the floor with a dry brush to pick up the dust; never put children on a dirty floor!" Similarly, workers in their letters to the editor also worry about the health risks involved in allowing dust to creep into domestic interiors. In the "Letters from Workers" from a 1925 issue of *Hygiene and Health in Workers' and Peasants' Family Life* there is a letter from a Leningrad worker entitled "Must help Ventilation" and explains how each workers' apartment must have "ventilation so that there will be no 'dust bloom.'"[101] The presence of dust within homes was to be avoided, if not feared; technologically advanced ventilation systems were seen as a means to combat its detrimental effects. Dust also indicated germs and microbes. In an article by Dr. V Bukhovetskii in *Hygiene and Health in Workers' and Peasants' Family Life* the dangers of breathing in dust are articulated. "Do Not Breathe in Dusty Air!" "In dust there are many microbes. Many of those microbes enter into our bodies, and might be the cause of our illnesses, like tuberculosis, and etc."[102]

Yet, it was not health alone that drew tastemakers to dust. Magazines often articulated very prescriptive notions of apartment aesthetics and how they should look in order to minimize the accumulation of dust: from furniture purchased to the placement of shelves; each act within an apartment had to be carefully considered to minimize the collecting of dust within the sanctuary of the home. In one particularly detailed piece on how to set up a worker's apartment, the author provides a detailed account of "what type of furniture should there be in a worker's apartment?"[103] It is introduced as an important social question. The apartment has "three rooms: dining and workers'; sleeping and kitchen," and should contain particular types of furniture in each of these three spaces. In each case, the emphasis is on wooden furniture, from the lacquered pine shelves in the dining room to the wooden bed frame in the sleeping quarters, all of which should be without flourish and without potential dust-accumulating surfaces.[104]

The interior of apartments, though, were not the only spaces implicated in harboring the dust of the past. If dust in apartment interiors contained the residue of the past, where did it come from? How did it enter the space of the home? The preoccupation with dust floating into apartments and hiding in velvety curtains emerged in discussions about shared domestic spaces, sometimes part of the interior of the apartments and other times shared external spaces, such as courtyards or staircases. The author of the prescriptive volume *Toward a Healthy and Cultured Everyday*, in the section on "Fleas and Bugs" at home, highlights this relationship between the domestic exterior and interior: "You may not introduce into the home on your feet dust and filth; you must first clean the filthy, dusty and sweaty feet before entering."[105] From this perspective, the interior of the home should be free from filth of the outside world; the outside should be kept outside. This was not always possible. Lurking right outside of the interior, there are "mice, cockroaches, etc." that you can see as well as the "bacteria" that you cannot see. The bacteria that enters the domestic sanctuary through the bottom of shoes or through the air is "most of all found in dust, dirt, and rotting garbage." Thus, the perimeter of residencies must always be cleaned to prevent the detritus from the outside getting inside.[106]

Similarly, in an article on the "Hygiene of the Bed," Dr. M. Dubianskaia advises of the dangers of dust as a metaphor for the past. "All parts of the bed – mattress, pillow, comforter, should be beat to get rid of the dust each day, in the fresh air, outside in the sun."[107] This type of advice abounds, including in the context of children's rooms and spaces: "The walls of the child's room should ideally be painted with oil paints so that they can be easily washed [and] do not collect dust."[108] In addition to modern, cleanable furniture, children should be dissuaded from the impulse to amass things:

In the child's room there must be few things. Things such as be drapes, rugs, pillows, screens, soft furniture—all of those are examples of what attracts/ the hotbeds of dust collection—it is firstly and secondly each thing disrupts/ displaces the quality of air, each decreasing the quality of air in various quarters in the room.[109]

Simple, plain wooden furniture with few nooks and crannies and little excess accumulation of stuff was necessary to avoid the impact of dust coming into the home or of dirt piling up. Children were imagined to be particularly vulnerable to dust on all counts because "illnesses caused by microbes from dust is damaging to children's young bodies."[110] In a short piece entitled "Child Care" there are a number of small drawings and bits of advice or steps offered; among these are: "Do not breathe in dusty air!"[111] or "Beware! Dust will get into the channels of the skin."[112] Dust brought danger to men, women and children alike: anyone who found themselves at home. The solution seemed to reside with technological advancement.

The interior spaces of daily life were central locations for the dismantling and rebuilding of society, whether urban or rural, efficiently and using modern technological devises. A popular rural-oriented prescriptive text from 1929 outlines how essential the transformation of the home was to the creating of modern subjectivity and the embracing of modern time.[113] In the chapter entitled "O bor'be za novyi byt," the authors highlight the obstacles in the way of improving everyday life in the Soviet Union. It asks: "what gets in the way of improving the everyday/byt? [...] and the answer revolves around the domestic sphere [...] there are often arguments within the home sphere and between husband and wife and between parents and children and children and parents [...] much of the conflict comes from the fact of the lack of space." It is the space itself and the lack of cleanliness that causes domestic discord. It is "the narrowness and muddledness of the home, the disorganization inside, etc."[114] Whether the dry dust is seen or not seen is not important, it has microbes. This text helps its readers learn how to combat the "dampness in the home" in an efficient and effective manner. By cleaning the corridors, the past is swept away with the broom and if the residence is clean, then Radchenko tells his reader: "there will be no dust."[115] Yet, the Soviet modern interior necessarily included residue of the past. It was in the specs of dust found in the corners of apartments, the cushions of sofas and the alleyways near *dvors*, where the past remained and flourished regardless of the efforts of Soviet tastemakers and propagandists to sweep it away.[116]

The past in the present: Soviet style

The crafting of the Soviet utopian domestic interior, in its communal form, involved an incorporating of the past, in both its working-class and elite guises. This could be found in both the revivalist folk art scene of the early revolutionary days and in the Retrospectivism of the reemergence of a Society for the Love of the Estate.[117] The working-class and even bourgeois communal apartment, in other words, existing alongside the embrace of an elite aesthetic and the endless fields and the antique clocks inside. The Soviets, in the early days, as Hilton has told us,[118] crafted an aesthetic sensibility that was meant to appeal broadly across populations. The task was not an easy or straightforward one. On the one hand, old monuments and symbols had to be destroyed to resurrect the new. On the other hand, there were "many forms of celebration [...] repeated forms and imagery of nineteenth-century peasant art, seasonal rituals and urban popular entertainment."[119] Many believed that the new "proletarian" symbolism was not enough to inspire the population more broadly. The context for the new regime's legitimacy entailed "the reconstruction of an identifiable Russian heritage" or a resurrection of national mythologies of the past in order to march toward the future.[120] Igor Grabar, who simultaneously played three roles—as an artist and art historian from the "World of Art" group; director of the Tretyakov Gallery; and head of the Commission for the Preservation of Artistic Treasures in 1919—described the importance of the past to the present in a pamphlet entitled "Why We Must Preserve and Collect the Treasures of Art and Antiquity." Even the "trifles of the past," he writes, present a vision of days gone by that should be preserved. The folk-art aesthetic was very much used and debated by the Soviet propogandists/constructivists, some of whom created a hybrid aesthetic meant to appeal to all constituencies. Agit-trains and steamboats, the quintessential Soviet modern industrial propaganda vehicles "futuristic in their décor," were often "toned down" in order to appeal to peasants. Aesthetics of narodnost, or folksiness, or an aesthetic that was "of the people," were trotted out in order to make soviet ideas and ideologies familiar and appealing to a broader population than those who resided in the urban industrial centers. "The ability to combine national traditions with modern functions was fundamental to early Soviet art policy."[121] Soviet tastemakers, artists and propagandists understood that older, traditional forms of art and aesthetics had to be repurposed in order to create a broad enough culture to be reachable and desirable to the population as a whole.

One such project was the renovation of the Kustar Museum in 1925. This opening indicated the central role that folk art would play in early Soviet visions of itself and its everyday. Vasilli Voronov, in his Museum guidebook, wrote: "The *kustar'* industry was and remains at the root of peasant art. Its further development under the new conditions of political and economic life must preserve these organic bonds and centuries of interwoven connections."[122] The art of collecting treasures of the past, and its movement, Retrospectivism, had a significant role to play in the years leading up to the revolution and across its borders. A collector and editor of a prerevolutionary publication and a 1914 primer for the novice collector *Sredi kollektsion*, Ivan Lazarevskii, describes how "Weary of the incessant modern racket, of the chaos of life in the big cities, of the clanking trams and the honking automobiles [...] we try to collect if only the crumbs of the beautiful past, to find rest, to reminisce over things that will never return."[123] Sometimes, too, the nostalgic romance with the past, even amidst revolutionary upheaval, would come in the form of the admiration of objects. Gregory Stroud points out that even by 1929, author Boris Pil'nyak waxes poetic about mahogany furniture of bygone years in his *Krasnoe derevo* [Mahogany]. "A master craftsman died," Pil'nyak explained, "but his works lived on for a hundred years in the country houses and estates. It was near to this furniture that people made love. They died on these sofas. They hid letters in the secret compartments of these secretaries."[124] He writes that although people die, objects continue to live. There were many who collected such things and who, after the revolution, continued to hang on to them as if celebrating the past and hanging on to its dusty threads. They also came in the form of an embrace of estates, both the exterior ground and the domestic interiors replete with all of the objects within.

The embrace of folk art and aesthetics from bygone years emerged among artists and propagandists alongside the impulse to celebrate eighteenth- and nineteenth-century estates in the years following the Bolshevik victory of the 1917 Revolutions. The aesthetic and ideological impulses of the glossy magazine detailed in the previous chapter, *Stolitsa i usadba*, reemerged and helped to inspire the creation of the Society for Gentry Estates in 1922. The utopian Soviet domestic interior, with its efficient layout and clean courtyards and stairs, with its dust-free air and up-to-date technologies, could not entirely shed the past.

A question that scholars have posed is whether the reemergence of the estate was itself a kind of rejection of Bolshevism per se or, rather, "it was seemingly at odds with everything modern—much less revolutionary—in Russia."[125] Of course the estate had been declining for decades and was already, when the Bolsheviks seized power, a thing of the past, decayed and often left fallow, haunted by Benjamin's ghosts. And yet, at least in the early years of the Revolution, the estate was revived among some of Russia's Moscow educated young people. There emerged an estate movement and embrace of the past in the 1920s. This included guides in period costume showing children the estates from bygone years to tours of the rural Pavlovsk palace grounds during the summer of 1922. These tours and many others were sanctioned by Anatolii Lunacharskii, the minister of the Commissariat of the Enlightenment and the Communist Party. This was part of a growing trend. The Russian gentry estate itself was among the earliest of Retrospective ruins. As we have seen in the previous chapter, it was already the subject of poetic nostalgia by the turn of the century and it continued to be a beloved artifact from the past, in its material and ideological forms, after 1917. It emerged as part of the overall impulse to create a future, which continued to reify the past.

The very existence of the Society of the Lovers of the Estate or OURI also reflects a kind of utopian vision of eighteenth- or nineteenth-century gentry domestic life, a celebration of past practices and the past that serves, in a sense, as a distraction from the inadequacies of the present moment. In the aftermath of the Civil War and the first years of the New Economic Policy, a small group of Moscow University students began to gather to immortalize and celebrate now faded estate life. Founded in December 1922, a group of young men, among them an art history graduate student, a literary scholar, a museum worker, a professional editor and a theater worker, began to meet in a typical old Moscow apartment building, the home of Vladimir Vladimiovich Zgura, and share their common love for the gentry estate. These eight initial members met to celebrate and explore the history of the Russian estate by embracing and studying the aesthetics of the fin de siècle publication *Stolitsa i usadba*. This group of young men aspired to turn their informal gatherings into an official society, sanctioned by the Soviet state. And, indeed, replete with bylaws and weekly meetings, in February 1923, they registered it as an official society with Narkompros, calling themselves Lovers of the Estate. This officially registered society existed as a registered and sanctioned group from December 1922 through 1930, whose membership included V.V. Zgura as president, I.V. Evdokimov as vice-president, among others.[126] Vladimir Zgura, the founding leader and main motor behind the group's inception, was just fourteen years of age at the time of founding. He was not alone in his youth, others in the leadership were between the ages of fourteen and twenty-two when the revolution happened. While the core group consisted of eight to ten individuals, primarily young educated men, the organizational meetings for the society attracted roughly a hundred members late into the 1920s. Thousands more casual participants attended lectures, toured the estates, and purchased guidebooks and short histories. It seems clear that the estate movement was not simply lingering, it was multiplying and reproducing. The impact was greater than the few who led.[127]

As further evidence of both the seriousness and the professional nature of this endeavor, around the same time, the members of OURI started a journal to chronicle their society and its activities, and opened up chapters outside of Moscow. These additional chapters flourished in a variety of cities including Leningrad (1925 with seven members); Smolensk (1925 with two members); Tambov (1925 with one member); Riazan (1925 with three members); and Kazan (1925 with two members). By the start of 1926, there were 127 members overall. The activities of the group increasingly included not only writings, a monographic series about estates called "Russkie usadby" and journal articles about the meetings and practices of preservation, but also excursions to the estates themselves, which engaged a broader public and were led by the group's leaders. Each of the side excursions was led by one of the group's leaders, and by the fourth year of the group's operations the members hatched a plan to publish a series called *Podmoskovnie muzei i usadby*. Like the official state sanction bestowed upon the organization itself, the state also blessed its publications. In 1926, the state supported the publication of a hefty catalog on *Museums and Sites of Moscow* (3,000 copies were printed), edited by Zgura and with many articles by members of OIRU singing the praises of Moscow's historical estates and sites. By 1926, as part of its efforts to reach out and engage with broader audiences, members of OIRU also created a two-year course of study, which initially was framed as a History of Art course but included sections on estate life and the art found on Russian eighteenth- and nineteenth-century estates. The interest in estate life of the bygone years began to grow, even as workers were cramming themselves into the corners of apartments in the new urban centers. What made this course of particular interest was not simply its deep dive into the domestic architecture of the rich but also the fact that it was the first free-standing course of study organized by this type of social organization.[128] Moreover, all courses were taught by the society members on topics ranging from the Russian domestic interior to the history of Russian art. The organization and its activities were totally sanctioned by the state in the early years of its existence, as it grew and reached into other arenas. Yet, ultimately, the repression of the late 1920s did not miss this organization. In the first quarter of 1928, the courses of the OURI closed down and by 1929 the final excursions took place. Although it is not clear precisely why this timing happened, it may have been due to a combination of the nascent capitalism in the excursions and the degree to which the particular embracing of the gentry past did not fit into the cultural revolution's stringent narratives.

Soviet time at home: The collective and the communal

There is, as outlined in Chapter 1, indeed, a consensus among scholars that in the early twentieth century, ideas about the past, present and future interacted to engender a new, novel, "modern" sense of time, in Russia and across Europe, whether within the interior or on the streets. The nascent Soviet state, in its first decade or so, operated according to a temporal logic that embraced utopian notions of time, including a sense of the collective. The future, thus, was always and necessarily "inherent in any Marxist society." [129] The early Soviet state was no exception. This investment in the future and embrace of utopian communal visions of an idealized tomorrow manifested in the everyday and its Soviet notions of *novaia zhizn*, not only on the street but also in the home. And in the home, as with utopian Soviet ideas elsewhere, these ideas were made concrete and became part of the imagined or lived experience of Soviets. In this sense, there was a push toward a domestic "concrete utopia" or a set of ideas that moved beyond the realm of the abstract, and ideas had become embodied by people and enacted in the everyday.

During the early Soviet era, much ink was spilled over the new emphasis on utopian collective visions of home. The impulse toward collective living and its related collective responsibility included practical and social elements. Writers described the dramatic ways in which communal arrangements impacted the everyday, from the number of meters allotted per person to the jolting experiences of being stripped of one's belongings. Mikhail Zoshchenko and Mikhail Bulgakov depict, in their acerbic ways, the impact on city living of the new official state decrees. Their words appear in the mid-1920s when, far from straight forward, housing ideas and housing itself was contested. It was the NEP years after all, when early Soviet ways receded, some even as they were being strengthened. Home itself embodied this contest, including the lacy curtains and the meager space allotment all at the same time. The reality of limited urban space and the push toward communalism marked, in many ways, the Soviet experience and reflected the entrenched nature of past notions and ideas that coexisted, cohabited, if you will, through the 1920s and beyond.

Mikhail Zoshchenko, whose narrators typically reside in communal apartments, is among the most popular satirists of the 1920s. Comfort itself seems no match for the efficiency and ideology of the shared living spaces in his stories. In his 1925 short story "The Crisis," Zoshchenko presents the saga of a husband and wife who are assigned a bathroom to live in with their newborn baby. While this living assignment has the advantage of their easily being able to give the baby a bath each day, it also means that their thirty-two apartment-mates gather to intrude on their small modicum of privacy to use the facilities themselves.[130] The following is from this short story that not only satirizes but also puts into full relief the challenges of communal living: "Now the bathroom really was classy. Everywhere you put your foot—a marble tub, a water heater, faucets. Incidentally, though, no place to sit. Try to sit on the edge and down you go, smack dab into the marble bathtub." Once the narrator accepts his fate, he describes his thoughts on the physical space of his new home, the water closet with its marble floors and modern plumbing, which belonged in prerevolutionary days to a formerly aristocratic family. He got married a month after accepting his situation, bringing his new wife into his bathroom home. Without quarters of her own, she accepts her fate: "Well, what the heck," she says. "Decent people live in bathrooms too. And in the worst case, [...] we can put up a partition." Within the first year in their happy home, the couple had a baby, Volodka, who also joined them, and they moved on with their life. "We gave him baths right there and went on living." Things were going just fine, with one rather large inconvenience: "in the evening the communal tenants would come barging in to the bathroom to wash up. Then the whole family had to move out into the hallway."[131] The cleanliness itself was a trade-off enough for the inconvenience of thirty-two individuals barging into their home each day. Ultimately, as Zoshchenko makes clear in his satire, collective living reflected deeply ingrained Soviet values.

While efficiency and cleanliness certainly resonated with the prescriptions of tastemakers from decades earlier, it was the emphasis on communal living arrangements and communal responsibility that emerged not only in Zoshchenko's and Bulgakov's satirical characters, but also in the everyday prescriptions that readers encountered in magazines and journals, from the sophisticated *Sovremennaia arkhitektura* to the more broadly read and distributed *Zhilishchnoe tovishchestvo*. Prescriptive texts heavily focus on "spaces of general use," which might include corridors, courtyards, stairwells and the like. In a 1924 issue of *Zhilits*, residents were schooled on how to maintain an efficient and cooperative sense of cleanliness in their shared living quarters. Early soviet women's magazines, housing journals and daily newspapers overflowed with advice on how to raise children, peel potatoes and clean the kitchen floors. Other, more professional and aesthetically minded journals (*Sovremennaia arkhitektura*) focused on issues of housing structure and furniture design. Regardless of the intended audience, however, there emerged a preoccupation with the collective responsibility of keeping the domestic spaces clean and up to date. And the early era also included much effort of building living spaces that reflected the ideology of the present, communal and shared, and efficient, if not always clean in reality.

In August of 1918, the newly minted Soviet regime initiated new policies vis-à-vis living spaces. This decree stated that old living spaces were to be divided up and shared among the many instead of enjoyed by the bloated few. And later in the post-civil war and NEP-era, on October 1, 1927, all soviet citizens were declared to have access to communal spaces. In the years in between, Soviet modernist planners and designers drew, discussed and in some instances built model communal domestic structures that were meant to reflect the new ideology of the everyday.[132]

It is collective living per se that brings the promise of health, both individual and social health for all. It was also imagined, of course, that collective arrangements would free women to more fully participate in Soviet life, as the cleaning and hygienic concerns would be met collectively rather than individually. In a 1925 issue of *Zhilishchnoe kooperatsiia* this relationship is explicit. Collective domestic living reflects perfectly this impulse, since "housing as the cornerstone of health" and old-fashioned arrangements inspire "the most unsanitary conditions," and the newly collective areas are therefore "dirty, the walls are flaking." The creation of Soviet modern domestic spaces must include a sense of shared collective responsibility, and this, the author believes, is precisely what is missing: "there is a frightening indifference and negligence when it comes to the performance of *krugavaia poruka* or collective responsibility," a notion that has a long and rich history in the Russian context.[133] There is a tension between the ideal of clean, efficient and collective, and the lived reality. "They [the collective] complains about the dirt on the stairs, the latrines and the corridors that go between your own apartment, your own room and the common spaces, and how it is not clean," but rather it is "infectious and infections travel into the individual rooms and throughout the apartments." The state and local authorities set up sanitary commissions, often composed of residents themselves, to cope with the problem of collective neglect of cleanliness, especially in the shared spaces of domestic life. It is the Sanitary Commission's job to help with this. "What does the commission do? Regular periodic inspections (once per month) in the interiors and the adjoining lands; these inspections include practical suggestions as to how to improve things."[134] There was always an intrinsic comparison with the mythical West. In a two-part article on "Living Habits in the West," published in 1926, the *Zhilishchnaia kooperatsiia* authors provide a gendered view of how workers in other nations to the west insisted on their rights and gendered equality in the creating of new, collective living spaces.[135] The Women's Section of the English Workers Party wrote a statute re living conditions (and the author of this Russian article, Alexander Blok, celebrates it).[136] His celebration, while lengthy and focused on the redirection of women's labor in the home, also attempts to undo the crimes of the past, which were perpetrated by the so-called bourgeoisie. "In the past, we have been slaves to the living quarters/domestic spaces and habits of the former epoch," Blok explains. In the German context, he writes, we must undo the past impulses and undo the "influence of the ruling *meshchanstvo* taste [...] in particular in the construction of living space." In its place must arise a plan/layout of the apartment to reflect the proper values. "The interior of the apartment matters," Blok notes.[137] After comparing Soviet and German living conditions, Blok returns to the problems intrinsic to building a modern Soviet society facing the future. The critique includes the fact that the residue of the past will not dissipate quickly enough. He bemoans "how much deprivation and sacrifice people have made in the past to shift/change their station! How many women's lives have been wasted in preserving and saving unnecessary things are wiping off their dust from an unending quantity of junk!"[138] "Authentic living culture requires the ridding of living spaces, such as junk."[139]

Right alongside the insistence on the efficient use of space and the decluttering of daily life in apartment buildings and complexes, "all residents of the home are obligated to maintain cleanliness in their domestic spaces and in the spaces of general use in the apartments." In order to ensure that the cooperative organization put out a set of rules and regulations for the collective to follow:

> a) regular cleaning of the occupied dwelling, not allowing any dust or dirt to accumulate; b) to pick up the space of general use in the apartment (kitchen, the corridors; laboratories); and also do not dirty the stairs, *ploshadka*, canopy and courtyard; c) dust when cleaning; and various forms of garbage that accumulate in the garbage bins and regularly throw it away in the designated place in the courtyard.[140]

In addition, "everyone living in the apartments has an obligation to keep the place warm and to keep out the moisture [...] and to not destroy the yard in the courtyard [...] there must be no repairs to the apartments without permission of the domestic committee."[141] The rules extended to socializing as well. There were some regulations on how to interact with your neighbors: "all residents must express an interest in each other and be respectful of one another's apartments."[142] The collective responsibility, thus, extended beyond the practical to the social. Efficiency, cleanliness and cordiality were required of each resident.

Such rules and regulations appeared with regularity. But one additional example is the 1929 Moscow prescriptive text, *Domovoe khoziastvo*, where there appeared a section entitled "Cleaner of the Household." Within this section were instructions on how to manage the domestic spaces of general use, including stairs/stairwells, the arrival *ploshadka* or the corridors in the residences.[143] The text states that there is an obligation to daily clean and sweep the collective floors and the latrines and the washrooms that are for general use, and also to clean at least once a week the front and back stairs and the adjoining area. During the winter months, there is the additional obligation of "cleaning the central heating system by the stairs not less than once every two weeks."[144] Moreover, one of the residents must daily wash and clean the bathrooms that are in general, such as the "toilets, toilet seats, urinals, washroom sinks and faucets."[145] Many communal apartments circulated the expected contribution for maintaining an efficient household. For example, in one instance there appeared "Measures against a Filthy Apartment," recorded when rules are not properly followed. The communal spaces demanded a certain vigilance:

> Stairs must be constantly maintained in cleanliness, and the following is absolutely required:
> a. Everyday sweep with a brush the grit and wet sawdust (on the stairs)
> b. Everyday open the staircase windows
> c. Clean the stairs with hot water no less than once per week
> d. Removal of dust and webs off the walls, clean the windows (except during winter time) not less than once a month.[146]

Each of these prescriptions relies on the notion that by attending to the communal spaces, by ensuring they are clean and efficient, daily domestic arrangements could be transitioned from the "individual to the collective" way of living, one where present-day and modern time were always at the fore. This was necessary in order to "beat back the old *byt*" and to reject "old customs and traditions" and build a modern Soviet now.[147]

Soviet authors, in conjunction with the emphasis on interior spaces, particularly concerned themselves with the outside and the *dvor* and the staircase, both of which were shared spaces that connected the exterior world with the domestic interior. In one article entitled "The Hygiene of the *Dvor*" readers are reminded how air must be fresh and the courtyard is, as a liminal space between the exterior street and the interior, at risk of being a conduit of dust and bacteria. "Dust causes the spread of a multitude of diseases" and must be prevented from coming inside the apartment. "Our staircases are mostly very dusty and dirty, and windows, window sills are covered with dust."[148] These must be monitored and cleaned on a regular basis as the dust and dirt always must be kept at bay:

> Do not forget about the cleanliness of the areas surrounding the person; the air in the domiciles, in the *dvor* and on the street. Air in the apartment cannot be clean, unless the *dvor*, the streets, the basement got rid of all of the dirt there [...] if stairs are dirty and poorly ventilated. All of that impacts [...] and elevates the likelihood of evil gasses dust, and microbes, corrupting the home.[149]

The *dvor* itself significantly impacted the interior residence, as the conduit from the exterior spaces to the interior ones, an area outside and yet private, often surrounding the residence on all sides; thus it had an impact on the air that gets into the interior; "all must be vigilant about the cleanliness of the *dvor*." The garbage pit, located within the *dvor*, was imagined as a factor. Great dangers lurked in the possibilities of odors and bacteria intensifying without proper ventilation. "If there is an opening that would allow the gasses to get into the homes, then the gasses and dust would spread from the *dvor*" into the inside of the apartments. Dangers lurk on both the inside and the outside in the battle to prevent the spread of dust of the past and the dirt of the present inside the homes of new Soviet citizens.

Tentative conclusions

The question of what makes modern time—with its efficiency and residue of the past—Soviet is not a straightforward one. On the one hand, the Soviet domestic tastemakers and experts touted the same qualities and goals that many across Europe elevated from the late nineteenth century forward: efficiency, technology and the modern ushering in of epochal transformation even as the past refused to go. Domestic space in Russia and then the Soviet Union, like many places across Europe, was shaped by an insistence on efficient daily public time. Yet, on the other hand, despite all of the parallels, Soviet temporal rhythms refracted through the domestic sphere had a particular dimension: at once collective in the present and future-oriented in general. In this sense, the past was always palpable in the early revolutionary Soviet temporal present; it would not recede despite the extreme urgency that it did so.

And yet, these tensions between new and old, the impulse to create modern spaces for families, do not have a unique place within the story of early Soviet domestic ideology. Late imperial tastemakers struggled with similar questions. The concern over dust, grime and even the preoccupation with efficiency and technology marked Russian culture from the late nineteenth-century days. How, if at all, did dust float across the revolutionary divide both in meaning and metaphor? In other words, what makes this particularly temporal framing Soviet? Maybe the answer resides not so much in the content of the prescriptions but in the form of their implementation. Much of the prescriptive literature from early revolutionary days involved how residents, at least in the Soviet imaginary, living as they were communally, could manage to keep their homes free from dust. For instance, in a 1924 edition of the journal *Bulliten zhilets* there appeared an article entitled: "What a (Communal) Resident Needs to Know." It advised that: "All residents are obligated to maintain cleanliness in each of their own apartments and in the places of general use." In practice this included "regular picking up" and avoiding "the accumulation of dust and dirt" in the places of "communal living."[150] The directives are clear: "You must pick up/clean/straighten the places of general use in the apartments and also do not dirty the stairs, the common squares, and the *dvor*."[151] It is the collectivity that is of the utmost importance: "all residents in their homes must keep in mind the interests of the other residents of their apartment and their apartment mates."[152] Of course there were endless disagreements among residents, which were recorded in reports and articles and letters to the editor (but that is for another day).[153] The main concern is for being considerate to others and together contending with the endless stream of non-efficient dust tracked into apartments, dragging the past along with it. Yet, there was an insistence on domestic collectivity, even if primarily (although not only) discursively, that distinguishes these prescriptions from modern temporal framings elsewhere. Moreover, the future, in part because of the Soviet penchant for utopian thinking, looms large as the past refuses to recede. Past, present and future meet in the walls and the corridors of the Soviet domestic interior.

There is a second way in which these prescriptions were Soviet. Within the Soviet ideological world, the urge toward collectivity was fundamentally a matter of freeing up Soviet citizens from the burdens of the everyday grind of housework. This weighed most heavily, if not entirely, on women. In an article in *Ogonek* by D. Mallory, entitled "Bor'ba za novyi byt,"[154] the correspondent describes a cooperative in Odessa in 1924, with the auspicious name Novyi Byt and explains how the new focus on collectivity frees women of their burdens. In the article, a worker is quoted as having said: "We must now release workers from the oppression of domestic caretaking." "It is our obligation to transform *byt*. We have organized in Odessa a 'Dom-Commune' called *Novyi Byt*. At this commune there will be a laundry, a cafeteria, a club. Coming from work, workers will find clean sheets/laundry, delicious lunch, warm room and a shower." This is the only such commune in Odessa, the article explains, but it is modeled on others elsewhere. The daily life reflects a profound break with the past:

> Now that they are living in the commune all of the women workers all strongly and vividly feel that the old form of daily life fettered them with new strength and inhibited cultural-moral work. How could a woman work at a club (educating others and learning herself) after bending over the stove or washing the walls, washing the laundry or scrubbing potatoes?

Rather, in this "House-Commune—you will see for the first time the real war with the OLD FORMS of domestic byt."[155] They write: "from morning until night you have the common table and helpers for the residents. You can eat the common food in the apartment or in the cafeteria. Tea kettle on all day. In the evenings – the cafeteria is lively. One hundred and nineteen rooms with 'modern accommodations'; no signs of old deprivations."[156] This time consciousness manifests in the urge to efficiency as well as in an awareness of large-scale epochal change. The author of a piece in *Zhilishchnoe tovarishchestvo* writes beautifully about the ways in which large-scale change is manifest in the material world.[157] The article is entitled "Decoration of Your Home":

> In every epoch and under the influence of one thousand elusive reasons, historical, societal and economical, each era creates its own style, not only in art, music, literature, theatre, architecture, but also the trivialities of clothing and decoration of the apartment; each epoch creates its new, which slightly resembles that which was done before, which was considered beautiful, graceful and comfortable in the recent past time.[158]

There too is a sense of the now and its particular relationship to the then:

> The era closest to our own before the revolution may be characterized in its relationship to domestic coziness [*Zhilishchnaia uiut*] like a bit of decline in taste and life reflecting the mediocrity of the petite-bourgeois taste.[159]

Temporal narratives reflect large-scale and small-scale habits and meanings, political, social and cultural alike. The battle against Soviet dust was one in which, at least in its prescriptive guise, women's lives would fundamentally change, time efficiency was internalized, the collective assumed the tasks once assigned to individuals and yet—like many other modern regimes, Russia included—the past stubbornly hung on for dear life.

Coda

Timelessness Today: A Few Observations

Time after time. Time is a strange subject for a historian: temporality and its history. It is a strange subject because it necessarily resides at the center of every historical study. Yet often unnoticed. Unsung. As Bill Sewell tells us in his pathbreaking set of essays, *The Logics of History*, historians know "how to think about the temporalities of social life."[1] Historians are necessarily engaged in questions of periodization and of cyclical and linear movement, whether with an emphasis on change over time or continuity, whether by exploring the cycles of an individual's life or the impact of a new moon. We too track large-scale temporal narratives, epochal change, whether famine, wars, revolutions and the like. This is our bread and butter. As Sewell highlights: "The common topic of historians is the unfolding of human action through time."[2] Sewell's main purpose in this particular essay is to illustrate how historians already and ahead of time have a theory or a set of conceptual and theoretical assumptions embedded within our discipline, ones premised upon temporal rhythms. Most historians, thus, already have an implicit "*theory* of social temporality." A set of theories that have "considerable subtlety and sophistication" and are attentive to time, although implicit rather than explicit. We all study some aspect of time. Sewell writes: "most fundamentally, I think we believe that time is *fateful*" and that the stories we research and reveal arrive in sequences and account for time, small and large.[3] Events are at the heart of our work, whether ritual ones such as bathing a child or catastrophic ones such as a hurricane or tidal wave or technological ones such as sending a person into space.

What then constitutes "the temporal turn," if anything at all?[4] It is, at least in part, to put time and temporality under the microscope, to explore how individuals and collectives define temporal rhythms and structure their—in this case—domestic interiors and homes around and through these very ideas. This book is an attempt to engage with the "temporal turn" in a Russian context at a moment of massive epochal change and change in everyday life. Each of the substantive chapters—nostalgia and the gentry estate, efficiency and the urban apartment, and utopia and the communal apartment—explores the ways in which time is refracted through the home. In a sense, *Modernity, Temporality and Domesticity in Russia: Time at Home* is a study of the spaces where public time and private time meet. By crossing the revolutionary divide, too, this study asks questions about how ideas and ideologies, whether centrally brewed and served up or plowed organically from below, or both, defined notions of time: private and public; intimate and civic; linear and cyclical.

These chapters have been preoccupied with the home and with the intersections of modernity, temporality and domesticity, and have attempted to look at time and temporality over several decades, from about 1900 to about 1930, at a crucial juncture in Russian history. Time logics have stood at the center of inquiry in order to understand how temporal narratives were refracted through the homescapes of Russian and then Soviet modern life. One recurrent theme is modernity. What constitutes modern time? Is it mechanical time and the ticking of the clock? Is it the invention of world uniform time, when all of the nations around the world began to share a common sense of time measurement? Does it have anything at all to do with the accounting for hours or days or even years? Or, as in the Soviet case, is it simply an internalizing of time obligations on the shop floor and in the communal kitchen? Some believe time primarily is to do with notions of accuracy and measurement, precision and the power of knowing and keeping track. There is a consensus that the fin de siècle moment in Europe brought with it new ideas about time and space, and that in addition to technological developments that "were revolutionizing the actual experiences of time and space, cultural changes were revolutionizing ways of perceiving and conceptualizing time and space across the cultural world."[5] The same was true of Russia, both before and after the revolutions. In this sense, to a large degree, this has been a story of continuities. From the early twentieth-century urban apartment of the now, clean, efficient and scientific, to the nostalgic gaze onto the past in the form of eighteenth-century estate life, with its echoes of temporal pastiche to the revolutionary dreams of communal tomorrows, each chapter has attempted to demonstrate the ways in which modern time itself is built upon the layering of the past, present and future.

Modernity has been defined, in part, by the ticking of the clock and the ways in which Russians and Soviets lived their lives according to mechanical (if internalized) rhythms, even as the dust of the past settles in through the apartment windows. Yet, this very notion of modern mechanical time is far from straightforward. Fast forward to the second decade of the twenty-first century. I do not think anyone would contest the "modern-ness" of Norway, and yet, there is a Norwegian Island, where its residents are rejecting the clock. On this island of Sommarøy with its 350 residents, everyone lives in perpetual sunlight for seventy days per year following the summer solstice. From May 18 to July 26, "darkness never falls across the sky." Residents have instituted a campaign "to do away with timekeeping on the island." Norway's parliament is considering the island residents' petition.[6] Does this make Sommarøy less than modern? Theirs is the desire to ignore convention and live according to the rhythms of the sun and not the technological hum of the clock. Theirs is also a desire to rid themselves of the illusion of objective time. As a recent article in *The Guardian* suggests, the proponents of this movement believe that "Time is an illusion. Lunchtime doubly so."[7] This claim, of course, presumes that individuals have not, without the external reminders, internalized Time's hold.

By contrast, as Chapter 4 has shown, the Soviet prescriptions for time efficiency often emphasized that individuals were meant to internalize time regimes and even adjust their movements to accommodate the most efficient way of dealing with domestic tasks; they were advised to collectively embody the Soviet time ideal. In an article on food preparation in the kitchen from 1928, entitled "The Economy of Time," for example, there appeared an emphasis on time efficiency, which, in part, was contingent on individuals' adjusting to how they occupied space within the domestic sphere to minimize extraneous movement: "It is very easy to spend a large amount of time on food preparation and so you must adjust your time expectations and your movements within the kitchen."[8] Time is, in this example, embodied and dictates its very movements. The physical space of the home too, as we saw, was set up—both before and after the revolution—to maximize efficient bodily movement. To create an efficient, time-saving conducive space, the homemaker needs "enough kitchen shelves for dishes and food" that are conveniently located to allow for minimal bodily movements, and she also should prepare meals in bulk, "as it is simply inefficient and ineffectual to do them day by day and one by one."[9] In this sense, rather than emphasizing the clock per se, these Soviet prescriptions highlight the importance of creating a proper environment and training the body to work efficiently and internalizing ultimately the power of the clock itself.

Another theme that has run though this story is the stubbornness of the past, its refusal to recede, whether manifest in the specs of dust of rapid apartment construction at the end of the nineteenth century highlighted in Chapter 2 or the dust floating inside through open windows and in the celebrations of eighteenth-century estate life both before and after the revolutionary upheaval, described in Chapter 3. The past was omnipresent, in the air that Russians breathed, no matter the deliberate attempts to push forward to the future in its Soviet communal utopian forms. One manifestation of the residual nature of the past was always nostalgia, a phenomenon that weaves its way through this story and seems to mark modern life from the start. Nostalgia, which resonates as much from the vantage point of 1900 as it does from 2019.

Time and Home have been at the center of Russia's great transformations over the course of the twentieth century, and they have been the subject of this book. In the Marxist tradition, of course, "the source of woman's backwardness was her confinement to the home and imprisonment by domestic labor." And, also, as Lenin wrote decades later, woman would "remain a domestic slave in spite of all liberating laws as housework remained isolated labor conducted in the home." And Susan Reid reminds us in her scholarship on the 1950s, Lenin famously wrote: "liberate woman, and reduce and eventually annihilate her inequality with man."[10] Although, of course, this never came to pass. Yet, by the 1950s, the ideologically motivated promise of communal living gave way to the huge construction campaign launched by Khrushchev in 1957 to allow a separate apartment for each family.[11] The communal ideal of the 1920s transformed. Yet, as Christine Varga-Harris explains, "unlike its American counterpart, the Soviet home in the 1950s represented neither the reinforcement of traditional family values and gender norms, nor a bastion of security in the face of potential nuclear annihilation. Rather, it signaled the dawn of a new era – a communist one."[12] The home in the 1950s, although now an individual family affair rather than a communal one, Varga-Harris explains, "gestured toward the tangible contrast between life before the Revolution, when the Russian proletariat was confined to slums, and after, when each worker could live in a humane manner." By the 1950s, at least ideologically speaking, "communist utopia [was] embedded in revolutionary promises for daily life [byt]."[13] Of course, it always was. The glance backwards and battle to shed the past never dissipated.

A brief fast forward to today. Or near today. We move past wars and regime changes and the rise of authoritarianism and its fall into something else. We pass by Khrushchev's embrace of the kitchen as a battlefield for the Cold War as well as the breakup of the Soviet system. We arrive at today and at daily life in Moscow's center, restructured and remade by Putin, endowed with all of the markers of late capitalism, from cash machines on every corner to yoga and pilates studios and vegan restaurants. But that is not all.

It is by now hackneyed to say that post-Soviet society is rife with nostalgia. From the nostalgia shops that crowd the ever-widening Moscow boulevards to the growing chains of restaurants that serve early twenty-first-century versions of "Soviet cuisine" and are decorated with pages of *Pravda* plastered on the walls. Or whose shelves are crammed with Soviet abacuses and scales, which were so ubiquitous in grocery stores of the past. In his recent essay on

"Second-Hand Nostalgia," Serguei Oushakine describes nostalgia as generational. He contends that scholarly observations—and nostalgia displays themselves—have moved beyond the initial wave of those who lived through the Soviet era and had an experiential attachment and brings his readers to the second wave "of post-communist nostalgia *without* [*sic*] relying on socialist experience as a key interpretive and explanatory frame." And Oushakine argues that it is this temporal, experiential, generational distance from the Soviet everyday that has inspired a particular materiality in this second wave's nostalgic sensibility. Experience is compensated "by the increasing visibility and importance of socialist *things* [*sic*]."[14] In this sense, my novice observations of contemporary Moscow align with Oushakine's claims.

Figures 5 to 14 were taken in May 2019 at various junctures on the Novyi Arbat, near the city center, where passersby did not even pause at the multiple past dreamscapes seen through the many restaurant and shop windows. The echoes of the Soviet—and also prerevolutionary—past are simply built into the fabric of big city life and, to some extent, now go unseen or imagined unremarkable.[15] This nostalgia industry—commodified and commercialized[16]—from the Soviet hats sold for the Maiskii holidays to the *Alyenka* candy (Figure 5) available at

Figure 5 Candy box. Rebecca Friedman (May 2019). Public domain.

every grocery, to the many varieties of the *avoska* bags found in the stores,[17] does not entirely discriminate, and there are signs of longing for Soviet objects as well as prerevolutionary ones, from the Russian peasant garb darned by waitstaff at restaurants to the chocolate bars and matryoshka dolls with the last of the Romanovs depicted. And sometimes it is difficult to discern which is which.

Figures 6, 7 and 8 were taken in May 2019 from within the Varenichnaya Resturant on Novyi Arbat and depict the material culture of the Soviet era to be consumed along with the dumplings themselves. Many of the objects, precisely the kind Oushakine writes about, mark today's "second-hand nostalgia." In this particular restaurant, and it seems all over the city, there are a multitude of time

Figure 6 Mechanical time. Varenichnaya Resturant on Novyi Arbat. Rebecca Friedman (May 2019). Public domain.

Figure 7 Alexander Herzen's literature. Varenichnaya Resturant on Novyi Arbat. Rebecca Friedman (May 2019). Public domain.

Figure 8 Pages of *Pravda*. Varenichnaya Resturant on Novyi Arbat. Rebecca Friedman (May 2019). Public domain.

pieces. Here we see the emphasis on mechanical time with the two clocks, one a child's and the other a small homelike alarm clock next to the photo picturing a domestic scene with the mother preparing food alongside her husband doing the dishes and overseeing their child helping likely to craft dessert. The book on the bottom shelf is by Alexander Herzen, often thought to be the nineteenth-century father of Russian socialism, a text likely to have been in every Soviet home. Yet, from the nineteenth century, the "sediments of time" in Koselleck's phrasing are evident here as three centuries overlap—the literary traditions of the nineteenth century, the pages of *Pravda* and the very fact of sitting in a customer-friendly restaurant amidst capitalist-tinged everyday life—creating a kind of timelessness that is so commonplace in Moscow today.[18] The eras blend into one another without distinction.

In her masterful work on the cultures of nostalgia, the late Svetlana Boym described the tenacity of this past imaginary. "After the October revolution, Soviet leaders performed one invisible nationalization—the nationalization of time. The revolution was presented as the culmination of world history to be completed with the final victory of communism and the 'end of history.'"[19] Because the revolution was conceived of as part of an inevitable teleology, "nostalgia," which necessitated some kind of cycling back to the past, was a bad word in these years. "The word 'nostalgia' was absent from the revolutionary lexicon [...] early revolutionary ideology is future-oriented, utopian and teleological." In this sense, the early revolutionary era, itself, full of inevitable contradictions, embraced temporal narratives from the past through the future that were often at odds with themselves. Soviet official discourse, for instance, "combined the rhetoric of revolution and restoration," and always embraced the past, present and future simultaneously as does the present-day Muscovite strolling on the Novyi Arbat.[20]

As the above stroll down Novyi Arbat makes clear, things Soviet are ubiquitous in today's Moscow. They do not even warrant a head turn. As Svetlana Alexievich highlights in her oral history on urban Russia today, *Second Hand Time*, "There's a new demand for everything Soviet. For the cult of Stalin. Half of the people between the ages of nineteen and thirty consider Stalin an unrivaled political figure. A new cult of Stalin, in a country where he murdered at least as many people as Hitler!?" She writes how everything Soviet is "back in style with 'Soviet style cafes' with Soviet names and Soviet dishes. 'Soviet' candy and 'soviet' salami, their taste and smell all too familiar from childhood."[21] The longing itself is nothing new or particular about today. "On the eve of the 1917 revolution," Alexander Grin writes, "and the future seems to have stopped standing in its proper place." "Now, a hundred years later, the future is, once again, not where it ought to be. Our time comes to us secondhand."[22] This notion of secondhand time—and second-hand nostalgia—reverberates in this particular moment in Russian urban development. And, in today's Moscow, the domestic imaginary occupies a particularly prominent place.

On this summer 2019 trip to Moscow, one I was determined to take even though I had finished the bulk of my research, my friend[23] and I happened upon a series of displays at the great nineteenth-century department store that sits exactly across from Lenin's tomb: GUM. GUM itself has a history that lives in the interstices between late nineteenth-century emergent, merchant capitalism, communism and today's commercialization of the past combined with a taste for today's luxury. On GUM's website the past is ubiquitous: "Today, GUM lives as it lived long ago in the ideal merchant city of Moscow."[24] Anyone with any Russian expertise or zest for travel who has been to Moscow will know precisely what we saw on that evening of May 1, 2019. Or more or less what we saw as we walked past Stolovaya 57 with its nostalgia narratives in foodstuffs and aesthetics, and as we stumbled into souvenir shops that sold peasant slippers or the Christion Dior shop where we could only dream on our two academic salaries. The Stolovaya 57 itself represents the multiplicity of temporal narratives in today's Moscow.[25] It is, on the one hand, "a self-service cafe modeled on a Soviet workers' canteen," a successful example of collective workers' dining, and at the same time, it is the creation of a luxury-oriented business group. Stolovaya 57, which opened in 2007, is "the brainchild of Bosco di Ciliegi, a Russian group with an Italian-inspired name that specializes in luxury shopping, it bills itself as an upgrade on the humble workers' cafeteria. As the cafe's website puts it: 'They dreamt about good food but cooked rather badly in Soviet canteens.'"[26] Not so in GUM's Stolovaya 57. Rather, it fits right in at GUM, which channels an idealized version of the Soviet Union alongside shops stocked with "Agent Provocateur lingerie, Coach bags, and Bose speakers." Like the "throwback grocery store called Gastronom №1" on the first floor of the luxury shopping arcade, Stolovaya 57 is a "kind of a nostalgic note for those people who would like to remember the old-style canteen and good times," while also experiencing an upscale feeling and consuming good fresh food.[27]

Stolovaya 57 was not the only echo from the past. Amidst these stores and ice-cream stands and movie theaters, stood a series of still-life pictures, three-dimensional and life-sized, of scenes that included: a family watching TV in their living room with a relatively modern-looking clock next to items that resonate with peasant designs (Figure 9); a book written by famous Soviet poet/playwright,

Figure 9 A family watching TV in their living room. Rebecca Friedman in GUM (May 2019). Public domain.

Vladimir Mayakovsky, who began writing before the revolution (Figure 10); a mother, father and child with a mechanical clock in the background (the mother is pregnant with the next generation and there are old photos of Moscow hanging in the background) (Figures 11 and 12); and finally, in another, still, there appeared a table all set in the background, while a daughter is staring at a phonograph with a Soviet-era Melodia record on the turn table (Figure 13).

These GUM displays, and many more in this series, in all their three-dimensional, life-sized glory, evoke a multitude of eras simultaneously. They reflect a certain timeless aesthetic, as these families might be listening to a record or sitting down to eat in 1989 or 1969 or even today. This timelessness seems the strange combination of a hyper-attentiveness to the measurement of time— the ubiquity of clocks and old photographs—and the somewhat careful and careless pastiche presented to passersby. This pastiche seems to indicate no one particular moment but many moments all at the same time. First of all, the very venue, GUM, has been around since the late nineteenth century and sports many

Figure 10 Book by Vladimir Mayakovsky. Rebecca Friedman in GUM (May 2019). Public domain.

temporal aesthetics, from nineteenth-century embellishments to twentieth-century themed restaurants to twenty-first-century luxury consumption. The displays of domestic interiors only added to the subtlety of this layering. For example, smushed in between Hugo Boss and Gucci, one finds a display, in the middle of the shopping center, of a mother and son sitting and watching an old-fashioned television (Figure 9), perhaps from the immediate postwar era or the 1970s when TV become more commonplace in homes. The TV sits near a shelf that carries a mechanical "modern-locking" clock. The aesthetics are mixed, the tableware on the shelf itself eclectic: porcelain to ceramic brown mugs with natural-like designs; a chess set; a pile of books by Frederick Engels. In a second window there is a mother, father and child (see Figure 12), who stand and sit

Figure 11 Mechanical clock. Rebecca Friedman in GUM (May 2019). Public domain.

with another mechanical clock in the background. The mother is pregnant with the next generation and there are old photos of Moscow hanging in the background. Here, in this photo, ideas about gender and women's roles as mother and wife resonate across eras, whether from the nineteenth century, the Soviet era or through to today. There were no working women or industrial workers of either gender to be found. Indeed, all of these images reflect traditional notions of gender, including pregnancy, which seems especially poignant given present-day anxieties about population decline and Putin's current pronatalist attempts to encourage women to be mothers.

Another one of these displays, still, has a table all set, with fruit in abundance, a daughter staring at a phonograph with a Soviet-era Melodiya record on the turn table (Figure 13). And also there are depictions of empire, which evoke a longing

Figure 12 Mother, father and child. Rebecca Friedman in GUM (May 2019). Public domain.

for the imperial past, albeit a domestic interior, with a table abundant with exotic foods and colorfully dressed guests. The evocation of "empire," and likely the nineteenth century, seems unmistakable. And finally, there is a home scene with photos on and cameras and a clock: layers and layers of moments in both individual and collective pasts. We see photo albums, old-fashioned cameras and a picture of child with a camera. The layers of eras are evident in each frame; each is yesterday, today and its location in the prestigious political center of the regime, also tell us, is tomorrow. What one sees in these domestic scenes is not a simple and straightforward Stolovaya 57 nostalgia. Instead, it seems much more embracing of a multitude of temporal frames, a nostalgia for the Soviet and pre-Soviet, and is a constant reminder of the hyper capitalism and consumerism of today. The Soviet, too, is heartily embraced, albeit aestheticized. Of course, there is nothing new about highlighting the prevalence of longing for the Soviet of the Imagination. Here it is the layers, intertwined and nonlinear, that produce a sense of timelessness.

Svetlana Boym describes how communist teleology was "extremely powerful and intoxicating; its loss was greatly missed by the post-communist world."[28] In other words, these days, the nostalgic person misses the Soviet past as it

Figure 13 A Soviet-era Melodiya record. Rebecca Friedman in GUM (May 2019). Public domain.

once was, despite its signs, amidst this new "post-communist lexicon." In these "post-communist days, everyone was looking for a substitute."[29] They search, Boym reminds us, for "another convincing plot of Russian development that will help make sense of the chaotic present." Liberals discuss rejoining the West, presenting the Soviet period as an aberration, while the conservatives wish to return to prerevolutionary Russia and its traditional values. The communists play their part and search for "the Russian-Soviet pastoral past as represented in musicals from the Stalin era."[30]

Perhaps this reemergence of the past in the present and the immediate "second hand" nature of the future, which itself appeared in the present, reflects one of modernity's gifts to us. When the Soviet Union was in its infancy and

Figure 14 Store front. Rebecca Friedman (May 2019). Public domain.

there were competing narratives of *byt'*, tastemakers felt free to interfere in the most intimate aspects of individuals' and collective lives. The lacuna between the should be and the was deepened as years progressed and finally as ideas themselves turned to dust. The past, the present and the future collided to create a particular sense of Soviet modern time, one intent on an embrace of a speedy and efficient today and ambivalently nostalgic about yesterday and with an aim toward a perfect and collective tomorrow. Today's sense of timelessness, focused on no single moment or frame, is reflected in the store front directly across from another friend's apartment last spring (Figure 14).

Here we see the combination of modern efficiency and technology (electrification), the Soviet anti-consumer impulse (the sign that simply says "Kitchen"), and the contemporary confusing and busy aesthetic evoking both modern and retro individual pieces to populate one's kitchen, still the most important room in the apartment. "If nostalgia is considered as a cultural practice, as a mode of actively engaging with the past by evaluating against the present and future, it involves an implicit element of contestation."[31] Here, in this photo, there is a contest. There is a "clash between the currently hegemonic capitalist versions of modernity and their obsolete and discredited socialist counterparts."[32] It is nostalgic sentiments that smooth over this clash and an emergent embrace of a certain timelessness that marks today's consumer-oriented—longing for the Soviet and tsarist past—present-day Moscow. Time and home—from 1900 through to today—sit at the nexus of Russia's modern self-definition, albeit in vastly differing apartments and imbued with a timelessness known, perhaps, only to the twenty-first century.

Notes

Introduction

1   Ana Menendez, *In Cuba I was a German Shepherd* (New York: Grove Press, 2001), 208.

2   Reinhart Koselleck, *Sediments of Time: On Possible Histories* (Palo Alto, CA: Stanford University Press, 2018), xii–xiii.

Chapter 1

1   Virginia Woolf, *To the Lighthouse* (Hertfordshire: Wordsworth Editions, 1994), 80.

2   Virginia Woolf, *Mrs. Dalloway* (London: CRW Publishers, 2003), 6.

3   William Sewell, *The Logics of History: Social Theory and Social Transformation* (Chicago: University of Chicago Press, 2005), 6.

4   Ibid., 6–7.

5   Ibid., 9.

6   A.R.P. Fryxell, "Time and the Modern: Current Trends in The History of Modern Temporalities," *Past & Present* 243, no. 1 (May 2019): 289.

7   Ibid., 289.

8   Michael David-Fox, *Modernity, Ideology, and Culture in Russia and the Soviet Union* (Pittsburgh, PA: University of Pittsburgh Press, 2015), 3.

9   David Hoffman, *Stalinist Values: The Cultural Norms of Soviet Modernity, 1917–1941* (Ithaca, NY: Cornell University Press, 2003).

10 Ibid., 7.

11 Ibid., 8.

12 Luba Golburt, *The First Epoch: The Eighteenth Century and the Russian Cultural Imagination* (Madison: University of Wisconsin, 2014), 3.

13 Ibid., 4.

14 Ibid.

15 Ibid., 7.

16 Ibid.

17 Ibid.

18 Ibid.

19 Russell West-Pavlov, *Temporalities (The New Critical Idiom)* (New York: Routledge, 2012), 46.

20 David Couzens Hoy, *The Time of Our Lives: A Critical History of Temporality* (Boston, MA: MIT Press, 2012), 59.

21 Ibid.

22 Hilary Fink, *Bergson and Russian Modernism, 1900–1930* (Chicago: Northwestern University Press, 2012), 4–5.

23 Ibid.

24 Ibid., 10.

25 Ibid., 11.

26 I would like to thank my colleague Bianca Premo for long ago introducing me to Palti's work.

27 Elias Jose Palti, "Time, Modernity and Time Irreversibility," *Philosophy and Social Criticism* 23 (1997): 27–62.

28 Hoy, *The Time of Our Lives*, vii.

29 Stephen Kern, *The Culture of Time and Space, 1880–1918: With a New Preface* (Cambridge, MA: Harvard University Press, 2003), 13–14.

30 Ibid., 17.

31 West-Pavlov, *Temporalities*, 53.

32 Palti, "Time, Modernity and Time Irreversibility," 29.

33 Ibid., 27–62.

34 West-Pavlov, *Temporalities*, 21.

35 Kern, *The Culture of Time and Space*, 13–14.

36 Ibid., 68.

37 Palti, "Time, Modernity and Time Irreversibility," 27–62.

38 Kern, *The Culture of Time and Space*, 29.

39 Reinhart Koselleck, *The Practice of Conceptual History: Timing History, Spacing Concepts* (Palo Alto, CA: Stanford University Press, 2002), 120–121.

40 Kern, *The Culture of Time and Space*, 19–20.

41 Ibid., 24.

42 Ibid., 27.

43 Ibid., 29.

44 Ibid., 26.

45 Ibid.

46 Svetlana Boym, *The Future of Nostalgia* (New York: Basic Books, 2002), xvii.

47 Ibid., xiv–xvi.

48 Ibid., 17–18.

49 Ibid., 30.

50 Thank you Mark Edele for pointing out this volume of *Past and Present* to me.

51 Stefan Hans, "The Fetish of Accuracy: Perspectives on Early Modern Time(s)," *Past & Present* 243, no. 1 (May 2019): 270.

52 Fryxell, "Time and the Modern," 289.

53 David Gange, "Time, Space and Islands: Why Geographers Drive the Temporal Agenda," *Past & Present* 243, no. 1 (May 2019): 302.

54 Fryxell, "Time and the Modern," 290–291, 296, 294.

55 Penelope J. Corfield, *Time and the Shape of History* (New Haven, CT: Yale University Press, 2007), xv.

56 Matthew S. Champion, "The History of Temporalities: An Introduction," *Past & Present* 243, no. 1 (May 2019): 247–254.

57 Peter Fritzsche, *Stranded in the Present: Modern Time and the Melancholy of History* (Cambridge, MA: Harvard University Press, 2010), 5.

58 Ibid., 1.

59 Ibid., 54.

60 Ibid., 8.

61 Ibid., 2.

62 Ibid., 8.

63 Vanessa Ogle, "Whose Time Is It? The Pluralization of Time and the Global Condition, 1870s–1940s," *American Historical Review* 118, no. 5 (December 2013): 1376.

64 Gerhard Dohrn-Van Rossum, *History of the Hour: Clocks and Modern Temporal Orders* (Chicago: University of Chicago, 1996), 3.

65 Ibid., 3.

66 Ibid., 368.

67 Michael Manchard, "Afro-Modernity: Temporality, Politics and the African Diaspora," *Public Culture* 11, no. 1 (1999): 245–268.

68 Mark Smith, *Mastered By the Clock: Time, Slavery and Freedom in the American South* (Chapel Hill: University of North Carolina Press, 1997), 2–3.

69 Ibid., 14.

70 Maria Todorova, "The Trap of Backwardness: Modernity, Temporality and the Study of Eastern European Nationalism," *Slavic Review* 64, no. 1 (Spring 2005): 140.

71 Ibid.

72 These long-standing narratives about Russian backwardness include the excellent *Russia Under the Old Regime* by Richard Pipes (New York: Penguin Books, 1997).

73 David Hoffman, *Peasant Metropolis: Social Identities in Moscow, 1929–1941* (Ithaca, NY: Cornell University Press, 2000).

74 On this see Laura Engelstein, "Combined Underdevelopment: Discipline and the Law in Imperial and Soviet Russia," *American Historical Review* 98, no. 2 (1993): 338–353.

75 Steven G. Marks, *How Russia Shaped the Modern World: From Art to Anti-Semitism, Ballet to Bolshevism* (Princeton, NJ: Princeton University Press, 2003), 1.

76 Andres Schönle, "Ruins and History: Observations on Russian Approaches to Destruction and Decay," *Slavic Review* 64, no. 4 (Winter 2006): 649–669. See also Andres Schönle, *Architecture of Oblivion: Ruins and Historical Consciousness in Modern Russia* (DeKalb: Northern Illinois University Press, 2011).

77 Schönle, "Ruins and History," 649–669.

78 Ibid., 652–653.

79 Gregory Stroud, "The Past in Common: Modern Ruins as a Shared Urban Experience of Revolution-Era Moscow and Petersburg," *Slavic Review* 65, no. 4 (Winter, 2006): 712–735. Like Schönle, Gregory Stroud describes the role that material objects from past eras played in the arts and in the cultural imaginary in the early years of the last century. He describes the emergence of a large-scale Retrospectivist movement, which reflected the proliferation of nostalgic impulses discussed in Chapter 3 of this book.

80 Mark Steinberg, *Proletarian Imagination: Self, Modernity and the Sacred in Russia, 1910–1925* (Ithaca, NY: Cornell University Press, 2002).

81 Ibid., 8.

82 Mark D. Steinberg, "Alexandra Kollontai and the Utopian Imagination in the Russian Revolution," *Vestnik of Saint Petersburg University: History* 62, no. 3 (2017): 438.

83 Ibid. Of the three utopian thinkers, Mayakovsky was the most focused on time and temporal narratives. He believed that "The old time was linked to the old *byt'*—the untransformed routines, habits, and conventions of everyday life." "The old *byt'* embodied the past in the present, the slow and repetitive march of ordinary time." By the late 1920s, this was the "time-the-reptile" and the "monster-*byt'*" that refused to die. As Trotsky and Kollontai would also find in their struggles against conventional *byt'* during the 1920s, the monster refused to die. "Mayakovsky worried about this in a melancholy poem he wrote toward the end of 1920, as the battles of the civil war were winding down but before the major compromises of NEP. 'The storms of revolution have subsided. / The Soviet muddle is covered in slime. / From behind the back of Soviet Russia / has crawled out / purring / the philistine.' Karl Marx, from his portrait on the wall, 'looks and looks all around, / and suddenly opens his mouth/and shouts: / "the revolution is snared in a web of ordinariness (*obyvatel'shchina*), / of a commonplace everyday life (*obyvatel'skii byt'*) more terrible than Wrangel"." The reptilian monster of normative time was all that remained. Life was fettered and chained to the present. A "leap" from necessity to freedom was impossible. See also Mark D. Steinberg, "Lev Trotsky and the Utopian Imagination in the Russian Revolution," *Vestnik of Saint Petersburg University History* 62, no. 4 (2017): 664–673, and Mark D. Steinberg, "Vladimir Mayakovsky and the Utopian Imagination in the Russian Revolution," *Vestnik of Saint Petersburg University History* 63, no. 1 (2018): 83–91.

84 Tim Harte, *Fast Forward: The Aesthetics and Ideology of Speed in Russian Avant-Garde Culture, 1910–1930* (Madison: University of Wisconsin Press, 2009), 3, esp. n2.

85 Ibid., 4.

86 Ibid.

87   Stephen E. Hanson, *Time & Revolution: Marxism and the Design of Soviet Institutions* (Chapel Hill: University of North Caroline Press, 1997).

88   Ibid., ix.

89   Ibid., xi.

90   Sally West, *I Shop in Moscow: Advertising and the Creation of Consumer Culture in Late Tsarist Russia* (Dekalb: Northern Illinois University Press, 2011), and Marjorie Hilton, *Selling to the Masses: Retailing in Russia, 1880–1930* (Pittsburgh, PA: University of Pittsburgh Press, 2011).

91   Diana Greene describes how a domestic ideology had made its way into Russia by mid-century; her work examines thick journals and children's magazines. "Mid-19th-Century Domestic Ideology in Russia," in Rosalind Marsh, ed., *Women and Russian Culture: Projections and Self Perceptions* (New York: Oxford University Press, 1998), 7897.

92   See, for example, Barbara Engel's seminal work on mothers and daughters among the nineteenth-century intelligentsia. She writes that Russia "never developed a comparable [to Western Europe] ideology of domesticity" because Russia lacked a bourgeoisie. As a result, she argues that mothers passed on their sense of morality to their daughters, who used that to justify their own process of radicalization and anti-government activities. Barbara Engel, *Mothers and Daughters: Women of the Intelligentsia in Nineteenth Century Russia* (Cambridge: Cambridge University Press, 1983), 6.

93   Mary Wells Cavender, "'Kind Angel of the Soul and Heart': Domesticity and Family Correspondence among the Pre-Emancipation Gentry," *Russian Review* 61 (July 2002): 391–408. So also Mary Wells Cavender, *Nests of the Gentry: Family, Estate, and Local Loyalties in Provincial Russia* (Newark: University of Delaware Press, 2007).

94   Rebecca Friedman, *Masculinity, Autocracy and the Russian University, 1804–1862* (London: Palgrave, 2005).

95   Jessica Tovrov, "Mother-Child Relationships among the Russian Nobility," in David Ransel, ed., *The Family in Imperial Russia: New Lines of Historical Research* (Urbana: University of Illinois Press 1978), 19.

96   Barbara Engel, *Breaking the Ties That Bound: The Politics of Marital Strife in Late Imperial Russia* (Ithaca, NY: Cornell University Press, 2013), 160.

97   Catriona Kelly, *Refining Russia: Advice Literature, Polite Culture, and Gender from Catherine to Yeltsin* (Oxford: Oxford University Press, 2001).

98   Engel, *Breaking the Ties That Bound*, 162.

99   Kelly, *Refining Russia*, 220–221.

100   Quoted in ibid., 171–172.

101   Svetlana Alexievich, *Secondhand Time: The Last of the Soviets* (New York: Random House, 2017), 4.

Chapter 2

1   *Zhenshchina* 9 (March 1, 1908): 1 and 4.

2   Ibid., 4.

3   I would like to thank the first-round anonymous reviewers and Mark Edele, in particular, for their detailed comments on this chapter.

4   Kern, *The Culture of Time and Space*; Koselleck, *The Practice of Conceptual History*; and Palti, "Time, Modernity and Time Irreversibility."

5   Harte, *Fast Forward*, 3.

6   Ibid.

7   Jane Gary Harris, "Countess Alexandra Zakharovna Muravieva," in Norma C. Noonan and Carol Nechemias, eds., *Encyclopedia of Russian Women's Movements* (Westport, CT: Greenwood Press, 2001), 44–45.

8   *Damskii Mir* 12 (December 1912): 25. *Damskii Mir* was published from 1907 to 1918 by Countess Muravieva; it began as a high-fashion magazine and morphed somewhat into a magazine meant to meet the needs of educated women in high society.

9   "Woman-Homemaker," *Zhenshchina* 9 (March 1, 1908): 1–4.

10 Rhonda Clark, "Women's Periodical Publishing in Late Imperial Russia," in Norma C. Noonan and Carol Nechemias, eds., *Encyclopedia of Russian Women's Movements* (Westport, CT: Greenwood Press, 2001), 106–109. On women, gender and journalism, see Barbara T. Norton and Jehanne E. Gheith, eds., *An Improper Profession: Women, Gender and Journalism in Late Imperial Russia* (Durham, NC: Duke University Press, 2001).

11 Jane Gary Harris, "Women's Periodicals in Early Twentieth Century Russia," in Norma C. Noonan and Carol Nechemias, eds., *Encyclopedia of Russian Women's Movements* (Westport, CT: Greenwood Press, 2001), 109–114.

12 Ogle, "Whose Time Is It?," 1376–1402.

13 Hilton, *Selling to the Masses*; West, *I Shop in Moscow*; and Louise McReynolds, *Russia at Play: Leisure Activities at the End of the Old Regime* (Ithaca, NY: Cornell University Press, 2002).

14 Kelly, *Refining Russia*, 158.

15 "A Humorous Album," *Zhenshchina* 3 (1907/8): 15.

16 Kelly, *Refining Russia*, 157.

17 Stephen Lovell, *Summerfolk: A History of the Dacha, 1710–2000* (Ithaca, NY: Cornell University Press, 2003), 58.

18 Hilton, *Selling to the Masses*; West, *I Shop in Moscow*; and McReynolds, *Russia at Play*.

19 Hilton, *Selling to the Masses*, 22–23.

20 Beth Holgrem, "Why Russian Girls Loved Charskaia," *Russian Review* 54, no. 1 (January 1995): 91–106.

21   McReynolds, *Russia at Play*.

22   Engel, *Breaking the Ties That Bind*, 160–161, and Kelly, *Refining Russia*.

23   Rose L. Glickman, *Russian Factory Women: Workplace and Society, 1880–1914* (Berkeley: University of California Press, 1986), 13.

24   James H. Bater, "Between Old and New: St Petersburg in the Late Imperial Era," in Michael Hamm, ed., *The City in Imperial Russia* (Bloomington: Indiana University Press, 1986), 56.

25   William Craft Brumfield, "Building for Comfort and Profit: The New Apartment House," in William Brumfield and Blair A. Ruble, eds., *Russian Housing in the Modern Age: Design and Social History* (Cambridge: Cambridge University Press, 1993), 56.

26   Joseph Bradley, "From Big Village to Metropolis," in Michael Hamm, ed., *The City in Imperial Russia* (Bloomington: Indiana University Press, 1986), 14–15.

27   Brumfield, "Building for Comfort and Profit," 75–77.

28   Bradley, "From Big Village to Metropolis," 35.

29   Brumfield, "Building for Comfort and Profit," 58.

30   Ibid., 65.

31   One of the earlier examples of more modest housing on a grand scale was L. Shishkovskii's eight-storey apartment house built for F.I. Afremov in 1904, located on Sadovyi-Spasskii Street. See Brumfield, "Building for Comfort and Profit," 75–77.

32   Brumfield, "Building for Comfort and Profit," 75–77.

33   Mark Steinberg, *Petersburg Fin de Siècle* (New Haven, CT: Yale University Press, 2011).

34   See Jeremy Aynsley and Francesca Berry on magazines and interior design in England in "Publishing the Modern Home: Magazines and the Domestic Interior 1870–1965," special issue of *Journal of Design History* 18, no. 1 (2005).

35   At the same time as Russians moved into their new urban spaces and began to ward off germs and other potential threats to hygiene and health, many took up dachas meant as a respite from the dangers of city living. Although an escape from the city overall, the dacha represented, for some, values attached to proper living that mirrored those in the urban apartments, "simplicity," "hospitality" and "modesty." See Lovell, *Summerfolk*, 99.

36   See Kelly, *Refining Russia*, esp. chs 3 and 4.

37   Norton and Gheith, *An Improper Profession*, 98.

38   Ibid.

39   Aynsley and Berry, "Publishing the Modern Home," 50. Aynsley quotes Roland Barthes who writes: "Each photograph is read as the private appearance of its referent: the age of Photography corresponds precisely to the explosion of the private into the public, or rather into the creation of a new social value, which is the publicity of the private: the private is consumed as such, publicly"

(Roland Barthes, *Camera Lucida: Reflections on Photography* [New York: Hill and Wang Publisher, 1982], 50.

40 Wayne Dowler, *Russia in 1913* (DeKalb: Northern Illinois University Press, 2012), 90.

41 Ibid., 96.

42 Ibid., 114.

43 Ibid., 253.

44 In her book *Refining Russia*, Kelly devotes several chapters to a discussion of the proliferation of prescriptive literature around the turn of the twentieth century.

45 There is a huge literature on these very tensions in the context of nations to the west, including most prominently Leonore Davidoff and Catherine Hall, *Family Fortunes: Men and Women of the English Middle Classes, 1780–1850* (New York: Routledge, 2003), and John Tosh, *A Man's House: Masculinity and the Middle-Class Home* (New Haven, CT: Yale University Press, 2008).

46 Hoy, *The Time of Our Lives*, 91.

47 Ibid., 43.

48 Henri Bergson, *Matter and Memory*, translated by Nancy Paul and W. Scott Palmer (New York: Double Day, 1959), 131.

49 See Dowler, *Russia in 1913*, on the significance of this year.

50 Dowler, *Russia in 1913*, 252–253.

51 *Zhenshchina* 9 (March 1, 1908): 3.

52 *Zhenshchina* 3 (January 1, 1908): 1.

53 Ibid.

54 *Zhenshchina* (January 1, 1908): 2.

55 Ibid.

56 Ibid.

57 There is a growing scholarship on the history of domestic interiors. Here I name only a few: Janet Bryden and Inga Floyd, *Domestic Space: Reading the Nineteenth Century Interior* (Manchester: Manchester University Press, 1999); Jeremy Aynsley and Charlotte Grant, eds., *Imagined Interiors: Representing the Domestic Interior Since the Renaissance* (London: Victoria & Albert Museum Press, 2006); Aynsley and Berry, "Publishing the Modern Home"; Penny Sparke, Anne Massey, Trevor Keeble, and Brenda Martin, eds., *Designing the Modern Interior: From the Victorians to Today* (Oxford: Berg, 2009); Deborah Cohen, *Household Gods: The British and their Possessions* (New Haven, CT: Yale University Press, 2009); Tony Chapman and Jenny Hockey, eds., *Ideal Homes? Social Change and the Experience of the Home* (New York: Routledge, 1999); Victoria Rosner, *Modernism and the Architecture of Private Life* (New York: Columbia University Press, 2008); Judith Flanders, *Inside the Victorian Home: A Portrait of Domestic Life in Victorian England* (New York: W.W. Norton, 2003); and Sharon Marcus, *Apartment Stories:*

City and Home in Nineteenth-Century Paris (Berkeley: University of California Press, 1999). On the subject of domestic as well as other spaces in the context of Russian, Soviet and Eastern European history, please see the two collections by Susan Reid and David Crowley: *Style and Socialism: Modernity and Material Culture in Post-War Eastern Europe* (Oxford: Berg, 2000), and *Socialist Spaces: Sites of Everyday Life in the Eastern Bloc* (Oxford: Berg, 2002), as well as the edited collection by Christina Kaier and Eric Naiman, *Everyday Life in Early Soviet Russia: Taking the Revolution Inside* (Bloomington: Indiana University Press, 2005).

58 Francesca Berry, "Designing the Reader's Interior: Subjectivity and the Women's Magazine in Early 20th Century France," *Journal of Design History* 18, no. 1 (2005): 61–79.

59 Ibid., 61.

60 Ibid., 63.

61 Jeremy Aynsley, "Graphic Change: Design Change: Magazines for the Domestic Interior, 1890–1930," *Journal of Design History* 18, no. 1 (2005): 43.

62 Bryden and Floyd, *Domestic Space*, 2.

63 Writing on the German context, Jeremy Aynsley describes similar patterns. Aynsley highlights how the interior was constructed through representations: "how periodic publications could both reflect and help to actively construct attitudes towards the interior in early twentieth-century Europe." In Germany, like Russia and elsewhere in Europe, women's periodicals tended to be eclectic. They "mixed the didactic with the entertaining, and the practical with the aspirational." The "heterogeneity of their content" meant that some magazines were discarded and others were meant to be collected (Aynsley, "Graphic Change," 43).

64 *Zhenshchina* 28 (July 2, 1908): 1–3.

65 Ibid., 1.

66 Elizabeth Hachter, "In Service to Science and Society: Scientists and the Public in Late Nineteenth-Century Russia," *Osiris* 17 (2002): 171–209.

67 Ibid., 207.

68 Daniel Beer, *Renovating Russia: The Human Sciences and the Fate of Liberal Modernity, 1880–1930* (Ithaca, NY: Cornell University Press, 2008), 11–13.

69 Bradley, "From Big Village to Metropolis," 35. In fact, there was a socio-economic urban geography developing, where elites occupied certain neighborhoods and housing in St. Petersburg. The Second Line on Vasilevskii Island had the largest concentration of merchants in the city, for example.

70 Sharon Kleinman, ed., *The Culture of Efficiency: Technology in Everyday Life* (New York: Peter Lang, 2009), 52.

71 Mariia Redelin, *Dom i khoziastvo: Rukovodstvo k ratsional'nomu vedeniiu domashniago khoziastva v gorode i v derevne*, vol. 1 (Moscow, 1889), 3.

72 *Dom i khoziastvo* 1 (January 3, 1904): 2.

73 Ibid., 5.

74 Ibid., 2.

75 Ibid.

76 *Sem'ianin* 5/6 (May/June 1894): 217. There are also discussions about curtains and differing seasons: It is best for people, who have the means, to have curtains that are for winter and summer ones. The winter ones would be made from "thick material" and in April would be replaced with summer curtains "striped with white and red or white and light blue." In the summer, then, the apartment will be "fresh and look fine."

77 Redelin, *Dom i khoziastvo,* 3.

78 Ibid., 3.

79 Ibid., 3.

80 Kelly, *Refining Russia,* 182.

81 Redelin, *Dom i khoziastvo,* 3.

82 Ibid., 3.

83 P.P. Andreev *Domovedenie. Rukovodstvo dlia khoziaek doma, domashnikh uchitelnits i guvernantok* (St. Petersburg, 1893), 1.

84 *Damskii mir* 12 (December 1912): 39.

85 Ibid.

86 Ibid., 25, 39.

87 *Zhenshchina* "Domashnyi stol" 6 (January 10, 1908): 1.

88 Ibid.

89 On this see Norma Noonan and Carol Nechemias, eds., *Encyclopedia of Russian Women's Movements* (Westport, CT: Greenwood Press, 2001), 112.

90 Ibid., 112.

91 See Cohen, *Household Gods.*

92 *Zhenshchina* 3 (January 1, 1908): 4.

93 Ibid., 2–4.

94 Ibid., 3.

95 Kelly, *Refining Russia,* 160.

96 Ibid., 162–164.

97 *Zhenshchina* 3 (January 1, 1908): 1.

98 Ibid., 4.

99 Ibid., 1.

100 *Zhenshchina* 1 (December 15, 1907/8): 1.

101 Redelin, *Dom i khoziastvo,* 29.

102 *Zhurnal dlia khoaziaek* (February 1, 1913): 4–5.

103 Redelin, *Dom i khoziaek,* 4–18.

104 *Zhenshchina* "Domashnii stol" 28 (June 24, 1908): 1.

105 Redelin, *Dom i khoziastvo*, 18.

106 Ibid., 21.

107 Ibid., 23.

108 *Zhenshchina* 7 (1908) 1–3.

109 Ibid.

110 Redelin, *Dom i khoziastvo*, 29–30.

111 Ibid., 33.

112 *Zhenshchina* 3 (1907/8): 1–5.

113 *Zhenshchina* 23 (November 15, 1908): 7–8.

114 Ibid., 8–9.

115 *Zhenshchina* 27 (June 17, 1908): 4.

116 Redelin, *Dom i khoziastvo*, 41.

117 *Zhenshchina* 2 (December 15, 1907/8): 8.

118 Ibid.

119 Ibid., 6.

120 Ibid.

121 Ibid.

122 *Zhenshchina* 3 (1908): 7–8.

123 *Dom i khoziastvo* 1 (January 3, 1904): 30.

124 Ibid.

125 Ibid., 30–31.

126 Ibid., 31.

127 Ibid.

128 *Zhenshchina* 3 (January 1, 1908): 9–10.

129 *Zhenshchina* 2 (December 15, 1907/8): 5.

130 *Zhurnal dlia zhenshchin* 4 (April 1915): 8.

131 Catriona Kelly, *Children's World: Growing Up in Russia, 1890–1991* (New Haven, CT: Yale University Press, 2008).

132 Ibid., 298 and 302.

133 Ibid.

134 *Zhenshchina* 10 (1908): 5–8.

135 Kelly, *Children's World*, 304–305.

136 *Zhenshchina* 2 (1907–1908): 7.

137 Ibid.

138 Ibid.

139 Ibid.

140 Ibid., 14.

141 Ibid.

142 Kelly, *Children's World*, 36.

143 Ibid., 570.

144 *Zhenshchina* 29 (July 2, 1908): 1.

145 *Zhurnal dlia zhenshchin* 10–11 (1918): 27.

146 *Damskii mir* 1 (January 1913): 43.

147 Kelly, *Children's World*.

148 *Zhenshchina i khoziaka* 4 (September 25, 1916): 9–10.

149 Ibid.

150 Ibid.

151 Ibid., 10.

152 *Zhenshchina* 1 (1908): 5–6.

153 *Damskii Mir* 1 (January 1913): 43.

154 Ibid.

155 Ibid., 42–43.

156 *Dom i semia* 1 (January 1910): 5.

157 *Damskii mir* 1 (January 1913): 42–43.

158 Ibid., 42.

159 Ibid.

160 *Zhurnal dlia khoziaek* 10–11 (October/November, 1918): 1–2.

161 Ibid.

162 *Zhurnal dlia khoziaek* 8 (April 15, 1913): 3–4.

163 Ibid., 20.

164 Ibid., 3.

165 Ibid., 20.

166 *Zhurnal dlia khoziaek* 10–11 (October/November, 1918): 8–10.

167 *Zhurnal dlia khoziaek* 8 (April 15, 1913): 19–20.

168 Ibid.

169 Ibid., 20.

170 *Listok for "Detskii mir"* 1 (November 22, 1903): 3.

171 *Listok for "Detskii mir"* 2–3 (November 27, 1903): 3.

172 Ibid.

173 Ibid., 5.

174 *Listok for "Detskii mir"* 10 (December 25, 1903): 4–6.

175 West-Pavlov, *Temporalities*, 17.

176 Mark D. Steinberg provides an extensive discussion in the introduction to his monograph entitled *Petersburg Fin de Siècle*, 3–5.

177 Steinberg, *Petersburg Fin de Siècle*, 3–5.

178 Mark Steinberg makes a similar observation and writes: "a recognition that these were fateful years was widely evident in public discussions of 'our times.'" Moreover, Steinberg describes how Russians' faith in the forward-moving progressive flow of history and its march forward was shaken in these years (*Petersburg Fin de Siècle*, 1).

Chapter 3

1   N.V. Polenova, *Abramtsevo: Vospominaniia* (Moscow: Izd. M. i S. Sabashnikovykh, 1922), 17–19.
2   Ibid., 20.
3   Leora Auslander, "Beyond Words," *American Historical Review* 110, no. 4. (2005): 1015–1045.
4   Koselleck, *The Practice of Conceptual History*, 120–121.
5   Koselleck, *Futures Past*, 240.
6   See Schönle, "Ruins and History," and Stroud, "The Past in Common."
7   The role of the eighteenth century in the nineteenth-century imaginary is discussed at length in Golburt, *The First Epoch*.
8   Golburt, *The First Epoch*, 4.
9   Ibid., 7.
10 Fink, *Bergson and Russian Modernism*, 5.
11 Boym, *The Future of Nostalgia*, 13.
12 Dowler, *Russia in 1913*.
13 Peter Fritzsche, *Modern Time and the Melancholy of History* (Cambridge, MA: Harvard University Press, 2010), 180 and 216.
14 Stroud, "The Past in Common," 713. See also Walter Benjamin, *Reflections: Essays, Aphorisms, Autobiographical Writings* (New York: Schocken Press, 1986), 106.
15 Golburt, *The First Epoch*, 14.
16 Ibid., 20.
17 Stroud, "The Past in Common," 716.
18 Schönle, "Ruins and History," 665
19 On this, see Richard Wortman, *Scenarios of Power: Myth and Ceremony on Russian Monarchy from Peter the Great to the Abdication of Nicholas II* (Princeton, NJ: Princeton University Press, 2000), 481. See also Stroud, "The Past in Common," 725.
20 Richard Wortman, "The 'Russian Style' in Church Architecture as Imperial Symbol after 1881," in James Cracraft and Daniel Rowland, eds., *Architectures of Russian Identity: 1500–Present* (Ithaca, NY: Cornell University Press, 2003), 114–115.
21 Boym, *Future of Nostalgia*, xiii–xiv.
22 Svetlana Boym, "Nostalgia and its Discontents," *Hedgehog Review* 9, no. 2 (Summer 2007): 13.
23 Steinberg, *Petersburg Fin de Siècle*.
24 Fritzsche, *Modern Time and the Melancholy of History*, 179–180, 4.
25 Ibid., 180.
26 Andrew Baruch Wachtel, *The Battle for Childhood: Creation of a Russian Myth* (Palo Alto, CA: Stanford University Press, 1990), 4.
27 Kelly, *Children's World*, 25.

28   Fritzsche, *Modern Time and the Melancholy of History*, 178.

29   Vladimir Nabokov, *Speak, Memory: An Autobiography Revisited* (New York: Vintage Books, 1989), 22.

30   Ibid., 79.

31   I would like to thank the anonymous reviewer for this insight.

32   P.P. Semenov-Tian-Shansky, *Epokha osvobozhdeniia krestian v Rossii v vospominaniiakh I* (St. Petersburg: Printing House of the Ministry of Railroads, 1915), 8.

33   Ibid., 8–10.

34   Ibid.

35   Konstantin Stanislavskii. *Sobranie sochinenii: v vos'mi tomakh*, vol. 1 (Moscow, 1954), 13–14, 32.

36   A.V. Shchepkina, *Vospominaniia Aleksandry Vladimirovny Shchepkinoi* (Moscow: I.I. Ivanov Publishers, 1915), 3.

37   Ibid., 3

38   Ibid.

39   Ibid., 5.

40   Stanislavskii, *Sobranie sochinenii*, vol. 1, 11.

41   P. Florinsky, *To My Children: Memoirs of Days Gone Past* (Moscow, 1916), 25.

42   Ibid., 35–36.

43   Ibid., 50.

44   Stanislavskii, *Sobranie sochinenii*, vol. 1, 8.

45   P.N. Miliukov, *Vospominaniia, 1859–1917* (New York, 1955), 13–14.

46   Stanislavskii, *Sobranie sochinenii*, vol. 1, 8.

47   V.H. Kharuzina, *Vospominaniia detskikh i otrocheskikh let* (Moscow: Novoe literaturnoe obozrenie, 1999), 17.

48   Ibid., 71–72.

49   Ibid., 181–182.

50   Ibid.

51   Ibid., 187–188. The house was pillaged in 1922.

52   Ibid., 103.

53   Ibid.

54   Ibid., 265. Kharuzina goes on to explain that from 1870 to 1879 she and her family would stay in Arkhangelsk for the summers with their aristocratic friends, the Yusupovs.

55   Ibid., 273.

56   Ibid., 286.

57   Ibid., 78.

58   Ibid., 193.

59   Ibid., 195.

60   Ibid., 163.

61   Ibid.

62   Ibid., 128.

63   Ibid., 70–71.

64   Ibid., 84–85.

65   Ibid., 19.

66   Ibid., 48.

67   Ibid., 164–168.

68   Ibid., 164.

69   Ibid., 177.

70   Ibid., 42.

71   Ibid., 152.

72   Ibid., 178.

73   Ibid., 127–128.

74   Ibid. 128.

75   There is a fairly extensive historiography on eighteenth- and nineteenth-century estate life in Russia. These works include: Thomas Newlin, *The Voice in the Garden: Andrei Bolotov and the Anxieties of Russian Pastoral 1783–1833* (Evanston: Northwestern University Press, 2001); John Randolph, *The House in the Garden: The Bakunin Family and the Romance of Russian Idealism* (Ithaca, NY: Cornell University Press, 2007); Wells Cavender, *Nests of the Gentry*; Priscilla Roosevelt, *Life on the Russian Country Estate: A Social and Cultural History* (New Haven, CT: Yale University Press, 1995); Lovell, *Summerfolk*.

76   Newlin, *The Voice in the Garden*, 5.

77   Ibid.

78   Michael Hughes, "The Russian Nobility and the Russian Countryside: Ambivalences and Orientations," *Journal of European Studies* 36 (2006): 115–137.

79   Newlin, *The Voice in the Garden*, 146.

80   Ibid., 146–147.

81   Anton Chekhov, *The Cherry Orchard*, in *The Essential Plays: The Seagull, Uncle Vanya, Three Sisters & The Cherry Orchard* (London: Modern Library Classics, 2003), 1.

82   Polenova, *Abramtsevo*, 5.

83   John Randolph, "The Old Mansion: Revisiting the History of the Russian Country Estate," *Kritika: Explorations in Russian and Eurasian History* 1, no. 4 (Fall 2000): 733. As Eric Hobsbawm describes for Britain, Germany and elsewhere around the same time, educated elites began inventing national traditions meant to sustain elites and rulers in times of uncertainty. See *The Invention of Tradition*, edited by Eric Hobsbawm and Terence Ranger (Cambridge: Cambridge University Press, 1992).

84   Gregory Stroud, "Retrospective Revolution: A History of Time and Memory in Urban Russia, 1903–1923" (PhD diss., University of Illinois, 2006), 28.

85 Many artists of the day saw the role that past and present played simultaneously. For example, in his discussion of ruins, scholar Andreas Schönle describes the work of Mstislav Dobuzhinsky, whose work embraced the intersections of then and now. Dobuzhinsky wrote that: "I think about modernity [...] I seek some kind of synthesis, which is there, at hand, near-by." In this rendition, the past and present are vulnerable to time's decay (Schönle, "Ruins and History," 652).

86 Schönle, "Ruins and History," 652.

87 Ibid., 665.

88 Fritzsche, *Modern Time and the Melancholy of History*, 213.

89 *Starye gody* (January 1910): 24.

90 Ibid.

91 Ibid., 24–31.

92 Roosevelt, *Life on the Russian Country Estate*, 327.

93 This quotation is from an excerpt of Vladimir Krymov's writings published in from *Новое русское слово* 10026 (July 21, 1934).

94 *Stolitsa i usadba* 6 (May 1, 1915): 4 and 33.

95 *Stolitsa i usadba* 1 (December 15, 1913): 1–2.

96 Ibid.

97 *Stolitsa i usadba* 69 (November 1, 1916): 9.

98 On melancholy, see Mark D. Steinberg, "Melancholy and Modernity: Emotions and Social Life in Russia Between the Revolutions," *Journal of Social History* 41, no. 4 (Summer 2008): 813–841.

99 John Randolph discusses the idea of the estate as a family archive in *The House in the Garden*.

100 *Stolitsa i usadba* 14, no. 69 (November 1, 1916): 7.

101 Ibid., 6.

102 Ibid., 6–7.

103 Ibid., 8.

104 *Stolitsa i usadba* 28 (February 15, 1915): 9.

105 Ibid., 9–13.

106 Ibid., 11.

107 Ibid.

108 Ibid.

109 *Stolitsa i usadba* 1 (December 15, 1913): 1–2.

110 Ibid.

111 *Stolitsa i usadba* 5 (February 1, 1916): 4–8.

112 Ibid.

113 Ibid.

114 *Stolitsa i usadba* 69 (August 15, 1916): 9–10.

115 Ibid.

116   *Stolitsa i usadba* 62/63 (August 1916): 14.

117   Ibid.

118   *Stolitsa i usadba* 57 (May 1, 1915): 3–4.

119   Ibid.

120   *Stolitsa i usadba* 63 (August 15, 1916): 9.

121   Ibid.

122   Ibid.

123   Ibid.

124   Ibid., 8.

125   Ibid.

126   *Stolitsa i usadba* 2 (January 15, 1914): 1–2.

127   *Stolitsa i usadba* 28 (February 15, 1915): 20.

128   *Stolitsa i usadba* 43 (October 15, 1915): 2.

129   Dowler, *Russia in 1913*, 251.

130   Wendy Salmond, *Arts and Crafts in Late Imperial Russia* (Cambridge: Cambridge University Press, 1996), 73.

131   John Bowlt, *Moscow & St. Petersburg 1900–1920: Art, Life, & Culture of the Russian Silver Age* (New York: Vendome Press, 2008), 131.

132   Ibid., 178.

133   Ibid.

134   Dowler, *Russia in 1913*, 251.

135   Ibid.

136   On the role of melancholy see Steinberg, "Melancholy and Modernity."

137   Dowler, *Russia in 1913*, 251.

138   Quoted in Alison Hilton, *Russian Folk Art* (Bloomington: Indiana University Press, 1995), 227.

139   Quoted in ibid., 229–31.

140   Quoted in ibid., 227. Original letter from Elena Polenova to P. Antipova, April 16, 1885, see E. Sakharova, ed., *VD Polenov-ED Polenova: Khronika semi i khudozhnikov* (Moscow 1964), 362.

141   Dowler, *Russia in 1913*, 251.

142   Ibid.

143   Sakharova, *V. D. Polenov-E.D. Polenova*, 50.

144   There is a substantial field on the Russian folk revival. See, for example, Hilton, *Russian Folk Art*; Salmond, *Arts and Crafts in Late Imperial Russia*; and Jonathan Mogul, "In the Shadow of the Factory" (PhD diss., University of Michigan, 1996).

145   Polenova, *Abramtsevo*, 50.

146   Quoted in Hilton, *Russian Folk Art*, 234–235.

147   Salmond, *Arts and Crafts in Late Imperial Russia*, 67–68.

148   Mogul, "In the Shadow of the Factory," 2.

149   Ibid., 267.

150   Ibid., 281.

151   Salmond, *Arts and Crafts in Late Imperial Russia*, 107.

152   Ibid., 102–103, 93.

153   Ibid., 73.

154   Sarah Warren, "Crafting Nation: the Challenge to Russian Folk Art in 1913," *Modernism/Modernity* 19, no. 4 (November 2009): 743–765.

155   Bowlt, *Moscow & St. Petersburg*, 178.

156   Ibid.

157   Debora Silverman, *Art Nouveau in Fin-de-Siecle France: Politics, Psychology, and Style* (Berkeley: University of California Press, 1992), 9.

158   Ibid.

159   Bilibin in *Mir iskusstva* 12, no. 1 (1904): 303–318.

160   Bilibin in ibid.

161   Bilibin in ibid., 303.

162   Bilibin in ibid., 303, 315.

163   *Mir iskusstva* 11 (1904): 108.

164   Ibid., 86.

165   Ibid., 163.

166   *Mir iskusstva* 4 (1900): 13–24.

167   *Mir iskusstva* 8, nos. 9–10 (1902): 213.

168   *Mir iskusstva* 12, no. 1 (1904): 267–270. See also page 285 of the same issue.

169   *Mir iskusstva* 1, no. 1 (1904): 285. On page 294 of the same issue, there is a picture of a seventeenth-century church.

170   *Mir iskusstva* 12 (1904): 298. There is a picture of an *izba* in Petrozavodsk county in Olonetskii province and another of the porch of the *izba* on same page.

171   Inside cover of *Russkaia usadba na stranitsiakh zhurnalov "starie gody" i "stolitsa i usadba"* (Moscow: MoscMeaning, Academy of Sciences, 1994).

172   Koselleck, *Futures Past*, 3.

173   Fritzche, *Modern Time and the Melancholy of History*, 165, 212.

Chapter 4

1   George Orwell, *1984* (Planet eBook. Available online: https://www.planetebook.com/free-ebooks/1984.pdf, accessed February 5, 2020), 44.

2   Vladimir Mayakovsky, *The Bedbug and Selected Poetry* (Bloomington: Indiana University Press, 1975); Mayakovsky, *Komsomolskaia*, 1924.

3   Susan Buck-Morss, *Dreamworld and Catastrophe: The Passing of Mass Utopia East and West* (Cambridge, MA: MIT Press, 2000), x–ix.

4   Ibid., 77.

5   This is cited in Engelstein, "Combined Underdevelopment," 343n21.

6   Buck-Morss, *Dreamworld and Catastrophe*, 71, 77.

7   Ibid., xi.

8   Ibid., 41.

9   "The year 1913 was the golden year of Cubo-Futurism, and of Russian Futurism in general, as an avant-garde force" (Anna Lawton, ed., *Russian Futurism through Its Manifestoes, 1912–1928* [Ithaca, NY: Cornell University Press, 1988]).

10 Filippo Tommaso Marinetti, *The Futurist Manifesto* (Society for Asian Art. Available online: https://www.societyforasianart.org/sites/default/files/manifesto_futurista.pdf, accessed February 5, 2020).

11 There is a tremendously rich historiography on gender in the early revolutionary years. For the most recent overview, see Amy Randall, "Gender and Sexuality," in Kees Boterbloem, ed., *Life in Stalin's Soviet Union* (London: Bloomsbury Press, 2019), 138–166.

12 Mark Bassin, Christopher Ely and Melissa Stockdale, eds., *Space, Place and Power in Modern Russia: Essays in the New Spatial History* (Evanston: Northern Illinois University, 2010).

13 Tracy McDonald, *Face to the Village: The Riazan Countryside Under Soviet Rule, 1922–1930* (Toronto: the University of Toronto, 2011).

14 In his *Peasant Metropolis,* David Hoffman highlights the experiences of peasants moving from the countryside to Moscow where they became a central component of the Soviet workforce.

15 *Dom i khoziastvo* 1 (1927): 1–2.

16 Ibid.

17 Eliot Borenstein, *Men without Women: Masculinity and Revolution in Russian Fiction, 1917–1929* (Durham, NC: Duke University Press, 2001).

18 A. Radchenko, *Domovodstvo vypysk 1: kak pravil'no vesti svoi dom* (Moscow, 1929), 11.

19 Ibid., 10.

20 Tricia Starks, *The Body Soviet: Propaganda, Hygiene and the Revolutionary State* (Madison: University of Wisconsin Press, 2008), 97.

21 Ibid.

22 Vladimir Mayakovsky, *The Bedbug and Selected Poetry* (Bloomington: Indiana University Press, 1975), 299.

23 Tom Cubbins, "Critical Soviet Design: Senezh Studio and the Utopian Imagination in Late Socialism" (PhD thesis, University of Sheffield, 2016), 56.

24 Tom Cubbins, *Soviet Critical Design Senezh Studio and the Communist Surround* (London: Bloomsbury Visual Arts, 2018).

25 Cubbins, "Critical Soviet Design," 59.

26 Ibid.

27 Ibid.

28 Ibid., 61.

29 Sheila Fitzpatrick discusses this notion of "always becoming" in her *Cultural Front: Power and Culture in Revolutionary Russia* (Ithaca, NY: Cornell University Press, 1992).

30 Djurda Bartlett, *Fashion East: The Spectre that Haunted Socialism* (Cambridge, MA: MIT Press 2010), 1–2.

31 Ibid.

32 Ibid., 13.

33 Ibid., 14.

34 Ibid., capitalization in the original.

35 *Sovremenaia arkhitetektura* 5 (1928): 160–162.

36 Ibid.

37 Ibid.

38 *Sovremennia arkhitektura* 4 (1929): 121–134.

39 Stephen E. Hanson, *Time and Revolution: Marxism and the Design of Soviet Institutions* (Chapel Hill: University of North Carolina, 1997), vii.

40 Cubbins, "Critical Soviet Design," 61.

41 Hanson, *Time and Revolution*, vii.

42 Kendall E. Bailes, "Alexei Gastev and the Soviet Controversy over Taylorism, 1918–24," *Soviet Studies* 29, no. 3 (July 1977): 373–394.

43 Ross Wolfe, "The ultra-Taylorist Soviet Utopianism of Aleksei Gastev" (*The Charnel-House*, December 7, 2011. Available online: https://thecharnelhouse. org/2011/12/07/the-ultra-taylorist-soviet-utopianism-of-aleksei-gastev-including-gastevs-landmark-book-how-to-work, accessed February 5, 2020).

44 Starks, *The Body Soviet*, 162.

45 Susan E. Reid, "Cold War in the Kitchen: Gender and the De-Stalinization of Consumer Taste in the Soviet Union under Khrushchev," *Slavic Review* 61, no. 2 (Summer 2002): 211–252.

46 "Besedy o domashnem khoziastve," *Dom i khoziastvo* 1 (1927): 1.

47 *Dom i khoziastvo* 1 (1927): 1–2.

48 Ibid.

49 *Dom i khoziastvo* 11, no. 45 (1928): 1.

50 Ibid., 4.

51 *Dom i khoziastvo* 41 (1928): 1.

52 *Dom i khoziastvo* 2 (1927): 2.

53 *Dom i khoziastvo* 41 (1928): 1.

54 *Dom i khoziastvo* 9, no. 43 (1928): 2–3.

55 Ibid., 2.

56 *Dom i khoziastvo* 4 (1928): 3.

57 *Dom i khoziastvo* 41 (1928): 1.

58 *Dom i khoziastvo* 8, no. 42 (1928): 3.

59 *Dom i khoziastvo* 41 (1928): 1.

60 *Dom i khoziastvo* 8, no. 42 (1928): 1.

61 *Dom i khoziastvo* 11, no. 45 (1928): 2.

62 Ibid., 3.

63 *Dom i khoziastvo* 15 (1928): 4.

64 *Dom i khoziastvo* 48 (1925): 1.

65 *Dom i khoziastvo* 15 (1927): 1–4.

66 *Dom i khoziastvo* 34 (1927): 2.

67 *Dom i khoziastvo* 48 (1925): 2.

68 *Za rubezhnoi* 2, no. 22 (1925): 44.

69 *Zhilishchnaia kooperatsia* 10 (1924): 14–16.

70 *Dom i khoziastvo* 28 (1928): 4.

71 *Gigena i zdorove rabochie i krest'ianskoi sem'i* 5, no. 12 (1924): 3.

72 Ibid., 3–4.

73 Benjamin, *Reflections*, xxxii.

74 Ibid., xxxiii.

75 Ibid., 125.

76 Ibid., 108–109.

77 Ibid., 108.

78 *Gigena i zdorove rabochie i krest'ianskoi sem'i* 5 (1926): 5.

79 *Bezhgodnik i stanka* (1926).

80 Reid, "Cold War in the Kitchen."

81 *Za zdorovnyi kulturnyi byt* (Moscow/Leningrad, 1931): 5.

82 *Za zdorovnyi kulturnyi byt*, 28.

83 *Dom i khoziastvo* 1 (1927): 1–2.

84 *Zhilishchnaia kooperatsia* 10 (1926) and 11 (1926).

85 *Zhilishchnaia kooperatsia* 11 (1926): 24–25.

86 Ibid.

87 Ibid.

88 Carolyn Steedman, *Dust: The Archive and Cultural History* (New Brunswick, NJ:
    Rutgers University Press, 2002), ix.

89 Steinberg, *Petersburg Fin de Siècle*, 49.

90 *Zhilishchnaia kooperatsia* 4 (1924): 20–22.

91 Ibid., 8.

92 *Za zdorovnyi kulturnyi* byt (Moscow/Leningrad, 1931): 5, 9.

93 *Za zdorovnyi kulturnyi byt*, 35.

94 *Gigiena i zdorove rabochie i krest'ianskoi sem'i* 24 (1925): 5.

95 *Gigiena i zdorove rabochie i krest'ianskoi sem'i* 4 (1926): 4–5.

96 *Dom i khoziastvo* 6 (1928): 3–4.

97 Ibid.

98 *Zhilishchno-sanitarnykh inspektorov* I & II (1921): 10–11.

99 *Gigiena i zdorove rabochie i krestianskoi semi* (1929): 3–4.

100 *Gigiena i zdorove rabochie i krestianskoi semi* 3 (1925): 3.

101 Ibid., 12.

102 *Gigiena i zdorove rabochie i krestianskoi semi* 3 (1926): 1–2.

103 *Dom i khoziastvo* 15 (1927): 2.

104 Ibid.

105 *Za zdorovnyi kulturnyi byt* (Moscow/Leningrad, 1931): 32.

106 Ibid., 35.

107 *Gigiena i zdorove rabochie i krestianskoi semi* 15 (1926): 5.

108 *Zhurnal dlia khoziaek* 6 (1926): 3–4.

109 Ibid.

110 Ibid., 4.

111 *Gigiena i zdorove rabochie i krestianskoi semi* 19 (1926): 13.

112 *Gigiena i zdorove rabochie i krestianskoi semi* 12 (1924): 2.

113 Radchenko, *Domovodstvo vynosk 1.*

114 Ibid., 3.

115 Ibid., 26, 30.

116 There was also a preoccupation with dampness: *Gigena i zdorov'e rabochie i krest'ianskoi sem'i* 3 (1926): 2. The article "The Dampness of Living Quarters" is about the dangers of dampness in an apartment.

117 Allison Hilton, "Reshaping Folk Art in the Soviet Era," in *Russian Folk Art in the Soviet Era* (Bloomington: Indiana University Press, 2011), 257–284.

118 Ibid.

119 Ibid., 258.

120 Ibid.

121 Ibid., 271.

122 V.S. Voronov, "Putevoditel po Kustarnomu muzeiu," 191, cited in Hilton, "Reshaping Folk Art in the Soviet Era," 272.

123 Stroud, "The Past in Common," 721. This quote is from Ivan Lazarevskii, *Sredi kollektsionerov* (1914; reprint, Moscow, 1999), 50.

124 Stroud, "The Past in Common," 721.

125 Stroud, "Retrospective Revolution," 3.

126 Other members included: B.P. Denike (scholarly secretary) and A.N. Trishevskii, I.A. Bakhrishin, A.N. Grech, I.M. Kartavtsov and S.A. Toropov, as members at large.

127 G.D. Zlochevskii, *Obshchestvo izucheniia russkoi usadby: ego deiatel'nost i rukovoditeli* (1920-e gody) (Moscow, 2011), 51.

128 Ibid.

129 Cubbins, "Critical Soviet Design," 55.

130   This is from the Kommunalka website, see Ilya Utekhin, Alice Nakhimovsky, Slava Paperno and Nancy Ries, "Communal Living in Russia: A Virtual Museum of Society in Everyday Life." Available online: http://kommunalka.colgate.edu/, accessed February 19, 2020.

131   Mikhail Zoshchenko, "The Crisis," a short story, translated by Charles Rougle (Moscow, 1925). Available online: http://kommunalka.colgate.edu/cfm/from_fiction.cfm?ClipID=565&TourID=940, accessed February 19, 2020.

132   Natalia Lebina, "Communal, Communal, Communal World," *Russian Studies in History* 28, no. 4 (2000): 53–62.

133   *Zhilishchnoe kooperatsiia* 18 (1925): 18.

134   Ibid., 18–20.

135   *Zhilishchnaia kooperatsiia* 10 (1926) and 11 (1926).

136   *Zhilishchnoe kooperatsiia* 18 (1925): 18–20.

137   *Zhilishchnoe kooperatsiia* 10 (1925): 26.

138   *Zhilishchnoe kooperatsiia* 18 (1925): 18–20.

139   Ibid.

140   *Zhilets* 5/6 (1924): 3.

141   Ibid., 4.

142   Ibid.

143   *Domovoe khozyaistvo* (Moscow: Iz-vo tsentrozhilsouza, 1929).

144   Ibid., 112.

145   Ibid., 113.

146   Ibid., 145.

147   *Za zdorovyi kulturnyi byt*, 5.

148   *Gigiena i zdorove rabochie i krestianskoi semi* 2 (1927): 8–9.

149   Ibid., 8.

150   *Biulleten' Zhilets* 5/6 (1924). In *Living the Revolution: Urban Communes & Soviet Socialism, 1917–1932*, Andy Willimott explores the politics and social lives of youthful enthusiasts building urban communes (London: Oxford University Press, 2019). See also Deirdre Ruscitti Harshman, "A Space Called Home: Housing and the Management of the Everyday in Russia, 1890–1935" (PhD diss., University of Illinois, 2018), which is another study that crosses the revolutionary divide.

151   *Bulleten Zhilets* 5/6 (1924): 3–4.

152   Ibid., 4.

153   There existed small-scale as well as more formally constituted groups that governed communal living spaces. There also was a proliferation of publications that were adjunct to these publications. These included, *Zhilishchie tovarischestvo*, for one.

154   D. Mallory, "Bor'ba za novyi byt," *Ogonek* 19 (1924): 1–2.

155 Ibid.

156 Ibid.

157 *Zhilishchie tovarischestvo* 8 (January 1923): 40–41.

158 Ibid.

159 Ibid.

Coda

1 Sewell, *Logics of History*, 6.

2 Ibid.

3 Ibid.

4 See "Viewpoints: Temporalities," *Past Present* 243, no. 1 (May 2019): 247–327.

5 Kern, *The Culture of Time and Space*, xii.

6 I would like to thank Dierdre Ruscitti Harshman for bringing this article to my attention. Josh Axelrod, "Meet the Residents of a Norwegian Island Who Want To Kill Time—Literally" (*NPR*, June 23, 2019. Available online: https://www.npr.org/2019/06/23/735191303/norwegian-island-wants-to-be-time-free, accessed June 24, 2019).

7 Julian Baggini, "An Island that Shuns Clocks? It Won't Stand the Test of Time" (*The Guardian*, June 24, 2019. Available online: https://www.theguardian.com/commentisfree/2019/jun/24/island-clocks-norway-time-free-sommaroy, accessed June 26, 2019).

8 *Dom i khoziastvo* 11, no. 45 (1928): 1.

9 Ibid.

10 Reid, "Cold War in the Kitchen."

11 Christine Varga-Harris, *Stories of House and Home: Soviet Apartment Life during the Khrushchev Years* (Ithaca, NY: Cornell University Press, 2015); Stephen E. Harris, *Communism on Tomorrow Street Mass Housing and Everyday Life after Stalin* (Baltimore: Johns Hopkins University Press, 2013); Susan Reid, "Everyday Aesthetics in the Khrushchev-Era Standard Apartment," *Etnofoor* 24, no. 2 (2012): 78–105, among Reid's other work.

12 Christine Varga-Harris, "Moving Toward Utopia: Soviet Housing in the Atomic Age," in Peter Romijn, Giles Scott-Smith and Joes Segal, eds., *Divided Dreamworlds?: The Cultural Cold War in East and West* (Amsterdam: Amsterdam University Press, 2012), 135.

13 Ibid.

14 Serguei Alex Oushakine, "Second-Hand Nostalgia: On Charms and Spells of the Soviet *Trukhliashchechka*," in Otto Boele, Boris Noordenbos and Ksenia

Robbe, eds., *Post-Soviet Nostalgia: Confronting the Empire's Legacies* (New York: Routledge, 2020), 39.

15   I am not the first to recognize this phenomenon of the commercialization of nostalgia: *The Guardian* wrote about the Kommunalka restaurant in 2016. "The design is so authentic that it's hard to believe you're in 2016. The restaurant is in a former communal apartment, with its original layout and even some of the décor. Walls are covered with 1970s newspapers and there's plenty of Soviet paraphernalia, including old radios, television sets, scales and jars with pickles scattered around" (Andrei Muchnik, "Moscow Restaurant Draws on Collective Soviet Nostalgia – and Adds a Salad Bar" [*The Guardian*, March 11, 2016. Available online: https://www.theguardian.com/world/2016/mar/11/moscow-restaurant-kommunalka-soviet-nostalgia, accessed February 5, 2020]).

16   There is a tremendous amount of writing on this queston of the nostalgia industry: Otto Boele, Boris Noordenbos and Ksenia Robbe, eds., *Post-Soviet Nostalgia: Confronting the Empire's Legacies* (New York: Routledge, 2020), is the most recent example. See also Sophie Pinkham, "No Direction Home" (*The New Republic*, May 3, 2018. Available online: https://newrepublic.com/article/147818/no-direction-home-post-soviet-countries-populism-nostalgia, accessed February 6, 2020); Sophie Armitage, "Why Russians Are Lining Up for Soviet-Style Canteens" (*Atlas Obscura*, February 7, 2019. Available online: https://www.atlasobscura.com/articles/soviet-restaurants-in-russia, accessed February 6, 2020); Jardine Bradley, "Back in the USSR: Finding Soviet Nostalgia in Moscow" (*The Moscow Times*, February 4, 2017. Available online: https://www.themoscowtimes.com/2017/02/04/in-the-shadow-of-empire-a57044, accessed February 6, 2020); and Brigid McCarthy, "Nostalgia for the Soviet Union" (*Public Radio International*, December 23, 2011. Available online: https://www.pri.org/stories/2011-12-23/nostalgia-soviet-union, accessed February 6, 2020).

17   Reid, "Cold War in the Kitchen."

18   Reinhart Koselleck, *Sediments of Time: On Possible Histories* (Palo Alto, CA: Stanford University Press, 2018), 3–9.

19   Boym, *Future of Nostalgia*, 59.

20   Ibid., 59–60.

21   Alexievich, *Secondhand Time*, 11.

22   Ibid.

23   Amy Randall and I spent May 2019 together in Moscow. Many of these observations are the result of our conversations that evening and subsequently. All errors are my own.

24   GUM, "GUM. Timeline: XIX Century" (n.d. Available online: https://gum.ru/history/, accessed February 6, 2020).

25   Armitage, "Why Russians Are Lining Up for Soviet-Style Canteens."

26   GUM, "GUM. Timeline."

27 Armitage, "Why Russians Are Lining Up for Soviet-Style Canteens."

28 Boym, *Future of Nostalgia*, 5.

29 Ibid., 59–60.

30 Ibid.

31 Otto Boele, Boris Noordenbos and Ksenia Robbe, eds., "Introduction," in
    Otto Boele, Boris Noordenbos and Ksenia Robbe, eds., *Post-Soviet Nostalgia:
    Confronting the Empire's Legacies* (New York: Routledge, 2019), 12.

32 Ibid.

Bibliography

Journals and magazines

Damskii Mir
Dom i khoziastvo
Mir iskusstva
Ogonek
Sem'ianin
Sovremenaia arkhitektura
Starye gody
Stolitsa i usadba
Zhenshchina
Zhenshchina i khoziaka
Zhurnal dlia khoaziaek
Zhurnal dlia zhenshchin

Books, edited collections

Alexievich, S. (2017), *Secondhand Time: the Last of the Soviets*, New York: Random House.

Andreev, P.P. (1893), *Domovedenie. Rukovodstvo dlia khoziaek doma, domashnikh uchitelnits i guvernantok*, St. Petersburg.

Armitage, S. (2019), "Why Russians Are Lining Up for Soviet-Style Canteens," *Atlas Obscura*, February 7, 2019. Available online: https://www.atlasobscura.com/articles/soviet-restaurants-in-russia, accessed February 6, 2020.

Auslander, L. (2005), "Beyond Words," *American Historical Review* 110 (4): 1015–1045.

Axelrod, J. (2019), "Meet the Residents of a Norwegian Island Who Want To Kill Time — Literally," *NPR*, June 23, 2019. Available online: https://www.npr.org/2019/06/23/735237020/meet-the-residents-of-a-norwegian-island-who-want-to-kill-time-literally, accessed June 24, 2019.

Aynsley, J. (2005), "Graphic Change: Design Change: Magazines for the Domestic Interior, 1890–1930," *Journal of Design History* 18 (1): 43–59.

Aynsley, J. (2005), "Publishing the Modern Home: Magazines and the Domestic Interior 1870–1965," special issue of *Journal of Design History* 18 (1).

Aynsley, J. and C. Grant, eds. (2006), *Imagined Interiors: Representing the Domestic Interior Since the Renaissance*, London: Victoria & Albert Museum Press.

Baggini, J. (2019), "An Island that Shuns Clocks? It Won't Stand the Test of Time," *The Guardian*, June 24, 2019. Available online: https://www.theguardian.com/world/2019/jun/20/sommaroy-island-norway-attempt-create-first-time-free-zone, accessed June 26, 2019.

Bailes, K. (1977), "Alexei Gastev and the Soviet Controversy over Taylorism, 1918–24," *Soviet Studies* 29 (3): 373–394.

Barthes, R. (1982), *Camera Lucida: Reflections on Photography*, New York: Hill and Wang Publisher.

Bartlett, D. (2010), *Fashion East: The Spectre that Haunted Socialism*, Cambridge, MA: MIT Press.

Bassin, M., C. Ely and M. Stockdale, eds. (2010), *Space, Place and Power in Modern Russia: Essays in the New Spatial History*, Evanston: Northern Illinois University.

Bater, J. (1986), "Between Old and New: St Petersburg in the Late Imperial Era," in Michael Hamm (ed.), *The City in Imperial Russia*, 43–78, Bloomington: Indiana University Press.

Beer, D. (2008), *Renovating Russia: The Human Sciences and the Fate of Liberal Modernity, 1880–1930*, Ithaca, NY: Cornell University Press.

Benjamin, W. (1986), *Reflections: Essays, Aphorisms, Autobiographical Writings*, New York: Schocken Press.

Bergson, H. (1959), *Matter and Memory*, translated by N. Paul and W.S. Palmer, New York: Double Day.

Berry, F. (2005), "Designing the Reader's Interior: Subjectivity and the Women's Magazine in Early 20th Century France," *Journal of Design History* 18 (1): 61–79.

Beumers, B. (2012), "National Identity Through Visions of the Past," in M. Bassin and C. Kelly (eds.), *Soviet and Post-Soviet Identities*, 55–72, Cambridge: Cambridge University Press.

Boele, O., B. Noordenbos and K. Robbe, eds. (2019), "Introduction," in O. Boele, B. Noordenbos and K. Robbe (eds.), *Post-Soviet Nostalgia: Confronting the Empire's Legacies*, New York: Routledge.

Boele, O., B. Noordenbos and K. Robbe, eds. (2020), *Post-Soviet Nostalgia: Confronting the Empire's Legacies*, New York: Routledge.

Borenstein, E. (2001), *Men Without Women: Masculinity and Revolution in Russian Fiction, 1917–1929*, Durham, NC: Duke University Press.

Bowlt, J. (2008), *Moscow & St. Petersburg 1900–1920: Art, Life, & Culture of the Russian Silver Age*, New York: Vendome Press.

Boym, S. (2002), *The Future of Nostalgia*, New York: Basic Books.

Boym, S. (2007), "Nostalgia and its Discontents," *Hedgehog Review* 9 (2): 7–18.

Bradley, J. (1986), "From Big Village to Metropolis," in M. Hamm (ed.), *The City in Imperial Russia*, 9–41, Bloomington: Indiana University Press.

Bradley, J. (2017), "Back in the USSR: Finding Soviet Nostalgia in Moscow," *The Moscow Times*, February 4, 2017. Available online: https://www.themoscowtimes.com/2017/02/04/in-the-shadow-of-empire-a57044, accessed February 6, 2020.

Brumfield, W.C. (1993), "Building for Comfort and Profit: The New Apartment House," in W.C. Brumfield and B.A. Ruble (eds.), *Russian Housing in the Modern Age: Design and Social History*, Cambridge: Cambridge University Press.

Brumfield, W. and B. Ruble, eds. (1993), *Russian Housing in the Modern Age: Design and Social History*, Cambridge: Cambridge University Press.

Bryden, I. and J. Floyd (1999), *Domestic Space: Reading the Nineteenth-Century Interior*, Manchester: Manchester University Press.

Buck-Morss, S. (2000), *Dreamworld and Catastrophe: The Passing of Mass Utopia East and West*, Cambridge, MA: MIT Press.

Champion, M. (2019), "The History of Temporalities: An Introduction," *Past & Present* 243 (1): 247–254.

Chapman, T., and J. Hockey, eds. (1999), *Ideal Homes? Social Change and the Experience of the Home*, New York: Routledge.

Chekhov, A. (2003), *The Cherry Orchard*, in *The Essential Plays: The Seagull, Uncle Vanya, Three Sisters & The Cherry Orchard*, London: Modern Library Classics.

Clark, R. (2001), "Women's Periodical Publishing in Late Imperial Russia," in Norma C. Noonan and Carol Nechemias, eds., *Encyclopedia of Russian Women's Movements*, 106–109, Westport, CT: Greenwood Press.

Cohen, D. (2009), *Household Gods: The British and Their Possessions*, New Haven, CT: Yale University Press.

Corfield, P. (2007), *Time and the Shape of History*, New Haven, CT: Yale University Press.

Cubbins, T. (2016), "Critical Soviet Design: Senezh Studio and the Utopian Imagination in Late Socialism," PhD thesis, University of Sheffield.

Cubbins, T. (2018), *Soviet Critical Design: Senezh Studio and the Communist Surround*, London: Bloomsbury Visual Arts.

David-Fox, M. (2015), *Modernity, Ideology, and Culture in Russia and the Soviet Union*, Pittsburgh, PA: University of Pittsburgh Press.

Davidoff, L. and C. Hall (2003), *Family Fortunes: Men and Women of the English Middle Classes, 1780–1850*, New York: Routledge.

Dohrn-Van Rossum, G. (1996), *History of the Hour: Clocks and Modern Temporal Orders*, Chicago: University of Chicago.

Dowler, W. (2010), *Russia in 1913*, Dekalb: Northern Illinois University.

Engel, B. (1983), *Mothers and Daughters: Women of the Intelligentsia in Nineteenth Century Russia*, Cambridge: Cambridge University Press.

Engel, B. (2013), *Breaking the Ties That Bound: The Politics of Marital Strife in Late Imperial Russia*, Ithaca, NY: Cornell University Press.

Engelstein, L. (1993), "Combined Underdevelopment: Discipline and the Law in Imperial and Soviet Russia," *American Historical Review* 98 (2): 338–353.

Fink, H. (2012), *Bergson and Russian Modernism, 1900–1930*, Chicago: Northwestern University Press.

Fitzpatrick, S. (1992), *Cultural Front: Power and Culture in Revolutionary Russia*, Ithaca, NY: Cornell University Press.

Flanders, J. (2003), *Inside the Victorian Home: A Portrait of Domestic Life in Victorian England*, New York: W.W. Norton.

Florinsky, P. (1916), *To My Children: Memoirs of Days Gone Past*, Moscow.

Friedman, R. (2005), *Masculinity, Autocracy and the Russian University, 1804–1862*, London: Palgrave.

Fritzsche, P. (2010), *Modern Time and the Melancholy of History*, Cambridge, MA: Harvard University Press.

Fritzsche, P. (2010), *Stranded in the Present: Modern Time and the Melancholy of History*, Cambridge, MA: Harvard University Press.

Fryxell, A.R.P. (2019), "Time and the Modern: Current Trends in The History of Modern Temporalities," *Past & Present* 243 (1): 285–298.

Gange, D. (2019), "Time, Space and Islands: Why Geographers Drive the Temporal Agenda," *Past & Present* 243 (1): 299–312.

Geraghty, C. (2007), "Re-examining Stardom: Questions of Texts, Bodies and Performance," in S. Redmond and S. Holmes (eds.), *Stardom and Celebrity: A Reader*, 93–105, London: Sage.

Glickman, R. (1986), *Russian Factory Women: Workplace and Society, 1880–1914*, Berkeley: University of California Press.

Golburt, L. (2014), *The First Epoch: The Eighteenth Century and the Russian Cultural Imagination*, Madison: University of Wisconsin Press.

Greene, D. (1998), "Mid-19th-Century Domestic Ideology in Russia," in R. Marsh (ed.), *Women and Russian Culture: Projections and Self Perceptions*, 78–97, New York: Oxford University Press.

GUM (n.d.), "GUM. Timeline: XIX Century." Available online: https://gum.ru/history/, accessed February 6, 2020.

Hachter, E. (2002), "In Service to Science and Society: Scientists and the Public in Late Nineteenth-Century Russia," *Osiris* 17: 171–209.

Hans, S. (2019), "The Fetish of Accuracy: Perspectives on Early Modern Time(s)," *Past & Present* 243 (1): 267–284.

Hanson, S. (1997), *Time & Revolution: Marxism and the Design of Soviet Institutions*, Chapel Hill: University of North Carolina Press.

Harris, J.G. (2001), "Countess Alexandra Zakharovna Muravieva," in N.C. Noonan and C. Nechemias (eds.), *Encyclopedia of Russian Women's Movements*, 44–45, Westport, CT: Greenwood Press.

Harris, J.G. (2001), "Women's Periodicals in Early Twentieth Century Russia," in N.C. Noonan and C. Nechemias (eds.), *Encyclopedia of Russian Women's Movements*, 109–114, Westport, CT: Greenwood Press.

Harris, S.E. (2013), *Communism on Tomorrow Street Mass Housing and Everyday Life after Stalin*, Baltimore: Johns Hopkins University Press.

Harshman, D.R. (2018), "A Space Called Home: Housing and the Management of the Everyday in Russia, 1890–1935," PhD diss., University of Illinois.

Harte, T. (2009), *Fast Forward: The Aesthetics and Ideology of Speed in Russian Avant-Garde Culture, 1910–1930*, Madison: University of Wisconsin Press.

Hilton, A. (1995), *Russian Folk Art*, Bloomington: Indiana University Press.

Hilton, A. (2011), "Reshaping Folk Art in the Soviet Era," in *Russian Folk Art in the Soviet Era*, 257–284, Bloomington: Indiana University Press.

Hilton, M. (2011), *Selling to the Masses: Retailing in Russia, 1880–1930*, Pittsburgh, PA: University of Pittsburgh Press.

Hobsbawm, E. (1992), *The Invention of Tradition*, E. Hobsbawm and T. Ranger (eds.), Cambridge: Cambridge University Press.

Hoffman, D. (2000), *Peasant Metropolis: Social Identities in Moscow, 1929–1941*, Ithaca, NY: Cornell University Press.

Hoffman, D. (2003), *Stalinist Values: The Cultural Norms of Soviet Modernity, 1917–1941*, Ithaca, NY: Cornell University Press.

Holgrem, B. (1995), "Why Russian Girls Loved Charskaia," *Russian Review* 54 (1): 91–106.

Hoy, D. C. (2012), *The Time of Our Lives: A Critical History of Temporality*, Boston, MA: MIT Press.

Hughes, M. (2006), "The Russian Nobility and the Russian Countryside: Ambivalences and Orientations," *Journal of European Studies* 36: 115–137.

Kaier, C., and E. Naiman (2005), *Everyday Life in Early Soviet Russia: Taking the Revolution Inside*, Bloomington: Indiana University Press.

Kelly, C. (2001), *Refining Russia: Advice Literature, Polite Culture, and Gender from Catherine to Yeltsin*, Oxford: Oxford University Press.

Kelly, C. (2008), *Children's World: Growing Up in Russia, 1890–1991*, New Haven, CT: Yale University Press.

Kern, S. (2003), *The Culture of Time and Space, 1880–1918: With a New Preface*, Cambridge, MA: Harvard University Press.

Kharuzina, V.H. (1999), *Vospominaniia detskikh i otrocheskikh let*, Moscow: Novoe literaturnoe obozrenie.

Kleinman, S., ed. (2009), *The Culture of Efficiency: Technology in Everyday Life*, New York: Peter Lang.

Koselleck, R. (2002), *The Practice of Conceptual History: Timing History, Spacing Concepts*, Stanford, CA: Stanford University Press.

Koselleck, R. (2004), *Futures Past: On the Semantics of Historical Time*, New York: Columbia University Press.

Koselleck, R. (2018), *Sediments of Time: On Possible Histories*, Palo Alto, CA: Stanford University Press.

Lawton, A., ed. (1988), *Russian Futurism through Its Manifestoes, 1912–1928*, Ithaca, NY: Cornell University Press.

Lebina, N. (2000), "Communal, Communal, Communal World," *Russian Studies in History* 28 (4): 53–62.

Lebina, N. (2016), *Sovetskaia posvednevnost: normy i anomalii*, Moscow: Novoe Literaturnoe Obozrenie.

Lovell, S. (2003), *Summerfolk: A History of the Dacha, 1710–2000*, Ithaca, NY: Cornell University Press.

Manchard, M. (1999), "Afro-Modernity: Temporality, Politics and the African Diaspora," *Public Culture* 11 (1): 245–268.

Marcus, S. (1999), *Apartment Stories: City and Home in Nineteenth-Century Paris*, Berkeley: University of California Press.

Marinetti, F.T. (n.d.), *The Futurist Manifesto*, Society for Asian Art. Available online: https://www.societyforasianart.org/sites/default/files/manifesto_futurista.pdf, accessed February 5, 2020.

Marks, S. (2003), *How Russia Shaped the Modern World: From Art to Anti-Semitism, Ballet to Bolshevism*, Princeton, NJ: Princeton University Press.

Mayakovsky, V. (1975), *The Bedbug and Selected Poetry*, Bloomington: Indiana University Press.

McCarthy, B. (2011), "Nostalgia for the Soviet Union," *Public Radio International*, December 23, 2011. Available online: https://www.pri.org/stories/2011-12-23/nostalgia-soviet-union, accessed February 6, 2020.

McDonald, T. (2011), *Face to the Village; The Riazan Countryside Under Soviet Rule, 1922–1930*, Toronto: University of Toronto Press.

McReynolds, L. (2002), *Russia at Play: Leisure Activities at the End of the Old Regime*, Ithaca, NY: Cornell University Press.

Menendez, A. (2001), *In Cuba I was a German Shepherd*, New York: Grove Press.

Miliukov, P.N. (1955), *Vospominaniia, 1859–1917*, New York.

Mogul, J. (1996), "In the Shadow of the Factory," PhD diss., University of Michigan.

Nabokov, V. (1989), *Speak, Memory: An Autobiography Revisited*, New York: Vintage Books.

Newlin, T. (2001), *The Voice in the Garden: Andrei Bolotov and the Anxieties of Russian Pastoral 1783–1833*, Evanston: Northwestern University Press.

Noonan, N., and C. Nechemias, eds. (2001), *Encyclopedia of Russian Women's Movements*, Westport, CT: Greenwood Press.

Norton, B.T., and J.E. Gheith, eds. (2001), *An Improper Profession: Women, Gender and Journalism in Late Imperial Russia*, Durham, NC: Duke University Press.

Ogle, V. (2013), "Whose Time Is It? The Pluralization of Time and the Global Condition, 1870s–1940s," *American Historical Review* 118 (5): 1376–1402.

Ogle, V. (2015), *The Global Transformation of Time: 1870–1950*, Cambridge, MA: Harvard University Press.

Orwell, G. (n.d.), *1984*. Planet eBook. Available online: https://www.planetebook.com/free-ebooks/1984.pdf, accessed February 5, 2020.

Oushakine, S.A. (2020), "Second-Hand Nostalgia: On Charms and Spells of the Soviet *Trukhliashchechka*," in O. Boele, B. Noordenbos and K. Robbe (eds.), *Post-Soviet Nostalgia: Confronting the Empire's Legacies*, 38–69, New York: Routledge.

Palti, E. (1997), "Time, Modernity and Time Irreversibility," *Philosophy and Social Criticism* 23: 27–62.

Pinkham, S. (2018), "No Direction Home," *The New Republic*, May 3, 2018. Available online: https://newrepublic.com/article/147818/no-direction-home-post-soviet-countries-populism-nostalgia, accessed February 6, 2020.

Pipes, R. (1997), *Russia Under the Old Regime*, New York: Penguin Books.

Platt, K. (2013), "Russian Empire of Pop: Post-Socialist Nostalgia and Soviet Retro at the 'New Wave' Competition," *Russian Review* 72 (3): 447–469.

Polenova, N.V. (1922), *Abramtsevo: Vospominaniia*, Moscow: Izd. M. i S. Sabashnikovykh.

Radchenko, A. (1929), *Domovodstvo vypysk 1: kak pravil'no vesti svoi dom*, Moscow.

Randall, A. (2019), "Gender and Sexuality," in K. Boterbloem (ed.), *Life in Stalin's Soviet Union*, London: Bloomsbury Press, 136–166.

Randolph, J. (2000), "The Old Mansion: Revisiting the History of the Russian Country Estate," *Kritika: Explorations in Russian and Eurasian History* 1 (4): 719–749.

Randolph, J. (2007), *The House in the Garden: The Bakunin Family and the Romance of Russian Idealism*, Ithaca, NY: Cornell University Press.

Redelin, M. (1889), *Dom i khoziastvo: Rukovodstvo k ratsional'nomu vedeniiu domashniago khoziastva v gorode i v derevne*, Moscow.

Reid, S. (2002), "Cold War in the Kitchen: Gender and the De-Stalinization of Consumer Taste in the Soviet Union under Khrushchev," *Slavic Review* 61 (2): 211–252.

Reid, S. (2012), "Everyday Aesthetics in the Khrushchev-Era Standard Apartment," *Etnofoor* 24 (2): 78–105.

Reid, S., and D. Crowley (2000), *Style and Socialism: Modernity and Material Culture in Post-War Eastern Europe*, Oxford: Berg.

Reid, S., and D. Crowley (2002), *Socialist Spaces: Sites of Everyday Life in the Eastern Bloc*, Oxford: Berg.

Roosevelt, P. (2005), *Life on the Russian Country Estate: A Social and Cultural History*, New Haven, CT: Yale University Press.

Rosner, V. (2008), *Modernism and the Architecture of Private Life*, New York: Columbia University Press.

Russkaia usadba na stranitsiakh zhurnalov "starie gody" i "stolitsa i usadba" (1994), Moscow: MoscMeaning, Academy of Sciences.

Sakharova, E., ed. (1964), *VD Polenov-ED Polenova: Khronika semi i khudozhnikov*, Moscow.

Salmond, W. (1996), *Arts and Crafts in Late Imperial Russia*, Cambridge: Cambridge University Press.

Schönle, A. (2006), "Ruins and History: Observations on Russian Approaches to Destruction and Decay," *Slavic Review* 65 (4): 649–669.

Schönle, A. (2011), *Architecture of Oblivion: Ruins and Historical Consciousness in Modern Russia*, DeKalb: Northern Illinois University Press.

Sewell, W. (2005), *The Logics of History: Social Theory and Social Transformation*, Chicago: University of Chicago Press.

Semenov-Tian-Shansky, P.P. (1915), *Epokha osvobozhdeniia krestian v Rossii v vospominaniiakh I*, St. Petersburg: Printing House of the Ministry of Railroads.

Shchepkina, A.V. (1915), *Vospominaniia Aleksandry Vladimirovny Shchepkinoi*, Moscow: I.I. Ivanov Publishers.

Silverman, D. (1992), *Art Nouveau in Fin-de-Siecle France: Politics, Psychology, and Style*, Berkeley: University of California Press.

Smith, M. (1997), *Mastered By the Clock: Time, Slavery and Freedom in the American South*, Chapel Hill: University of North Carolina Press.

Smith, V. (2007), *Clean: A History of Personal Hygiene and Purity*, Oxford: Oxford University Press.

Sparke, P., A. Massey, T. Keeble and B. Martin, eds. (2009), *Designing the Modern Interior: From the Victorians to Today*, Oxford: Berg.

Stanislavskii, K. (1954), *Sobranie sochinenii: v vos'mi tomakh*, vol. 1, Moscow.

Starks, T. (2008), *The Body Soviet: Propaganda, Hygiene and the Revolutionary State*, Madison: University of Wisconsin Press.

Steedman, C. (2002), *Dust: The Archive and Cultural History*, New Brunswick, NJ: Rutgers University Press.

Steinberg, M. (2002), *Proletarian Imagination: Self, Modernity and the Sacred in Russia, 1910–1925*, Ithaca, NY: Cornell University Press.

Steinberg, M. (2008), "Melancholy and Modernity: Emotions and Social Life in Russia Between the Revolutions," *Journal of Social History* 41 (4): 813–841.

Steinberg, M. (2011), *Petersburg Fin de Siècle*, New Haven, CT: Yale University Press.

Steinberg, M.D. (2017), "Alexandra Kollontai and the Utopian Imagination in the Russian Revolution," *Vestnik of Saint Petersburg University: History* 62 (3): 436–448.

Steinberg, M.D. (2017), "Lev Trotsky and the Utopian Imagination in the Russian Revolution," *Vestnik of Saint Petersburg University History* 62 (4): 664–673.

Steinberg, M.D. (2018), "Vladimir Mayakovsky and the Utopian Imagination in the Russian Revolution," *Vestnik of Saint Petersburg University History* 63 (1): 83–91.

Stroud, G. (2006), "The Past in Common: Modern Ruins as a Shared Urban Experience of Revolution-Era Moscow and Petersburg," *Slavic Review* 65 (4): 712–735.

Stroud, G. (2006), "Retrospective Revolution: A History of Time and Memory in Urban Russia, 1903–1923," PhD diss., University of Illinois.

Todorova, M. (2005), "The Trap of Backwardness: Modernity, Temporality and the Study of Eastern European Nationalism," *Slavic Review* 64 (1): 140–164.

Tosh, J. (2008), *A Man's House: Masculinity and the Middle-Class Home*, New Haven, CT: Yale University Press.

Tovrov, J. (1978), "Mother-Child Relationships among the Russian Nobility," in D. Ransel, ed., *The Family in Imperial Russia: New Lines of Historical Research*, 15–45, Urbana: University of Illinois Press.

Utekhin, I., A. Nakhimovsky, S. Paperno and N. Ries (n.d.), "Communal Living in Russia: A Virtual Museum of Society in Everyday Life." Available online: http://kommunalka.colgate.edu/, accessed February 19, 2020.

Varga-Harris, C. (2012), "Moving Toward Utopia: Soviet Housing in the Atomic Age,"
in P. Romijn, G. Scott-Smith and J. Segal (eds.), *Divided Dreamworlds?: The Cultural
Cold War in East and West*, 133–154, Amsterdam: Amsterdam University Press.

Varga-Harris, C. (2015), *Stories of House and Home: Soviet Apartment Life during the
Khrushchev Years*. Ithaca, NY: Cornell University Press.

Wachtel, A. B. (1990), *The Battle for Childhood: Creation of a Russian Myth*, Palo Alto,
CA: Stanford University Press.

Warren, S. (2009), "Crafting Nation: the Challenge to Russian Folk Art in 1913,"
Modernism/Modernity 19 (4): 743–765.

Wells Cavender, M. (2002), "'Kind Angel of the Soul and Heart': Domesticity and
Family Correspondence among the Pre-Emancipation Gentry," *Russian Review*
61 (July): 391–408.

Wells Cavender, M. (2007), *Nests of the Gentry: Family, Estate, and Local Loyalties in
Provincial Russia*, Newark: University of Delaware Press.

West-Pavlov, R. (2012), *Temporalities (The New Critical Idiom)*, New York: Routledge.

West, S. (2011), *I Shop in Moscow: Advertising and the Creation of Consumer Culture in
Late Tsarist Russia*, Dekalb: Northern Illinois University Press.

Willimott, A. (2019), *Living the Revolution: Urban Communes & Soviet Socialism,
1917–1932*, London: Oxford University Press.

Wolfe, R. (2011), "The Ultra-Taylorist Soviet Utopianism of Aleksei Gastev,"
The Charnel-House, December 7, 2011. Available online: https://thecharnelhouse.
org/2011/12/07/the-ultra-taylorist-soviet-utopianism-of-aleksei-gastev-including-
gastevs-landmark-book-how-to-work как-надо-работать, accessed February 5,
2020.

Wood, E. (1997), *The Baba and the Comrade*, Bloomington: Indiana University Press.

Woolf, V. (1994), *To the Lighthouse*, Hertfordshire: Wordsworth Editions.

Woolf, V. (2003), *Mrs. Dalloway*, London: CRW Publishers.

Wortman, R. (2000), *Scenarios of Power: Myth and Ceremony on Russian Monarchy from
Peter the Great to the Abdication of Nicholas II*, Princeton, NJ: Princeton University Press.

Wortman, R. (2003), "The 'Russian Style' in Church Architecture as Imperial Symbol
after 1881," in J. Cracraft and D. Rowland (eds.), *Architectures of Russian Identity:
1500–Present*, 101–116, Ithaca, NY: Cornell University Press.

Zgura, V. V. (2016), *Dvevnikovyi zapiski*, Moscow: Minuvshee.

Zlochevskii, G. D. (2011), *Obshchestvo izucheniia russkoi usadby: ego deiatelnost
i rukovoditeli (1920-e gody)*, Moscow: Rossiiskii *issledovatel'skii institute kul'turnogo i
prirognogo nasledeniia imeni* D. S. Likhacheva.

Zoshchenko, M. (1925), "The Crisis," a short story, translated by Charles Rougle,
Moscow. Available online: http://kommunalka.colgate.edu/cfm/from_fiction.
cfm?ClipID=565&TourID=940, accessed February 19, 2020.

Index

Abramtsevo estate 81–2, 104, 117–24, 146
advertising 44, 56, 59, 63
advice literature 47, 51, 58–63, 67, 75–6, 79–80, 162
Aksakov family and estate 81–2, 125
Alexievich, Svetlana 34, 176
Andreev, P.P. 58–60
antiques 59
apartment living 3–5, 41–3, 52, 57–60, 66, 72, 131–2, 139, 147, 149, 152–4, 163–5, 171
apartments, transformation of 86
Apollon (journal) 84
Archangelsk 96
archival discoveries 109
Art Nouveau 106, 122
artistic goods 50
autobiographical writing 87, 89, 92–3
Aynsley, Jeremy 52

backwardness 27–8, 102, 128
Ballets Russes 91
Bartlett, Djurdja 136
bathrooms 161
Bauman, Zygmunt 13
bedrooms and bedding 65–8, 74–8
Benjamin, Walter 21, 28, 84, 128, 147, 149, 157–8
Benois, Alexandre 91
Bergson, Henri 16, 18, 48, 82–3
Berry, Francesca 52
Bershtein, A.N. 71
Bezgodnik 148
Bilibin, Ivan 117, 123
Bloch, Ernst 136
Blok, Alexander 162
Bogdanov, Alexander 130
Bogrodskoe Workshop 121
Bol'shakov, A.M. 13
Bolshevism 30, 127–8, 133, 138, 146–7
Bosco di Ciliegi 177

bourgeois society and culture 8, 30–3, 46, 51
bourgeoisification 40
Boym, Svetlana 21, 83, 176, 181–2
Bradley, Joseph 42
Buck-Morris, Susan 128
Bukharin, Nikolai Ivanovich 27
Bukhovetskii, V. 153
Bulgakov, Mikhail 160–1
Bulliten zhilets 166
bureaucratic procedures and categories 13

calendars 24, 128
capitalism 26
cast iron dishes 61
Catherine the Great 115
Chekhov, Anton 39, 86, 103–4
Chernyshevsky, Nikolai 131
The Cherry Orchard 86, 103
childhood 69–73, 86–92, 100
childrearing 70–1, 78
children, physical domestic space available to 73–5, 78; *see also* games for children
children's furniture 146
children's rooms 69, 73–8, 154–5
Christianity 18
cleaning 64–7, 77, 141–4, 164
clocks 17–18, 22, 25, 47, 174–6, 179–80
collective living 33, 160–8; *see also* communal living
comfort and coziness 150
communal living 33, 142–3, 172; *see also* collective living
communalism 6, 8
consumer-oriented society 56
consumerism 40
contextualization 11, 79
contingency of the present moment 79
Cornfield, Penelope J. 23
Cubbins, Tom 136
curtains 57

Damski mir (magazine) 36–7, 59–60, 74–5
David-Fox, Michael 13
Dehrn van Rossun, Gerhard 25
department stores 40, 177
"Detskii Mir" exhibition 78
Diaghilev, Sergei Pavlovich 15
dining rooms 64
Dior, Christian 177
Dobuzhinsky, Mstislav 84
Doktor Nikolia 70
Dom i khoziastvo 56, 133, 142–5
domestic science 55
domesticity 30–2, 92; cult of 31,
    41
Dowler, Wayne 45
dreamscapes 173
dreamworlds 128–9
Dubianskaia, M. 153–4
"duration" concept 16, 29, 83
Durkheim, Émile 19
dust 150–5, 168, 171

Einstein, Albert 20
Eisenstein, Sergei 129
electrification 142
elite groups 12, 43, 104, 108
"emotional hygiene" 70
Engel, Barbara 31, 41
Engelgardt, V.A. 110
Engels, Frederick 179
English Workers Party 163
Enlightenment thinking 11, 13
epochal change 48, 53, 65, 70, 79, 165, 169
estates: cultural and social meanings of
    101; interest in and studies of 6, 27, 86,
    107–13, 157–9; resurgence of 100–4
Europe, Russia's place in 14
Evdokmov, I.V. 158
everyday life 50–1, 92, 94, 97–8, 102, 155,
    162, 173–4
exceptionalism, Soviet 13
experts and expertise 67–9, 75–7

factory-made goods 50, 65
family life 30
fin de siècle nostalgia 82–5, 89
First World War 84
Florinsky, P. 91–2
folk art 123, 156–7
France 52, 145, 122

"Frederik" 142
French Revolution 23–4, 128
fresh air 62–3, 72, 152, 165
Fritzsche, Peter 23–4, 83, 85, 105
Fryxell, A.R.P. 12
furnishing of apartments 143, 145
furniture design 65–6, 143–5, 149, 152–7
futurism 130

games for children 71
Gange, David 22–3
Gastev, Aleksei 140
Gastronom No. 1 (grocery store) 177
gendered concepts 33, 96–7, 133–5
Germany 52, 122, 144, 163
Giddens, Anthony 13
Gigena i zdorov'e rabochie i krest'ianskoi
    sem'i (journal) 147
Golburt, Luba 14–15, 82, 84
"Golden Age" of the nobility 4, 102
Goldman, Wendy 130
Golitsyn estate 105–6
Gomel'skaia 109
Goncharov, Ivan 131
Gorky, Maxim 50–1, 55
Grabar, Igor 156
Greenwich Mean Time 11
Grin, Alexander 176
The Guardian 171
GUM (department store) 177–82
Gundobin, N.P. 78

Hanson, Stephen E. 29, 139–40
Harte, Tim 28–9
heating and ventilation systems 56–8, 66,
    153, 164–5
Heidegger, Martin 15, 47
Herzen, Alexander 128, 175–6
Hilton, Alison 117
historians 10–11
"historical consciousness" 83
historicism and historicity 20–1, 82
"historicist turn" 14–15
Hoffman, David 13–14
home: as a healthy environment 72; as a
    place to define oneself 43–4, 48, 51;
    visions of 160
household manuals 57–8, 64
housekeeping and housework 141–5, 172
housing stock in Russia 41–3

Husserl, Edmund 47–8
hygiene and hygienic practices 45, 52–64, 67–78; for children 78; relationship with death 78
hygiene committees 72

Iakunchikova, Maria F. 120
Iakunchikova, Maria Vasilevna 123–4
"industrial" and "pre-industrial" time 25
industrialization process 23, 85
infantilization 119
International Women's Day 147
intimacy, emotional 91, 99
Ireland 122

Kataev, Valentin 139–40
Kay, Ellen 69
Kelly, Catriona 31–2, 38, 41, 62
Kern, Stephen 20, 47
Kharuzina, Elena Afenas'evna 100
Kharuzina, Vera Nikolaevna 92–100
Khomyakov, Aleksey 16
Khrushchev, Nikita 172
kitchens and kitchen gadgets 54, 60–4, 142–3
Kollontai, Alexandra 28, 133
Koselleck, Reinhart 5, 18, 22, 125, 176
Krichinskii, Stepan 84–5
Krisman, Oscar 70–1
Krupskaya, Nadezhda 133
Krymov, V.P. 106
Die Kunst (journal) 124
kustar industries and Kustar Museum 120–1, 123, 157

lags in development 26
Lazarevskii, Ivan 157
leisure pursuits 40–1
Lenin, Vladimir 24, 27, 29, 127–9, 134–5, 147–9, 172
Lermontov, Mikhail 110–11
lifestyle and lifestyle magazines 44–6, 51; *see also* magazines for women
living rooms 64
love of nature 95
Lovell, Stephen 39, 101
Lunacharsky, Anatoly 134, 158

magazines for women 4–6, 35–8, 44–5, 49–53, 58–63, 77, 106–8, 132, 135, 140, 142, 161–2
Mallory, D. 167
Mamontov, Savva and Elizaveta 81–2, 117–20, 124
Manchard, Michael 25
Marinetti, Filippo 28, 130
Marks, Stephen 27
Martynovna, Anna 97
Marx, Karl 16, 29, 135–6
Marxism 172
material culture 27
Mayakovsky, Vladimir 28, 35–6, 127, 135–6, 177–9
McDonald, Tracy 131
memoirs 91–3, 96, 100
memory 94
Menendez, Ana 1
micro-time 50
middle classes 31–2, 38–45, 52, 61, 64–5, 79, 86
migration 41, 48, 79, 86, 132
Mikhailovka estate 111–13
Miliukov, P.N. 89–92
Mir iskusstva 84, 91, 105, 115, 122–4
modernity and modernism 7, 9–24, 27–8, 38, 45–8, 57, 69, 71, 78–81, 83, 95–6, 121–2, 129, 132, 146, 160; definitions of 11, 13–14, 170; Russian and Soviet 12–16
mortality in childhood 72
Moscow 42, 46, 79, 84, 86, 95, 106, 109, 132, 147, 176–7
Moscow Society for Neuropathology and Psychiatry 71
Muir & Mirrieless (department store) 40
Muranovo 112
Muravieva, Alexandra Zakharovna 36–7

Nabokov, Vladimir 88
national identity 23
natural world 95
New Economic Policy (NEP) 135–8, 158, 160
Newlin, Thomas 101
Nicholas II, Tsar 27
Nietzsche, Friedrich 21
Norway 170–1
nostalgia 3, 6–7, 19–23, 32, 80, 82–8,

92–3, 96, 99, 103–7, 116–17, 171–3, 176–7; "public" 84–5; *restorative* or *reflective* 21
Nussbaum, Dr. 67

Odessa 167
Ogle, Vanessa 24–5
Orthodox belief 16
Orwell, George 127
Oushakine, Serguei 173

Palti, Jose 17–19
parental nearness 92
Pasad, Sergei 121
past, sense of 84
pastoral ideal 101–3
peasants and peasant traditions 26–7, 41, 49, 55, 67, 79–80, 86, 104, 114–25, 132, 146, 157
pedagogy 70–1
pediatricians 69
Peter the Great 15, 123
Peter III, Tsar 101
Pil'niak, Boris 157
Poland 122
Polenova, Elena 117–20, 123–4
Polenova, N.V. 104
political consciousness 44
politicized texts 52
postmodernism 27
Pravda 172, 176
"precariousness" 45
psychiatrists 77
Pushkin, Alexander Sergeyevich 88
Putin, Vladimir 172, 180

"racial time" (Manchard) 25
Radchenko, A. 134, 155
Randall, Amy 130
Randolph, John 101
Ransel, David 30–1
reclining chairs 67
Redelin, Maria 4, 32, 55, 58–67
Reid, Susan 33, 140, 172
"representational strategies" 51
Retrospectivism 115, 156–7
revolutionary moments 135
revolutionary movements 128–31, 176
Ricoeur, Paul 136
Riumini mansion 108

Robotnitsa (magazine) 6
Romanov anniversaries 84–5
Roosevelt, Priscilla 101
ruins 27
Russian Revolution 24, 33, 128

St Petersburg 41–3, 46, 69, 79, 84, 86, 91, 106, 132, 151
sanitary commissions 162–3
Schönle, Andreas 27, 105
self, sense of 51
self-improvement 45
Sem'ianin (magazine) 57
Senezh Studio 136
"separate spheres" doctrine 32
Serf Emancipation Act (1861) 101
Sewell, William 10, 169
sexuality 71
shared experiences 99
shared space external to apartments 154, 164–5
Shchepkina, Alexandra 90
shops 40; *see also* department stores
sibling relationships 97
simultaneity 20, 29
slavery 25–6
Smith, Mark 25–6
social memory 21
social mobility 39
social transformation 13
Society for Gentry Estates 157
Society for the Study of the Russian Estate 6, 125
Society of the Lovers of the Estate (OURI) 158–60
soft furnishings 65
Solemenko 122
Sommarøy 170–1
Soviet ideology 131, 156, 162, 165–7, 182–3
Sovremennaia Arkhitektura (magazine) 138–9, 161
sovremennost 79–80
speed 28–9, 35–6
spiritual life 77
Stalin, Joseph 29; cult of 176; era of 182
Stalinism 135
Stanislavsky, Konstantin 90–2
Stankevich family 90
Starks, Tricia 134

Starye gody (magazine) 105, 122
Steedman, Carolyn 150–1
Steinberg, Mark 27–8, 43, 79, 85, 151
Stolitsa i usadba (magazine) 106–8, 157–8
Stolovaya café 177
Stolypina, A. 110–11
Stroud, Gregory 157
Style Moderne 6, 42, 106, 115, 121–4
sunlight 55, 66–7, 72, 76–7

technological advancement 62
temperature in rooms 75
temporal efficacy 32
temporal rhythm 49
"temporal turn" 9, 169
temporality 7–23, 27–8, 82, 169;
    philosophers of 16–17, 47;
    "theoreticians" of 10
Tian-Shansky, P.P. Semenov 89
time 9–11, 16–22, 25–34; conceptions
    of 2–3, 9–11, 17, 19, 22, 29, 46, 140,
    170; consciousness of 47–8, 50, 69, 76,
    79–80, 84; different kinds of 16, 19;
    inside the home 30–4; internalized
    26, 29; irreversibility of 10, 17–21;
    "nationalization" of 176; non-linearity
    of 16; *past, present* and *future* 47–9;
    public and *private* 47, 170; "real" 83;
    refracted through the home 169–70;
    Russian and Soviet 26; standardization
    of 25, 80
time-saving products and practices 55–7,
    62, 73, 140–6, 171
time-space compression 28, 35–6
time-space nexus 20
timelessness, sense of 183

Todorova, Maria 26
Tolstoy, Lev 16, 87, 92
toska 94
"tough love" 70
Trotsky, Leon 27–8, 128
Turgenev, Ivan 30
Turino Exhibition of Decorative Arts
    (1902) 124

urbanization 43, 86, 116
utopianism 6–8, 28, 138–9, 160, 166

Varenichnaya Restaurant 174–5
Varga-Harris, Christine 172
Voronov, Vasilli 157

washing machines 63, 143
Wells Cavender, Mary 101
women, role and status of 31, 33, 36–40,
    45, 52, 60, 133–5, 147–50, 162, 167–8,
    172
Woods, Elizabeth 130
Woolf, Virginia 9–10, 12
working classes 38, 156
World of Art movement 15, 115, 122

Yusupovs' palace 96

Zgura, Vladimir 158–9
Zhenotdel, the 133
Zhenshchina (magazine) 35–9, 49–53,
    60–7, 70, 73, 75
Zhurnal dlia khoziaek (magazine) 6, 52,
    76–7
Zhurnal dlia zhenshchin (magazine) 52
Zoshchenko, Mikhail 160–1